MAYDA .....
CALLING MAYDAY

A Story Of Rescue

by
Joyce Millard

With best wishes
Joyce Millard
14 January 1997

The author, Joyce in Uniform

© Joyce Millard 1995
ISBN 0 9527335 0 1

All rights reserved.
No part of this publication may be reproduced, stored in a retrieval system or transmitted in any form or by any means, electronic, mechanical, photocopying, recording or otherwise without prior written permission from the author.

Published in Great Britain by
BLUEBELLE BOOKS
160 Colneis Road, Felixstowe, Suffolk IP11 9LJ England

Printed in England by
Printwise (Haverhill) Limited
8 & 10 Hollands Road, Haverhill, Suffolk CB9 8PP

Cover Picture by Mark Coomber

COMMENTS FROM WWII FIGHTER PILOTS

F/LT. BILL COOK (COOKIE) DFC - NO. 421 SQDN. KENLEY CANADIAN WING 1943.
"I do not think anyone who was in aircrew will ever forget the contribution made by those like yourself, who were always on call to get us back to base or out of the 'Drink'."

HON. SEC. OF THE GOLDFISH CLUB - JOHN C. FRENCH - 1992
"I share your sentiments about the lack of recognition shown to WAAF D/F operators. Had they not done their job efficiently, hundreds of us would not be here today. In my own case, I'm sorry to say, you did not hear us - my SOS was picked up loud and clear by a German D/F operator in the Frisian Islands and we were duly dragged away from our aquatic antics and invited to spend the rest of the war in a purpose-built Gasthaus."

LADDIE LUCAS CBE DSO DFC. COLTISHALL WING LEADER 1943.
"Let me say at once what a splendid job the Fighter Command pilots felt the WAAF's on Direction/Finding Stations did for all of us. When I returned from the Malta battle, I remember so well the excellent service rendered by the D/F Stations near the coast. We had 140 miles of sea between East Anglia and north Dutch coasts and many were the times when we had to get fixes for our ditched comrades on the way home. No one will know this better than Johnnie Johnson who has written the Foreword for your book (which I am so glad you have written). Johnnie often used to come up to Coltishall with his Canadians from Kenley and work with us."

W/CDR. JOHNNY CHECKETTS DSO DFC. AMERICAN SILVER STAR & POLISH CROSS OF VALOUR. C.O. 485 (N.Z) SQDN. & HORNE WING LEADER
"I was very interested to read about your book. I knew that many men were rescued from the 'Drink' but did not know how many. There is no doubt that a considerable number of these were the result of fixes from our D/F Stations. I was one! I was shot down half-way between Boulogne and Dungeness on 2nd May 1942 at 20.30 hours. Reg Baker of 485 gave a fix on my position and I was rescued by the Navy an hour later, just as night was falling. I was lucky. Generally, the R/T was very good, especially for Homing and Mayday fixing. We had great confidence in the R/T operators in England and the fixing stations saved many lives, mine among them."

W/CDR. HUGH C. GODEFROY DFC - (TOOK OVER KENLEY CANADIAN WING FROM W/CDR. 'JOHNNIE' JOHNSON IN SEPTEMBER 1943)

"Yes, I am anxious to thank you girls for your devotion to helping us and this is the first opportunity I have had to communicate my gratitude. Once after the invasion, I very much needed your help but my R/T was dead and I was unable to give a MAYDAY. I had to bail out with the Channel lashed by a Force 8 gale, where I earned my membership in the Goldfish Club. Fortunately, I was seen on fire by a small returning vessel who pulled me out of the water half-drowned."

THE HON. MR. JUSTICE DOUGLAS R. MATHESON - EX-F/LT. NO. 411 (CAN) SQUADRON

"I join with you in your pique about the failure of any officialdom to properly record and acknowledge the tremendous service to airmen provided by D/F Stations and R/T operators . . . Many times I blessed those people who were able to give us a vector when we were in trouble . . . I was once caught in a London fog and the next thing I was seeing Barrage Balloons on all sides. Indeed it was a dicey few moments. I frantically called for a Homing and was promptly told to get up to a safe altitude in the fog and I was then given a couple of headings which brought me dead over Hornchurch airfield with a ceiling of about 500ft. and to a safe landing. Let me assure you that to hear those lovely voices of our Controllers giving us those vital vectors when we needed them most, was music to our ears and if 'the powers that be' have failed to recognise the vital role that you and your colleagues played during those years, they have indeed missed acknowledging your contribution, which was second to none. I wish you every success with your proposed book."

W/CDR. ROLAND 'BEE' BEAMONT, CBE, DSO, DFC, - NEWCHURCH WING

"You girls probably helped many of us that summer. Perhaps you were 'fixing' me when I Mayday'd on 8 June 1944 after being shot up by a 109 near the Beachhead. We got three 109's and I made a slow crossing home to Newchurch with a large hole in my right wing. Many thanks for all your vital help to us in those great days."

F/O HUGH ROSS - TEMPEST PILOT NO. 80 SQUADRON

"I read your letter in Intercom with considerable sympathy, as one of those who called MAYDAY. We were all grateful to those who helped to get us back but there was no way of passing on our thanks and I for one would enjoy reading some account of the work done by D/F Stations."

(Hon.) LT. COL. THOMAS WHELER MBE DFC CD. CHAIRMAN - CANADIAN FIGHTER PILOTS ASSOCIATION, ONTARIO WING.

"I joined 411 at Redhill in early 1943 and stayed with them through Staplehurst, Biggin Hill, and Tangmere and I'm sure you vectored us around the skies then and I'm thankful you did. You ladies were magnificent to say the least - a true example of the unbeatable English spirit. I was shot down in August 1944 when based in France but managed to escape three times and finally got back to England. Take care and many thanks to you and your special group of people."

W/CDR. DOUGLAS (GRUBBY) GRICE MBE DFC (BATTLE OF BRITAIN PILOT 32 SQDN)

"I too am surprised that D/F operators have not received the recognition they deserve for the part they played in the Fighter Command set-up. Without them the whole system of controlled interception would have been impossible and their accuracy in monitoring Mayday calls must have helped to save countless pilots."

CLIFF BURKETT - HEREFORD

"I too was a D/F operator (W/T) before my three years in A/S/R so I understand your feelings about lack of recognition. We have to obtain our satisfaction from the knowledge that we were part of one big team - the best Air Force there has ever been - but nevertheless, it would be nice to have just a little praise directed our way amongst the millions of words written in hundreds of books."

CONTENTS

			Page No.
		FOREWORD	VII
		INTRODUCTION	VIII
Chapter	1	GREENHORNS IN BLUE	1
	2	CRANWELL AT LAST	7
	3	EN ROUTE FOR KENLEY	14
	4	EVERY DAY A FIELD DAY	21
	5	PLAYING THE FIELD	39
	6	TWO OF OUR AIRCRAFT ARE MISSING	46
	7	THE AIR RESCUERS	49
	8	THE DAY I REMEMBER THE SIXTH OF SEPTEMBER	66
	9	PRESSING ON REGARDLESS	77
	10	LISTENING IN AND OUT	96
	11	'SCREWBALL' BEURLING	106
	12	CHRISTMAS IN HOSPITAL	111
	13	THE END OF AN ERA - KENLEY TO GO	117
	14	EUROPE TO BE LIBERATED	125
	15	THE V-1 ONSLAUGHT	138
	16	NO ODDS TOO GREAT FOR POLES	156
	17	GOODBYE WITTERSHAM	160
	18	WELL, HELLO TOLLY	164
	19	BATTLING AGAINST ALL THE ODDS	175
	20	THE END IN SIGHT	189
	21	THE BEST MAY-DAY OF ALL	199
	22	IN LIMBO	212
	23	I WANT OUT	218
	24	AFTERTHOUGHTS - THEN AND NOW	234

FOREWORD
by

Air Vice Marshal J.E. 'Johnnie' Johnson, C.B., C.B.E., D.S.O., D.F.C., D.L.

When, in the high Summer of 1943, I was leading the Kenley (Canadian) Wing and my New Zealand friend Al Deere was leading the Biggin Hill Wing, we were the spearheads of a great organisation which included all those airmen and airwomen who, often with great devotion, toiled on the ground to get our Spitfires into the air, to help us in our fight against enemy fighters and to bring us safely home sometimes - in badly shot-up Spitfires.

For all those fighter pilots who, as the author says, had to cross the Channel several times a day (eight times on D-Day) in their single engine Spitfires, it was a great comfort to know that watching over us were young girls like Joyce Millard, aged 19, who were right on the ball when things went wrong. I can still remember how she and her colleagues at their Direction Finding Station helped to rescue a great Canadian fighter pilot. Squadron Leader 'Buck' McNair, after he bailed out of his Spitfire just a few miles off the French coast. Thanks to Joyce and her friends, the Controller and his WAAF's in the Kenley Ops Room and the gallant Air-Sea Rescue crew in an old slow Walrus, collected Buck from under the very noses of the Germans and two weeks later he was back on Ops.

I commend the author's splendid account of those stirring days in Fighter Command when we were all part of a highly successful team.

INTRODUCTION

When I was eventually demobbed from the Women's Auxiliary Air Force at the end of the Second World War, a chapter in my young life ended and like millions of ex-Service personnel, I returned to civilian life full of hope and expectation of a bright future in a peaceful world. I put away my memorabilia, including diaries and in the following decades, I seldom thought or spoke about those exciting years I spent on a Direction/Finding Station in the south-east corner of England, attached to the two most famous Fighter Aerodromes in the country - Kenley and Biggin Hill.

It was the 50th Anniversary of the Battle of Britain that sparked off a re-awakened interest in my war-time occupation and it was about that time that I was due to have one of those rare re-unions with two long-time WAAF chums who were part of our 4-woman crew and with whom I shared a billet. These were the only occasions my war-time diaries saw the light of day and I usually took them along but busy chatting, we invariably forgot to refer to them. Instead of putting them away again this time, I decided to have a nostalgic re-read right through - something I had never bothered to do before because I thought they mostly contained girlish trivia. During war-time, we were not supposed to keep a diary - or at least, not to record anything that 'might be useful to the enemy' and on Direction/Finding Stations, we were housed in civilian billets, with the additional risk of prying landladies, who may well have been more interested in our off-duty activities than in our work, had we inadvertently forgotten to keep our diaries out of sight. I was gratified to find that I was not such a dumb-belle after all and had sneaked in some interesting clues and shorthand notes relating to operational rescues I had worked on. Covering late 1942 to part 1946, they provided my bed-time reading for several weeks and I had many a chuckle at my youthful escapades. Diaries certainly make memories come alive - so many incidents I thought long since forgotten were recalled to mind by just a brief reference and then I was able to remember the rest quite clearly but a few names and recorded facts gave no hint of any recognition. By the time I had re-lived a second time, my far from mis-spent youth, I had developed a keen interest in wanting to find out the facts behind some of those RAF rescue operations we worked on, that we were never told about at the time.

Without a doubt, we had one of the most worthwhile and rewarding jobs in the WAAF's - helping to save the lives of countless aircrew who had to bale out over the English Channel and North Sea . We were tuned in to the radio frequency of the Ops Room Controller and fighter pilot and took bearings on the voice transmission from the aircraft nearly every time the pilot spoke, with Mayday distress calls given top priority. The Air/Sea Rescue Service performed some courageous deeds during the recovery world-wide of some 13,000 airmen from the sea and approximately half of those were picked up in 'Home Waters'. High Speed Launches often snatched aircrew from their dinghies in close proximity to the enemy coast, running the risk of being within range of German gunfire and possible attack by the Luftwaffe. The air rescues were mainly performed by Walrus amphibian aircraft, alighting on the water to pick up survivors, sometimes in foul weather and rough seas. The English Channel and North Sea were inhospitable places to ditch, all alone in a dinghy, very often with neither friendly or enemy land in sight and many a pilot, not knowing whether his Mayday had been heard or his position 'fixed', must have thought that an untimely end was his inevitable fate. In those hostile waters, there can have been no more heart-warming sight for a downed pilot than to watch the approach of a High Speed Launch with its RAF roundel and white painted identification number on the bow, ploughing through the waves towards him, or to hear the drone of a trusty old Walrus hovering overhead, about to land nearby.

    I trained as a VHF/RT/DF (Very High Frequency/Radio Telephone/Direction Finding) at Cranwell, and at the end of the course I was posted to Kenley Fighter Station - then on to one of their D/F Stations on the south coast, near Rye. In our small circular Tower, situated in the middle of a field we kept a 24-hour vigil in shifts, monitoring the position of various fighter squadrons and the Mayday bearings we took were the initial key factor in many a search - helping the Flying Boats and High Speed Launches to find them as speedily as possible. WAAF D/F operators can rightfully claim a helping hand in the overall team effort of Air/Sea Rescue who successfully plucked hundreds of aircrew from the sea around the south-east corner of England. During two years of active air operations, I listened to the intercom of fighter pilots in combat with the Luftwaffe, strafing targets along the coast of Occupied Europe and chasing and shooting down 'Doodlebugs'.

    At our Reunion, I realised that Joan Wedgbury and Eileen Bond had fared no better in finding any recorded reference about our D/F involvement and we often wondered whether those aircrew who were saved from the sea - when less pre-occupied with their own important survival, ever reflected on the organisation that led to their recovery. Certainly the rescue of one fortunate pilot was entirely due to Eileen's excellent hearing. Way back in July 1943, when we were all on duty as part of the same crew, Eileen was the only person on her frequency to hear a faint Mayday call from a pilot about to bale out and he was located and rescued a few miles from the enemy coast on the strength of that single bearing.

The 6th September 1943 must have been the busiest day ever for Air/Sea Rescue when 118 American Fortress aircrew were picked up from the Channel after a disastrous mission to Stuttgart. Kenley Ops Room and D/F Stations participated in 85 of those rescues and our operators received a generous tribute from the Commanding Officer of No. 11 Group, thanking us 'for our efficiency in fixing' etc. I have a copy of the letter and noted a few facts about the events of that day in my diary.

By the end of the war, WAAF personnel had risen to 155,000 but surprisingly only an infinitesimal number of books have been written or published by ex-WAAF's during the last half century. Whatever the reason for the poor output, it means that factual information on how we lived and coped with the challenge of the many and varied tasks we undertook, will not be recorded in the vast history of the Second World War. The generation of women who served in the Forces, proved that we could do many men's jobs that we had not been given the chance to undertake before, just as efficiently and did we not pave the way for more equality for women after the war in pay, employment and the opportunity of higher university education?

Joan, Eileen and I decided that it would be a pity if the important work of D/F Stations was not recorded and we thought we had sufficient material to give an accurate and genuine account but between the three of us, I was the only one who owned a typewriter with years of secretarial experience and it was my diaries containing all the facts. We had all completed our adult education in that war-time Service School of life experience, whose main teaching I had rigidly adhered to . . . . 'Never Volunteer for Anything!'. I realised I was being pressurised into taking on the task and I was also being out-voted.

Until recently, I have rarely spoken about my war-time occupation and as a general rule women are reticent to indulge in self-promotion but during my research, I found no Sector maps depicting the position of Kenley and Biggin Hill's D/F Stations or any evidence that the WAAF D/F operators who manned them, ever existed! That was the incentive to goad me into action and join the increasing number of ex-Service 'bods' who are taking a nostalgic backward glance at their war effort and now have the time to commit thoughts and memories to paper. Fortunately, fifty years later, I have not had to rely entirely on regurgitated memory. The brief notes in my diaries about Mayday calls are accurate, further authenticated by my research of details in squadron records and that has enabled me, in several instances to add a personal account of their ordeal by the pilots involved. It has been an enlightening and rewarding experience finding out the 'end of story' behind the Mayday rescues I took part in. However, I would like to add that the views and opinions expressed are entirely my own and any discrepancies in the narrative are quite unintentional. To avoid embarrassment, I have not commented on the description or character of friends and people I met.

    I am dedicating this book to the women who served with me and to all the forgotten WAAF's on D/F Stations who were engaged in the team effort of helping to save the lives of our gallant fighter pilots and bomber crews:-

Joan Wedgbury	Eileen Bond	Curly Dunsmuir and Jay
Donnie Mayhew	Lilian Thornton	Joan Bellinger
Peggy Clinker	Mary Reynolds	Rhona and Sybil
Doris Martin	Connie Short	Beryl and Frankie
Polly Pollard	Eileen Miller	Sheila and Nora
Auntie Joan Palmer and All!		

Chapter 1

GREEN-HORNS IN BLUE

In the early years of the war, three of my sisters were already serving in the WAAF's, so when I was old enough to join, it was predictable that I would follow suit. I volunteered in 1942, rather than wait to be drafted, which gave the opportunity of stating a preference for the Service of your choice, whereas waiting for your call-up summons, meant being drafted into any one of the Women's Services, the Land Army, NAAFI, or even into munitions. My oldest sister was a Plotter in the Operations Room at Digby in Lincolnshire and she told me about a new trade only recently available to WAAF's, who were now being trained to replace airmen for overseas D/F duties. My other two sisters were doing Admin. secretarial work - one was stationed at Cardington in Bedfordshire, where the WAAF personnel numbered over 1,000 - a very suitable place for a sister about to be married but I had set my sights on hopefully being selected for this new trade, which would almost guarantee being posted to a fighter aerodrome and getting involved in a bit of the action. Four sisters serving in the WAAF's during the war was probably quite exceptional but it did not occur to any of us at the time.

A few days before Christmas 1942, I set out from my home in Wembley, a north London suburb, for the Recruiting Office in Kingsway and as instructed, I reported to Victory House, along with a number of other new recruits and from there we were taken to Paddington, en route for Gloucester. We began to sort ourselves out in small groups and at the station, the five I had been speaking to, got a compartment to ourselves and we became good friends during those first weeks. Gloucester was a WAAF Recruiting Centre where we were issued with our uniforms, underwent medicals and had various tests to determine fitness and I.Q. rating. My sisters gave me some useful tips to ease the rookie initiation - take a pillow, a hot-water bottle, marking ink and a bath plug - all essential items in a WAAF survival kit. Every item of clothing needed to be marked with one's name - less likely to get 'nicked' and a good case for a claim if it was! Why everyone needed to possess their own bath-plug was one of the many irritating quirks of service life but it seemed that the insolvable method of securing a plug on a chain to a bath that could not be pinched, had not yet been mastered!

The Forces failed completely to convert me to the virtues of the bright and early start - I was more for 'burning the mid-night oil' and sleeping until

I was good and ready to face the day. At 6 a.m. in December it was still pitch dark when that dawn Tannoy blasted its 'Wakey, Wakey - Rise and Shine' command through every hut on the campus. The light in our hut would be turned on and with only my head protruding outside the bedclothes, I knew how freezing it was when I saw my warm breath creating a cloud of steam, as it collided with the chill air inside the hut. The thought of putting warm feet on ice-cold lino, while in a dazed stupor fumbling for slippers, was enough to make me fully submerge under the bedclothes again. Joining up over the Festive Season did help to make the early bird lark more of a gradual process, as on Christmas Day we were allowed the special treat of a lay-in until 8 a.m. and on Boxing Day 7 a.m., leading up to the pre-dawn 4 a.m. rising two days later for departure to Morecambe. At this stage, we were not yet indoctrinated into the Service way of doing things and still thought with a civvie mind - even had the audacity to pose the question "Why was it necessary to get us up at the unGodly hour of 4 a.m. and then keep us hanging about on a bitterly cold station in the dark for over two hours?". We soon learned another important Forces lesson - "Ours not to reason why - ours but to do . . ."

Nothing could dampen my spirits though - I was told on only my second day that I had passed the Intelligence and Trade Tests and had been accepted for the 2-month course at Cranwell. I did not expect it would be that easy or quick.

Morecambe in January was rather a dreary place and I have never had the slightest inclination to pay a return visit. We were there for three weeks but it seemed a lot longer, attending those tedious lectures and parades that all new recruits had to endure. Who in the Forces will ever forget their first inoculation at the hands of the sadistic medic whose smile broadened as the needle got blunter - maybe not so indelibly printed in the memory as mine! We were all lined up, eventually getting to sit on a bench with left sleeve rolled up to expose an accessible bare upper arm and as we got nearer I could see the pained look on the face of the girls in front who'd had their jab and although I was still three females away from the dreaded needle, the smell of the antiseptic got to me, the room began to sway and faces became blurred as I lunged forward and landed on a heap on the floor. When I came round, someone was pushing my head in between my knees and I was also relieved to find that I had 'been done' while I was out cold on the floor! Then 'rigor mortis' gradually set in for the next 24 hours and any attempt to try and raise the arm more than a few inches made undressing, combing hair, bra fastening and knife and fork eating, a bit of an effort.

I had never seen so many females amassed in one place but it was some consolation to have five nice friends to knock around with and one of us could usually be relied on to see the funny side of any situation. We reckoned that if there were any fellas in Morecambe, they were probably afraid to go out alone at night! Late passes were easy to get but seldom needed! We were often marched in squads around the streets of Morecambe, much to the delight of the children, who would jeer and make faces at us, especially when we had gas mask drill and couldn't tell them off. During the final week, we were given our postings - sadly all to different destinations as we were hoping that some of us at any rate, might stay together. I wonder what happened to the girls of Hut 31 - Maureen, Nicki, Pam, Jose and Joan? We exchanged addresses and fully intended to write but somehow we did not manage to keep in touch.

I was sent to No. 16 Maintenance Unit, Stafford - a temporary posting I was told until there was a vacancy on the RT/DF course at Cranwell . . . I might have guessed there would be a snag somewhere. Had I known that 'temporary' was going to be 2½ dreary months at that cheerless Maintenance Unit, I might have become very depressed but like having a carrot dangled in front of me, I was ever optimistic that it wouldn't be much longer, when the weeks turned into months. I was not at all pleased at being stuck behind a typewriter again, taking down shorthand dictation in the Admin. Office at half the pay I was getting in civvie street. My reason for escaping from the solicitor's office in Wembley was the opportunity of doing something more interesting and challenging for my war effort. Career prospects for women pre-war were so limited - secretarial and office work, teaching, nursing, shop assistant or domestic work just about covered them all, so the many and varied trades in the Women's Services were opening up a lot more opportunities. I was also rather unfortunate to be working for a man like Sharratt, who was an awkward cuss with a nasty temper. I forget his actual rank but whatever it was, he revelled in his bit of authority and power to make his underlings grovel. If someone wanted an overnight pass, a 48 or leave, he would predictably say 'No' without even considering why he couldn't say 'Yes'. Sometimes he would retract a little and say he would give it some thought, leaving the hopeful person in suspense until the last minute, unable to make any firm plans. Apart from being a veritable P in the A, the best thing about him as far as I was concerned, was that he was frequently out of the office - all day sometimes but when he returned, I would be given a double load of dictation and he would expect me to finish it in one day. I don't know how I stuck it . . . or him! The irony was that I was summoned before the WAAF Offficer, who enquired whether I would like to re-muster to Clerk General Duties - in other words, desk and typewriter bound - rather than proceed with the course at Cranwell. I must have kept my cool and answered politely "No thank-you Ma'am" but goodness knows how I kept from blurting out what I really thought about the proposition and all its implications. I did wonder whether Sharratt had anything to do with the suggestion but if he had, I am sure it wasn't because he thought I was an efficient secretary - more likely the tormentor losing his favourite victim!

Soon after I settled in at Stafford, I was eligible for a 48-hour pass and I paid my first visit home since joining up. Peter Noble, a Beaufighter pilot I had been going out with in pre-WAAF days was also on leave. I had met his parents and visited their apartment in Dolphin Square, Victoria and that evening they took us both out to dine at the Trocadero. Peter and I spent the next day together and he came to Euston to see me off on the mid-night train to Stafford. I reached camp about 6 a.m. - had breakfast and then went to work. It was the first of many times during my Service life when I skipped a night's sleep but it always caught up with me in the end.

My particular chum at Stafford was a girl called Garland, or Gay for short, and she was also waiting for the Cranwell course. We were always on the look-out for a bit of fun to relieve the monotony of life on a dull Maintenance Unit and one night we got a bit more than we bargained for!

St. Mary's Church, Stafford

We thought we would take a look at Wolverhampton on our day off and the quickest way back to 16 M.U. from the centre of Stafford was through a churchyard, just behind the main shopping area. It was late and had we thought about it, I suppose it was quite eerie, walking through a cemetery on a cold January night with the wind rustling the branches of the trees but Garland and I were quite oblivious of our surroundings amid all those departed spirits (just so long as they had all departed!)

The place was quite deserted and we were busy chatting, when in the distance we could see a man on his own, approaching from the opposite direction. As he got nearer, we could see it was an airman in uniform and when he stopped in front of us, more or less blocking our path, we thought he was going to ask us something - well, he did, but not quite what we were expecting! He opened the front of his great-coat - shone a torch on what was dangling from his open flies and said "Have you ever seen such a beauty?" . . . . . and went on his way. I was absolutely speechless but Garland, who was never at a loss for words, uttered a stream of invective I had never heard pass her lips before! I was incensed that we were subjected to such a confrontation and I wanted to go back to the High Street and look for a couple of RAF S.P's or if we couldn't find any, report him to Stafford Police Station but Garland was a few years older than I was, with a level head on her shoulders, and said "Let's think about this for a minute." Obviously weighing up the pro's and con's, she looked at her watch and then realised that we only had twenty minutes before curfew time "If we hang about in Town, we are going to get into trouble for being late back into Camp and if we try and explain the reason, who is going to believe us - it will just sound like a lame excuse 'cos we're late. If he's caught, he will be on a very serious charge, maybe a Court Marshal, which we would have to attend as witnesses. Now, I didn't actually see his face in the dark, did you?" "Well, no, not exactly, I guess my gaze was elsewhere" I had to admit! . . . So continued Garland "There's only one part of his anatomy that we could identify and we are not likely to be asked to do that! The best thing we can do is to forget it. Besides, any involvement in a tribunal might well delay us getting to Cranwell and our course could come through any day." I could see the sense of her argument and she was right of course but I felt uneasy that he might take matters further, should he meet a girl on her own.

(In all my four years journeying around the country, hitching rides in various modes of transport and out walking, very often by myself in the black-out, this was the only 'nasty' incident of unwanted attention from a complete stranger that I ever experienced. One time I remember, I was rather indignant when a driver expected a kiss in return for giving me a lift, as I got out of the car - that was a one-off incident too - he did ask first . . . and he did accept 'No' as an answer! Doesn't that speak volumes about the decent behaviour of men of that generation towards women and the freedom of movement we were able to enjoy without fear of being molested. The drastic change over the last five decades is hard to fathom.)

****

A few years ago, I happened to be visiting the area for the first time since 1943 and out of curiosity, I wondered whether I would be able to find the churchyard again. It was a Sunday, with no parking restriction in the centre of Stafford's deserted shopping area. The first person I asked, put me in the direction of the only church he knew of, near the Town centre, St. Mary's - but on first appearance, it wasn't quite how I remembered it - there were no grave stones and no overhanging trees. It seemed a lot larger with more open space and a wider paved area. I wasn't at all sure it was the right churchyard but after all these years, was my memory at fault? There were two elderly gentlemen sitting on a seat and when I spoke to them, they told me that this path was the way to the Maintenance Unit and I assumed from the signpost to No. 16 M.U. nearby that it was still an RAF camp. I mentioned to the two gents how I remembered it during the war (but not the reason why!). What I hadn't noticed in the shadows, until they pointed them out, were the headstones standing vertically against the boundary fence. I was told they had been removed from the graves many years past and placed there, some barely readable now. Several trees had also been dug up to make room for a wider pedestrian footpath.

Several questions came to mind standing there and recalling that incident all those years ago. I wondered how long and how often the RAF 'flasher' went on his nightly prowls and whether any other females were confronted along that lonely sinister path among the gravestones? And more importantly, was he ever caught in the act? I certainly hope so. In those days, it was called 'indecent exposure' and men who indulged in that sort of odd behaviour were considered a bit cranky but mostly harmless.

I must have been too embarrassed as a rather naive 18 year old to give explicit details in my diary. I had only written 'Had an experience I'll never forget walking back from Stafford. Thank heavens I was with Garland. The air was blue' - ending with lots of exclamation marks.

Chapter 2

CRANWELL AT LAST

The training for becoming a Radio Telephone/DF Operator was a 2-month course at Cranwell in Lincolnshire, more renowned for its College of Air Training - the RAF equivalent of the Army's Sandhurst Academy and the Navy's Dartmouth College, but during the war other courses were held there. At Radio School we attended classes on Procedure and Technical subjects, including the Morse Code and we were given an insight into the improved methods for recovering pilots who had baled out or crashed into the sea. which increased our enthusiasm for the minor but important role we were being trained for. To prepare aircrew for flying duties involved lengthy and costly training and it was essential to have an efficient rescue service to save as many lives as it was humanly possible to do, but with a lamentable lack of foresight for a sea-encompassed nation, the need for such had not been envisaged in the early stages of the war. The whole question of Air/Sea Rescue had been sadly neglected until it became all too obvious during the Battle of Britain and at Dunkirk, that a large number of our scarce resources of fighter pilots were being lost through drowning, who might well have been saved with better facilities. Before dinghies were standard issue, their survival time in the water was only as long as they could remain afloat in their Mae Wests. Aircraft from their own squadron might mount a search and if located, the nearest sea-going vessel in the vicinity would be contacted to pick up the survivor, or sometimes the local lifeboat would be called out, if within a reachable distance of the shore.

The first steps towards a co-ordinated rescue organisation were soon taken when it became known that over 200 aircrew had been lost in the area of the English Channel by mid-July 1940. Assuming that a percentage of those reported 'Missing' sank in their aircraft, unable to get out in time, or already mortally wounded, it can still only remain conjecture how many might have ejected safely, with or without dinghies, only to succumb in the end to dehydration, exposure, exhaustion, starvation or just the hopelessness of not being found. But fully functional units were not operational until well into 1941. The RAF were allotted the task of controlling air searches with Lysander and Walrus aircraft based at intermittent coastal airfields around our shores and the Royal Navy were responsible for directing the operations of the High Speed Launches based at naval ports - they performed regular patrols and could be directed to the position of a 'ditched' pilot. These Marine Craft Units formed a chain around the coast with an important centre at Dover.

We had been at war for over a year before this amount of progress had been achieved, whereas the German Air/Sea Rescue 'Seenotdienst' was an efficiently run organisation prior to the outbreak of the war, geared to maximise the chances of survival. The Luftwaffe High Command had realised the importance of retrieving trained aircrew from the sea to fight again and their satisfactory recovery rate was a great boost to the morale of their pilots. By mid-1940, German A/S/R units were soon established at the newly captured Channel Ports operating Heinkel 59 Float 'planes, in conjunction with fast rescue launches and their pilots were issued with one-man dinghies, many months before similar types were supplied to the RAF. The Germans pioneered several ingenious pieces of equipment to aid recovery - the bright yellow scull cap pilot's wore, could be more easily spotted bobbing up and down in the sea and they were supplied with a fluorescent dye for staining the water around the dinghy a vivid green, also clearly visible from the air by the regular patrols on the look-out for 'ditched' pilots. In fact, the German Air/Sea Rescue service picked up more British and Commonwealth aircrew in the early years, than our own inadequate recovery service and although they spent several years behind the wire of PoW camps, they did at least survive.

With the ever increasing air traffic flying over the water ways, it became a matter of extreme urgency for the rescue facilities to be improved and expanded to cope with the large number of Allied bombers, often with fighter escorts, who might crash land on the sea after returning from round-the-clock raids to all parts of Occupied Europe and deep into Germany too. In addition to attack from German fighters, they encountered heavy coastal and inland flak from well-defended targets and as one pilot aptly said "The Ack Ack was the heaviest I have ever seen. You would not think an aircraft could fly through it without being cut to pieces." It was no longer just a single fighter pilot who might need rescuing, but a bomber crew of 7/10 men.

Gradually, the service became more efficient - increased numbers of faster launches with trained crews, were put into action - life jackets were improved and in addition to the single rubber dinghy, which inflated automatically on hitting the water, came the larger tent-type dinghy with a tarpaulin cover, big enough to accommodate a whole bomber crew. These were equipped with emergency rations, water purifying tablets, signalling flares, protective clothing etc. Trained Rescue Officers ran special courses for aircrew to improve their chance of survival after abandoning their aircraft. The time factor was crucial because once an aircraft hit the water, the weight of the engine alone, soon made it submerge into the depths. Radios on aircraft had an emergency push button Channel for transmitting a Mayday distress call before baling out - providing there was time - and if the radio was still in a serviceable condition. Aircrews were also given advice on various ways of evading capture, should they parachute down over enemy territory. Those first few hours were also vital because there was always the chance of being found by a member of the Resistance in Occupied Countries and whisked away to a 'safe house' before the Germans were able to track him down, and then joining an escape line back to England.

Peter Noble - Beaufighter pilot 254 Sqd.

I thoroughly enjoyed the work part of the course at Cranwell - there was so much to learn and most of it completely different from anything I had ever done before but the rigid discipline was a bit hard to stomach. I was put on more 'charges' in the two months I spent there, than the rest of my four years' service. Peter Noble, the Beaufighter pilot I'd known in civvie street, was stationed at North Coates, near Grimsby - about 40 miles from Cranwell - and when he got a few days leave, he came over to see me and stayed at the Officers Mess on Camp. Keeping up with the work on the course had kept me fully occupied and I'd had little time to visit the places of interest in the area. On his first day, Peter and I went into Sleaford, had a walk down by the river and dinner at the Lion Hotel. The next day I wasn't free until early evening but we headed for Lincoln, where we had a look around the impressive Cathedral, dined at the Great Northern Hotel, ending with drinks at the Saracen's Head - a favourite haunt of aircrew from the many bomber aerodromes in Lincolnshire and the 'boys in blue' were there in force that night. On Peter's last day, we went into Sleaford and took a train to Boston - it was a lovely May day and we sat in the park all afternoon - I don't remember him sending me the photos my diary tells me he took. From there he caught the 7 p.m. train up the coast to North Coates.

When I got back to Cranwell, I was told that I was in trouble and had been reported for walking hand-in-hand with an RAF Officer within the Camp area. I really thought someone was pulling my leg and at first I didn't believe them but it was true - somewhere in that vast RAF Manual of umpteen 'Rules and Regs' it stipulates that Officers and 'other ranks' should be 16 inches (or was it 18?) apart at all times on RAF establishments. The fact that I had only been in the WAAF's for a few months and had never had a sight of, let alone a chance to study my subservient status in the Air Force Commandments, was apparently no grounds for extenuating circumstances and being a first offence, did not warrant being let off with a caution either. At Cranwell, discipline was strictly by the book and I was hauled before the 'Queen Bee' to receive my punishment for such 'improper behaviour'. When the charge was read out, I was asked if I wanted to say anything in my own defence. I took a deep breath, giving me extra courage to ask if the other party in this 'hand-holding' crime would be similarly charged. I was told not to be impertinent and I could see she was annoyed that I had had the audacity to speak out, which was no doubt the reason I was given a rather severe punishment for such a trivial matter - three days Confined to Camp and 14 days privileges stopped, which meant being deprived of attending any camp dances or entertainment. When I told Peter over the 'phone, he thought it a bit steep and rather unfair but I didn't expect or get much sympathy from him. He only offered to come over and hold my other hand while I was doing my fatigues!

In defiant mood, I wasn't going to miss Garland's 21st birthday celebrations and a few days later I sneaked out of camp without a pass. Garland, Mary and I caught the bus into Sleaford, where we had a slap up meal and a few drinks. Then we walked to Leasingham to a dance where we met some RAF fellas from Cranwell and when the dance ended, they helped me get back into Camp by the 'back door' - in other words, under the barbed wire! So much for RAF security during war-time, eh? That little unofficial outing went undetected but I came unstuck over a couple of others. I continued attending Camp dances while still 'serving my sentence' - S.P's (Special Police) used to pay regular visits during the evening, and their presence made recalcitrant offenders like me hot under the collar but with so many personnel at Cranwell, they would not have known by sight, those who ought not to have been there. It was imperative though to be back in the billet and under the bedclothes by 9.30 p.m. when the 'duty waller' came round to check that you were being a good girl and conforming to the punishment - then when they were out of sight, I emerged again from the bed fully clothed and back to the dance. WAAF's were billeted in the two-storey houses of the pre-war Married Quarters and we had ways and means of quick exits and entries via the back garden and holes in the fences

- all a bit of a lark really! One evening however, a 'keen-type' Corporal decided to do a double check and returned at 10 o'clock and my bed was empty. I had to admit it was a fair cop and of course it meant another charge. 'One damn thing after another' I complained to my diary.

We were tested quite often and at various stages through the course and I managed to stay in the top half but when competing with a clever dick-ess, who in one test got 90% in one subject and 98% in the other, I always felt I was struggling, only managing an average 76%. In another test, I was joint top of the class with 92% and I have no doubt the other one was 'clever clogs'.

In our gang at Cranwell, we had another little ruse going which had been working well right until the final week of the course. On early morning Parade, we used to take it in turns to answer 'Present' for each other, so that a couple of us could have a longer lay-in or a last minute swat before a test. During the last week the system broke down and I was marked 'Absent' because the person who should have replied . . . didn't! She probably forgot who she ought to have been saying 'Present' for. We often wondered why the person in charge, never counted the number of WAAF's on Parade, to see if they tallied with the number on their list - but they never did.

My misdemeanors were beginning to snowball and I was again summoned to appear before Miss Deal at 13.15 and Miss Dawson at 15.30 the same afternoon to receive sentencing for my last two offences. In the morning, we had had our end of term results and whatever punishment they meted out, nothing could dampen the elation I felt at having got through the course with quite respectable marks. Between the two Queen B . . . . 's I was given 'jankers' and Confined to Camp for two days, which meant that I wouldn't be able to go on leave the next day with the rest of my course, but would have to spend an extra day at Cranwell until 24.00 hours. My fatigues included cleaning the upstairs of the Guard Room, scraping black paint off Miss Jones' window and scrubbing out the coal bunker! There were some right twisted minds in authority in the Air Force who thought up some of these absurd punishments - polishing dustbin lids was another. I wasn't supervised while doing the coal bunker chore, so I just threw a bucket of water over the floor and stayed out of sight having a crafty fag. Another favourite fatigue was cleaning out the ablutions - I'm glad I was spared that.

I just do not know how I managed to end up in the top seven at the end of our course, with all the distractions I had to cope with, when I knew I ought to be studying. No. 1 WAAF sister used to cycle over from Digby aerodrome to see me quite often and I don't suppose she realised how many times she interrupted my good intentions. No doubt she wanted to keep a watchful eye on how little sister was coping in the Services and whether I was behaving myself. I bet I never told her the half of it! One of my favourite expressions was "I'll worry about that tomorrow" - Scarlett O'Hara's philosophy in "Gone With the Wind". Those who failed the course by a small margin were given a second chance by repeating it all again with the following course. Perish the thought of having to spend another 2-months at Cranwell, I wrote! The failures were re-classified to another trade. Being one of the lucky seven who got over 60% in our final exams, we were automatically promoted from Aircraft Woman 2nd Class to A.C.W. 1st Class - the first rung up the ladder of promotion but even more welcome, a slight improvement in the pay stakes.

On the morning of Thursday 27 May 1943, all the 'good girls' in our class were allowed to go home on leave and those left behind reluctantly bade them farewell. Among the naughty were a few being punished for coming in only half an hour late from our Passing Out Parade Dance (not among the guilty that time') and the nasty Queen B . . .'s were not allowing them to leave until 5.30p.m. My opinion of WAAF Admin. Officers inexorably 'soured' from then on, plus my own experience at their hands. Petty deprivations to try to instil discipline, usually had the reverse effect by producing unco-operative rebels and that is probably the reason I became one!

While I was just killing time that last day with absolutely nothing to do, I called in at the C.D Office to try and discover my posting destination. At some stage on the course, I believe we were asked to state a preference for a posting but I couldn't remember where I had applied for. Not that it usually made a lot of difference because if you asked for a posting to the south of England - you were more than likely to be sent to the north of Scotland. After all my recent problems, I just could not believe my good fortune when I was told I had been posted to Kenley in Surrey and that marvellous news cheered me up no end and made having to spend an extra day at Cranwell tolerable. Kenley was one of the most famous fighter aerodromes in the country and still in the forefront of operational activities in Fighter Command - within reasonable access of home too.

I had been corresponding with another pre-WAAF boyfriend I had met in London - a Canadian Sgt. Pilot called Stanley Atkinson from Kapuskasing, Northern Ontario. He was a Wellington pilot, stationed in Yorkshire, so didn't come south very often. He had arranged his leave to coincide with mine at the end of my course so I was very much looking forward to that . . . if only I could get away from this wretched place! We tried to plead and cajole the Guard Room 'bods' into giving us our clearance and railway warrants early because it was such a waste of time idling about but they would not relent. No doubt the Queen B. . . .'s gave strict instructions not to allow us to leave until midnight . . . and midnight it was. I can't remember why Vera and Vi were being kept back but the three of us were really 'cheesed-off' at the petty mindedness of making us stay until the bitter end, that we ordered a taxi to be at the Camp gates at one minute past midnight, for a quick get-away. It cost us thirty shillings but well worth not having to stay there any longer than was necessary. At Grantham Station, I saw Vera and Vi off on their north-bound train and then I waited in the Church Army Canteen for the London train which was due at 1.18 a.m. I can still recall the joy and utter relief, when the train began to get up steam as it left Grantham Station, that I was finally escaping from Cranwell and those beastly Queen B. . . 's with their nasty stings! When I got to Kings Cross, I had to wait an hour there for the Underground trains to start but a kind S.P. helped me with my kitbag and took me for a welcome cup of tea in their office, as nowhere else was open at that early hour. I eventually arrived home at Wembley about 6 a.m. and headed straight for bed as I was shattered from the events of the previous 24 hours and lack of a night's sleep.

****

I did attempt to find the correct clause in the RAF Manual for my 'sin' of holding hands with an officer - I felt sure that a similar restriction would still be in force today to prevent close contact between the sexes while walking about Camp. I 'phoned Wattisham, my nearest RAF establishment and spoke to an airman in the Guard Room but when I explained the information I was seeking, I believe he thought I was 'having him on'. I suggested he ask the Duty Sergeant and I would ring back later. When I did so, he announced (I thought with some degree of satisfaction. that he'd found an easy solution which didn't involve him in any aggro:) - "In them days" he told me "it would have been King's Regulations - we only have Queen's Regulations now". I pointed out to the 'not very bright' young man that when there was a change of monarch, they didn't change all the rules - they just changed the title from King to Queen's Regulations! And that was as far as I got with that . . . .

Chapter 3

EN ROUTE FOR KENLEY

How tranquil it was to be able to relax at home after the pace of my troubled life at Cranwell but I had already forfeited one of my precious seven days leave for my sins. I also caught up on my lost night's sleep and by the morning post, I had a letter from Stan suggesting a time to meet him in London the following afternoon. In those days, Wembley was a very pleasant suburb of London in which to live. The garden of our house backed on to the large G.E.C. Sports Ground, which was the length and breadth of several football pitches and the G.E.C. factory area bordered the opposite side. Earlier in the war, while I was still living at home, the G.E.C. complex had a miraculous escape during a German air-raid - the first bomb dropped on the North Wembley side, missing the Wrigley Spearmint Factory and the next cluster of bombs dropped diagonally across the sports ground, causing five or six craters from corner to corner and just missed the G.E.C. Factory. As far as I remember it was an early morning raid and as the explosion of each bomb came nearer and louder, we really thought our end had come! The G.E.C. Sports Pavilion wasn't hit either - it was a sturdy brick-built building and had been requisitioned for occupation by a platoon of Irish Fusiliers. During 1941/2 my local girl friends and I were often invited to dances there and we got to know quite a few of these lads who weren't much older than we were - when I was 'sweet sixteen' I had a crush on an Irish charmer called Michael O'Brien Tippett - a name that just seemed to roll off the tongue. It was an extraordinary coincidence that I would meet up with him again in Hastings in 1943.

My leave did not run as smoothly as planned. When Canadian Stan Atkinson arranged his leave to coincide with mine, I didn't think there was any chance of Peter being in London, as in his letters he had only recently had a leave. I met Stan as arranged and the following morning I received a telegram from Peter asking me to meet him at Kings Cross at 6 p.m. as he had got a 48hr. pass and I was supposed to be meeting Stan at 5.30. I don't quite remember how I wriggled out of that tricky situation but Peter only had two days and I spent some time with each, so it must have sorted itself out, as I was still writing and receiving letters from both afterwards.

When it was time to head for Kenley, my young brother Derrick helped me with my kit-bag as far as London Bridge. It was not a direct route from Preston Road, with several changes so I was grateful for his help. At London Bridge I met Doris Martin, who was on my course at Cranwell and we travelled down together, spending the first night at Kenley 'A' Camp, the name for the main part of the airfield. It was inevitable that Kenley and Biggin Hill would be singled out for attack by the Luftwaffe and both aerodromes were raided frequently in the early war years. Kenley suffered considerable damage but still managed to remain functional. They were dangerous times for RAF personnel on any aerodrome on the south coast.

Since the outbreak of the war in 1939, the Air Force in its wisdom had been acquiring premises in and around Kenley and many RAF staff were being housed in requisitioned civilian billets, scattered over a wide area - a precautionary measure against possible loss of life of skilled personnel from air-raids when concentrated in one place. A shop in the main Caterham shopping area was already being used as a mock Operations Room for training Ops Room staff and this became temporary accommodation for Kenley Sector Operations Room, while the more permanent premises of "The Grange" at Old Coulsdon were being suitably converted. It was from the temporary Caterham shop premises that RAF operations were controlled during the crucial months of August and September 1940 at the height of the Battle of Britain. Air Chief Marshal Dowding, Lord Beaverbrook and Winston Churchill were among those who visited at various times to observe first hand the progress of the Battle. Passers-by doing their shopping, would have been very surprised had they known what was going on behind those closed doors in Godstone Road.

The other 'sprogs' and I spent our first day at Kenley running around getting our 'arrival' chits signed and we were told to report for duty the following morning at the Ops Room at "The Grange", Old Coulsdon, about three-quarters of a mile from Main Camp. It was a rambling old 17th century Manor House, used as the local court-house but since 1940, became the Kenley Sector Operations Room.

We duly reported at 09.30 at the Reception Desk where RAF Military Police were on duty, vetting all those who entered and we assembled there waiting for someone to show us around. The centre of the first floor had been removed, leaving a perimeter gallery where the Controller and nine of his staff could see at a glance the overall picture on the Ops Room table below, which was a giant map of the south-east corner of England, divided into sections with grid reference numbers - known as No. 11 Group. There were about a dozen WAAF's positioned around the table, receiving up-to-date information from various sources, such as the Observer Corps, Filter Room, Radar plots and D/F Station 'fixes' on RAF squadrons. Plotters wore head-phones and chest mouth-pieces and transferred the information they

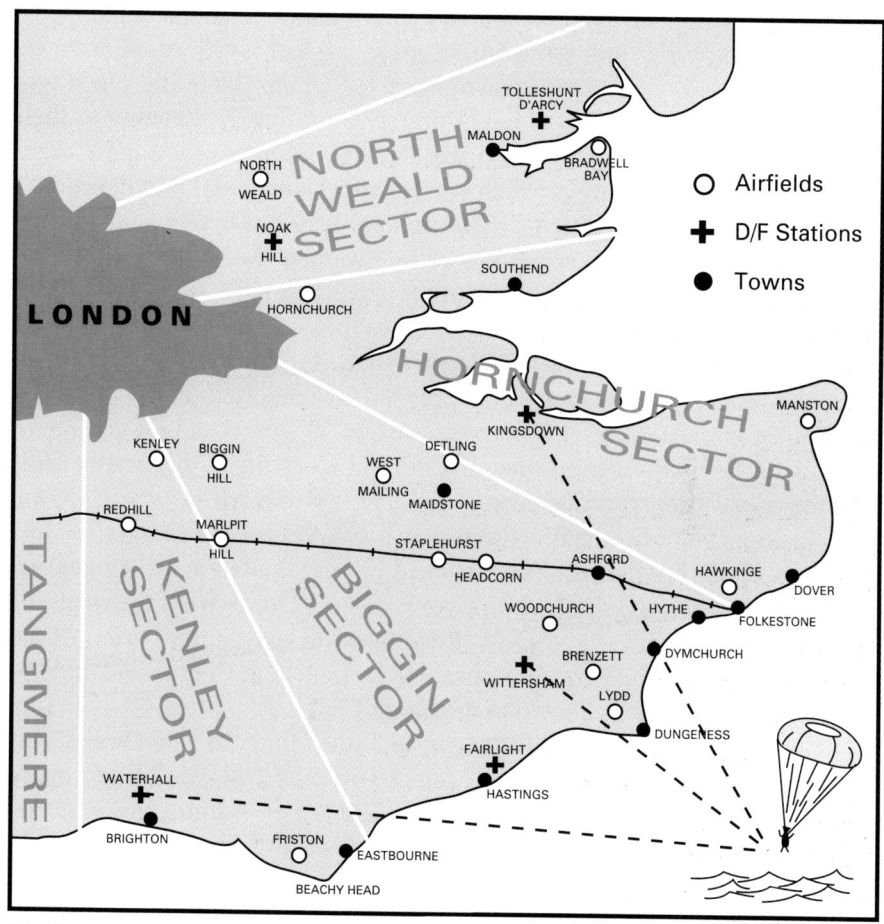

No. 11 Group Sector Map

were given on to the table, wielding their croupier type magnetic rods. All raids were numbered and the strength and height of approaching enemy aircraft were identified on the markers by 'H' (for hostile) or little swastikas and our own aircraft were shown as 'F' (for friendly) with the number of the squadron. Allied aircraft were fitted with the IFF device (identification friend or foe), which altered the shape of the 'blip' on a radar screen, so the operators could distinguish between friendly and enemy aircraft. This was standard practice by 1942 and any doubtful radar 'blips' were classified as 'bogeys' - unidentified aircraft. Fortunately Britain had a head start in radar development and managed to maintain that superiority throughout the war years.

This was my first glimpse of how an Operations Room functioned - D/F operators were under the jurisdiction of Kenley Signals Officer, Sqd./Ldr. Howard, who sat on the right of the Controller. The place was buzzing with industrious 'bods' intent on the job in hand, attending to their own part in the overall operation. I was suitably impressed and quite eager to join this large organisation which was playing such a vital role in the war. We were witnessing a very busy morning of Ops Room activity and no-one seemed to have the time to spare to deal with us then, so we were allowed to go home. On our return 36 hours later, decisions had been made as to where we were going - some WAAF's were being posted to D/F Stations right away but I was rather pleased to be staying and working at "The Grange" to learn a bit more about the Ops Room procedure. I reported for duty the next morning at 07.30 hours and became part of 'B' crew. The Ops Room complex was spread over an area around Old Coulsdon - the nearby Golf Clubhouse had been commandeered and that was our Mess, where we ate and where dances were held. There was a NAAFI within the golf course grounds and our billets were requisitioned private houses in an unmade up road alongside and overlooking the golf course. Guess what the name of my house was called . . . . 'Cranwell Cottage'? I am just not going to be allowed to forget! The Orderly Room was in Coulsdon Court Road and the whole establishment was known as 'C' Camp.

Things were looking up I thought, as I got settled in - this was a vast improvement over life in huts on Main Camp and I could foresee many advantages - a lot more freedom for a start and not an Admin. Queen B . . . in sight! As we were working shifts, including night duty, it was impractical to enforce any sort of curfew on us, all spread out in different houses and there would be less disturbance for sleep after night duty than in a camp hut - we might even be able to have a lay-in on our day off - a perk not allowed in a hut, where all beds had to be made and 'biscuits' and bedding stacked for daily inspection.

At 'The Grange' we worked in a room off the Controller's gallery, listening to the intercom channels and writing down in abbreviated long-hand the instructions and rapport between the Controller and fighter pilots. The following are a few examples:-

'Are you receiving me?' was written down as . . . . 'R U R Me'
A = Angels = height in thousand feet. A15.
'Bandits at 10,000ft. Can you see them?' as . . 'Bdts at A10 - Can U C them?'
'Message received and understood. Listening out' as . 'Msg rcd & u/std. L/O'
A lot of it was repetitive jargon and it didn't take long to get the hang

of it, inserting obvious abbreviations of anything unusual as you went along. Being a stenographer, I was often tempted to revert to shorthand but no-one else would have been able to decipher it. Swear words were either included as a blank or the first and last letter, with dots in between. Before long, we had a complete vocabulary of the current swear words in use on both sides of the Atlantic, as the intercom we most frequently listened to was on the Canadian squadrons in the two Spitfire Fighter Wings in No. 11 Group - Nos. 401, 403,* 411, 412, 416* and 421*. Those marked * belonged to the Canadian Wing at Kenley and during the Spring and Summer of 1943 were led by Wing Commander 'Johnnie' E. Johnson. Wing Leaders had their own aircraft with their initials painted on the fuselage, as well as their own personal call-sign. 'Johnnie' Johnson's was GREYCAP which he used throughout the war and we always knew when he was leading the Wing.

Joan Wedgbury was logging the intercom when W/Cdr. Paddy Finucane was shot down in July 1942. He was one of our most famous and highly decorated fighter Aces and received a lot of publicity in the press. He was leading his Wing during a large mass attack by fighters on targets in France and as he flew low over a machine-gun post, the gunner got in a lucky shot which punctured the radiator of his Spitfire. Almost immediately the engine temperature began to rise and was turning too slowly for him to gain height. He reached the Channel but was too low to bale out and he was seen to open his sliding hood, in readiness for an attempted crash landing on the water but the Spitfire sank like a stone, allowing no time for Finucane to get out. The crash may have knocked him unconscious. On his way to the target, Joan heard him say "Take the right target, chaps. Here we go" and the last message she logged was "This is it, chaps". His fellow pilots circled the sea for a long time afterwards but all that surfaced was a slowly widening streak of oil which floated on the water. He was only 22 and in his short and eventful career as a Spitfire pilot, he had been awarded the D.S.O., D.F.C., and 2 bars and in two years combat he shot down at least 32 enemy aircraft which was the highest score to date in 1942, although this was equalled by 'Sailor' Malan the following year and was ultimately surpassed by our own 'Johnnie' Johnson who, by the end of the war had notched up 38 enemy aircraft.

We were within easy walking distance of the Ops Room and on my first day, I was on morning shift and night duty from 20.30 hours until 07.30 the next morning. I can't remember how many WAAF'S were on each crew for the whole Ops Room but I was told they used to assemble for duty and march in a squad along the streets to 'The Grange' until one day they were strafed by a marauding Luftwaffe fighter and suffered some casualties. Thereafter, staff were instructed to make their own way on duty.

At the top of 'The Grange' were several attic bedrooms which contained a couple of RAF issue beds, where WAAF's during their break on night duty could have a wee kip for an hour or so. There were bars across the windows of these rooms which may have been used as a nursery in days gone by. Joan Wedgbury well remembers the commotion she caused up there one night. She was reading a book about the Spanish Inquisition and nodded off to sleep still thinking about the dreadful tortures they inflicted on prisoners. She dreamt she was being put into a wooden cage with bars, which was being lifted off the ground when she woke up, repeatedly crying out "I am innocent". The Army had a Liaison Room on the same floor and when one of the soldiers rushed in to find out what all the shouting was about, he found Joan standing at the window with her 'passion killer' knickers showing below her WAAF shirt, trying to prize open the bars to escape! Others had also heard the commotion and when they arrived on the scene, they found the soldier with his arms around Joan and not realising that he was only trying to calm her down, jumped to the obvious but wrong conclusion that he was forcing his attentions on her and she was shouting for help! The poor soldier must have been equally bewildered when he was dragged away from Joan, who was still not wide enough awake to realise what was happening. In typical Air Force fashion, an official enquiry over the rumpus was called for, which Joan and the soldier had to attend. She had to produce the book as evidence and the relevant chapter was read out which satisfactorily explained the whole matter and the soldier was fully exonerated but the Board of Enquiry had difficulty in stifling the sniggers at the picture it all conjured up in their minds!

There were plenty of places to visit in the area on our days off and we used to get invited to Canadian Army Dances at Lingfield, with transport provided there and back. Somewhere in the vicinity was a place we frequented, called the Cider Mill and my verdict on the fairly potent brew they sold was 'pretty hot stuff', which they were not supposed to sell to the Canadians, my diary informed me. At the Britannia Club in Croydon in 1943, I had a meal of pork sausages, new potatoes, fresh garden peas, followed by strawberries and cream, all for 'a bob' (one shilling or five new pence). The aptly named 'Kitbag' was another haunt. Dances were often held at the Golf Club for Kenleyites and after one of these 'Do's', I was escorted home on a warm moonlit summer night by a Canadian called Bernard who wanted to show me the 19th hole on the golf course. (Being unfamiliar with that sport, I didn't find out until much later that there were only 18!). Maybe that is why it took us until 3 a.m. to reach the door of my billet.

[In my diaries, I frequently omitted to mention the surnames of many people I met and now that I am delving into my past in some detail, it is probably just as well there can be no positive proof of identity!]

Working in the Ops Room at Old Coulsdon and living in private billets, it was seldom necessary to go to Main 'A' Camp, except for collecting railway warrants, passes or to see the M.O. or dentist. My next visit there, was when I was being sent on an internal posting to one of Kenley's D/F Stations at Wittersham, a small village just north of Rye.

Chapter 4

EVERY DAY A FIELD DAY

I was the only WAAF being posted to Wittersham so I had to find my own way and after leaving Rye Station with my kitbag, I didn't know quite how to get there as the buses weren't very frequent. Eventually I hitched a lift in an RAF Regiment car and without the help of the driver, I might never have found the place as the D/F Tower was in the middle of field, some way beyond the village.

Joan Wedgbury

Eileen Bond

Joan Wedgbury and Eileen Bond were already installed at Wittersham a few weeks before I arrived and I was put in their billet. They were among the first batch of WAAF's who were sent to replace the airmen for overseas duties. The RAF D/F operators were mostly in the older age group, many of whom were married and being in civilian billets at Wittersham, their wives would have been allowed to stay or visit frequently. They weren't going to relinquish this comparatively cushy war-time number for unknown destinations abroad if they could help it and they thought by causing as much mayhem as they dared to the equipment and setting all the dials wrongly, that women would be found incapable of doing their job and they'd be allowed to stay. Good try fellas - but it didn't work!

The small circular D/F Tower was situated in a field on high ground, as the additional height extended our reception range. We also manned two mobile trucks with 'H' type aerials protruding from the roof, known as Green Tender and A/S/R 111 and these units gave us facilities to be operational on three different frequencies at once. The work places were rather cramped but we also had a larger brick-built Rest Hut in the same field, equipped with a couple of camp beds, a coke/wood stove which, if we could make it really glow, made excellent toast for supper - or a missed breakfast. With a lot of patience, we could also heat soup or things like baked beans on it but when you were really hungry, it seemed to take forever. We also had tea making facilities and a table and chairs, where many a game of Canasta was played.

The Rest Hut - Wittersham (20 years later)

From the Rest Hut, we would get a summons by telephone to man the Tower or mobile trucks at any time of the day or night and when it was extremely urgent, such as a Mayday call, like the pilots, we 'scrambled'. The equipment we used was a dial controlled Receiver Set R.1132, about 6ft. high in three sections, with the power unit below. If the mains supply failed, we also had accumulators to provide standby power. We sat at a sturdy table top bench, operating a horizontal wheel about the size of a truck steering wheel, which rotated the aerials. Above this was a solid wooden sensing plate, slightly smaller than the wheel, which when turned 10 degrees off the dead space, was pressed down. If the signal reduced in volume, the bearing was 'correct' (not true which could mislead as being True North). If the signal increased in volume, then the bearing was a reciprocal, i.e. 180° out. Over the sensing plate was the cursor wheel divided into 360°. The cone above held the lower shaft bearing and there was another one in the top of the Tower holding the upper bearing. The sensing plate controlled mechanically operated switches - when the plate was depressed, this caused the reflector switches to open, physically reducing the length of the reflectors and if they were no longer reflecting, the signal strength dropped, indicating a correct bearing. Sometimes if the transmission was almost beyond our range or from a low flying aircraft, then we would only receive a faint signal and if we were uncertain whether we had a correct bearing or not, we would say so. Invariably, one of the other D/F Stations would be nearer to the aircraft and be able to give a positive bearing from a louder signal. To change the frequency, we inserted a four digit crystal somewhere in the range of 5750 / 6537.5 / 6612.5 K/cs etc. as far as I can remember.

We worked three regular shifts - afternoon from 13.30 to 21.00 hours.

D/F Tower in a field

Direction/Finding Equipment - Receiver Set (Photo M. Howard)

Next morning from 08.30 to 13.30 and then on night duty the same day from 21.00 hours to 08.30 a.m. This was our day off but mostly we had to catch up on lost sleep first and then we were free until afternoon shift the next day. These hours were flexible between ourselves - if someone wanted to go to a dance and come late on duty, the afternoon shift would stay on. The D/F Station was manned 24 hours a day and any crew on duty were obligated to stay until they were relieved.

We could not transmit or speak to pilots - we could only receive the intercom transmitted between the Controller and the pilots and at the same time as taking a bearing, we logged what that bearing was in a record book. We had earphones and a breast-plate mouth piece and by a direct land line, we were permanently in touch with a WAAF in the Operations Room at Kenley and later Biggin Hill. The bearing we took on the pilot's voice transmission would give the direction from our Tower at Wittersham and the aircraft sending the signal would lie somewhere along that line. On a pre-arranged frequency and at the same time, two other D/F Stations in the Sector would do likewise and these bearings were passed to the Triangulator Room in the parent Sector Operations Room and displayed on a Triangulator Table - the point of intersection of these direction lines would give the position of the aircraft. The resultant 'fix' was then immediately passed to a plotter seated around the Ops Room table, who would place a relevant marker in the appropriate reference grid square. The Controller in the gallery above would then know exactly where his squadron aircraft were. If an aircraft was lost or uncertain of his position, the pilot would ask for a 'fix' and if every section was 'on the ball' a pilot was often given a Vector to steer within a minute of asking for it. Maydays were given priority and we concentrated on taking a bearing on every transmission until the pilot abandoned his aircraft.

During the winter months, it was often bitterly cold working in those unheated Mobile Trucks, especially during the night and we would sit huddled in a blanket to keep warm - or with a hot water bottle, if we'd had time to fill one before a summons. There were often animals in the field - either sheep or cows and in the black-out we never knew whether we might stumble on a squatting animal or step in what they had left behind. A moonlit night was always welcome. Sometimes we were up to our ankles in mud crossing the field and it was six months before we were issued with battledress tunic and trousers and Wellies. Around dawn if all was quiet, we were often on the verge of dozing off - then the cows would begin to stir and our trucks were a favourite place for them to have their early morning scratch. They would give a vigorous and prolonged heave-ho on the corner and almost rock the truck on to two wheels, giving the occupant inside a bit of a fright. They never actually managed to overturn it, although we always expected they would eventually.

Direction/Finding equipment with operator (Photo M. Howard)

Our toilet facilities on duty were very primitive - a non-flush Elsan portable, in a partition inside the passage between the outer brick wall barricade and the Tower. It was the chore of the morning shift to empty it. Two WAAF's could be seen crossing the field every morning carrying the unsavoury container by its handles and those with weak stomachs (nearly all of us!) would tie a large handkerchief under their nose, dabbed with a little perfume. We also had to dig our own holes to dispose of the contents too. When the first WAAF's arrived they found those spiteful chauvinist airmen had left another unwelcome surprise for them - they had purposely not emptied the Elsan for many days.

I was under training for a short spell before I was allowed to operate by myself and I looked forward to the challenge of every duty because the work was extremely interesting and rewarding. We were all fully dedicated to the job of helping to save pilots' lives and we worked well as a team.

The massive air offensive reached its peak during the summer of 1943 and was a period of maximum activity in Bomber, Coastal and Fighter Commands, as well as the USAAF. Bomber Command often sent a thousand bombers at a time on raids into Occupied Europe and penetrating further into Germany too. The aim was to progressively undermine their military might by constantly and systematically destroying their economic and industrial war capability, before an invasion attempt could have a reasonable chance of successfully liberating the rest of Europe. The type of operation the fighter squadrons were engaged in (and we listened to the intercom of) came under special code names for different types of sorties. The Canadian version is in brackets.

CIRCUS   - a large fighter escort accompanying bombers to Europe, hoping to attract Luftwaffe response (Come out and play)
RAMROD - escort of bombers to or from a target. (Hovering over the heavies)
RODEO   - a fighter sweep for the purpose of destroying enemy fighters. (On the war-path looking for trouble!)
RHUBARB - a small number of fighters engaged in low level attacks on opportune ground targets.(Trimming the trees with your radiator and catching French girls cami-knickers off the clothes line with your tail wheel!)

    During sweeps over enemy occupied territory, any target was lawful prey to marauding fighter pilots - swooping low over Jerry Aerodromes and raking their aircraft on the ground with cannon and machine gun fire - destroying canal barges - train busting - dodging high tension cables, hedge-hopping or flying 'on the deck' to avoid ground defences and Radar detection. On the way home they might look for E-boats and other shipping in coastal ports or out in the Channel. At high speed, spontaneous re-actions and great skill were needed to perform such feats - all adding to the exhilaration of being able to exercise personal initiative in the face of danger.
    When escorting bombers to long range destinations, Spitfires did not have the fuel capacity to stay with them all the way to target - they would turn back, refuel and rendezvous with the bombers on withdrawal. This meant that fighter pilots would often fly over the hostile waters of the North Sea/English Channel at least four times a day - maybe more, if on extra ops the same day. Engine trouble, especially glycol leaks and oil pressure problems, were often as common a reason for 'ditching' as being shot down

by enemy fighters or flak. The Air/Sea Rescue Service was increasingly in demand and during July 1943, 196 airmen baled out over the sea and 139 of those were saved. We dealt with the highest number of Mayday calls during the summer and autumn of 1943.

The rescue of one fortunate pilot was due entirely to the excellent hearing of a WAAF on our crew. On 25 July 1943, Eileen Bond was the only person to hear a faint Mayday call on her frequency and a rescue facility was sent out along the direction of that single bearing - he was located and picked up just off the French coast, so Kenley Ops Room told us at the time. Eileen couldn't remember the the call-sign or exact time and all I had entered in my diary when we were on duty that day between 13.00 and 21.00 hours was . . . . "B-crew congratulated. Eileen was the only one to hear a Mayday on a chappie who baled out a few miles off the French coast". On one of my visits to Public Record Office at Kew, I tried to find out who that pilot might have been but there were several 'ditchings' on that particular afternoon, so his identity not satisfactorily established. I found details of four but there may have been more -

1. Sq/Ldr. Jack Charles, the Canadian C.O. of 611 Squadron was rescued despite his proximity to the enemy coast. He baled out after being attacked by German fighters, while escorting bombers to Holland. A dozen pilots of 611 hovered over him until a Walrus arrived to pick him up.
2. 8 aircraft of 411 Sqdn escorted a Walrus from Shoreham in an attempt to rescue a Mustang pilot shot down approx. 11 miles off the French coast at Etretat. After a two hour search the missing pilot could not be found and due to approaching darkness, it was called off.
3. F/O B.W. Anthony of 168 Sqdn. crashed in the English Channel 60 miles south of Selsey Bill at 17.30 - picked up by A/S/R Shoreham.
4. 132 Sqdn. took off at 13.45 and crossed the enemy coast east of Ostend. F/Sgt. Rupert W. Munson's Spitfire was hit by flak but he managed to get 12 miles out to sea before being forced to bale out. After about 3 hours in his dinghy, he was picked up by Naval launches and spent the night at Manston before returning to his base.

It was unlikely to have been No. 1, as with all that activity over his dinghy, other D/F stations would have heard the Maydays transmitted by the pilots watching over him. (Two months previously, Sq/Ldr. Jack Charles had shared the prize of shooting down Biggin Hill's 1,000th Hun with Cdt.

Rene Mouchotte - on page 48). If it was a High Speed Launch that picked up F/O Anthony, Nos 2 & 3 might have been the same rescue. No. 4 also a probable candidate.

Four bombers were also reported missing on 25 July, presumed lost at sea.

During the war, the 'powers that be' never told any particular section more than they thought they needed to know and on D/F Stations, we were only given the call-sign of the squadrons we were to work on - never the squadron number, or the names of any of the pilots. We would be asked to listen out for call-signs such as Delta, Sunrise, Bambi or Keyboard aircraft and squadrons were divided into Red, Blue, Yellow or White Sections. From little pieces of information, we were able to put a lot of 'two and two's' together and some of the various accents we heard were fairly easy to identify. There were only two French fighter squadrons at that time and we had no difficulty in recognising the excitable Polish chatter when their squadrons were airborne. It was the squadrons of the two Canadian Wings that we regularly listened to and I soon linked up a few of their names because my eldest WAAF sister was a plotter in Digby Operations Room and had met quite a few of them. Some of the Canadian squadrons were stationed there before coming south to Kenley and Biggin Hill Sectors. During a scrap in the air, they would sometimes let a christian or surname slip out, and I recorded several times when two of the most well-known Spitfire pilots of the Kenley Wing were airborne - Buck McNair and 'Screwball' Beurling. In fact, I was on duty and involved with Sq./Ldr. Buck McNair's Mayday when he baled out on 28 July 1943 and my sister remembers me telling her afterwards what I had heard him say just before he went down. I think she had a bit of a crush on him at Digby! He was the C.O of 421 and the squadron had taken off from Manston just after 14.00 hours, acting as withdrawal cover to Fortresses on their return from the Ruhr, to rendezvous over Rotterdam. McNair developed engine trouble when off the coast at Knocke and decided to turn back. P/O Tommy Parks escorted him as he left the Wing but at 20,000ft. he began to lose height and when they got as far as 12 miles off

W/Cdr. 'Buck' McNair

the coast at Dunkirk, his engine caught fire - he lost control and his aircraft dived towards the sea. As I was taking the last bearing before he abandoned his Spitfire, his final message was "So long you guys - I'm really gonna get my feet wet this time". I now know that he baled out at only 5,000ft. and fell another few thousand feet while trying to get his parachute to function which took him down to 75ft. and he fell from that height into the sea. His parachute release gear partially fused together and his dinghy had been burned - he was floating in his Mae West. Tommy Parks stayed with him, hovering overhead and giving further Maydays, so other D/F Stations would have got accurate bearings also. Then Spits from 411 relieved Parks, who had been circling McNair for over an hour and was getting low on fuel. Meantime, when the rest of 421 learned that their 'Chief' was down in the 'drink' awaiting rescue, they landed at Manston, refueled and joined the rescue team.

At 13.00 hours, Sq/Ldr. Grace and his Walrus crew from Hawkinge, were 'scrambled' to a position 40 miles east north-east of North Foreland, escorted by four aircraft of 501 and McNair's 421 squadron. He was located in a position 30 miles north of Dunkirk and the Walrus landed and picked him up from a very choppy sea. He was burned on his face and very cold. Once safely on board he was stripped of his wet clothing, wrapped in blankets and massaged. Gentian violet was immediately applied to his burns. The Walrus landed back at Hawkinge at 15.20 and after a medical check in Sick Bay, he was later transferred to Canterbury Hospital.

He was obviously a very popular C.O. to warrant such a response from the boys in his squadron who flew back to join in the search but sometimes such a scene of activity alerted the Luftwaffe that an important RAF ace or Senior Commander was being watched over and they have been known to hinder a rescue by intercepting the hoverers and attacking the defenceless pilot in the water, but on this occasion they were unmolested.

Sq./Ldr. Robert Wendell McNair spent two weeks in hospital and returned to his unit quite recovered and in good spirits. He then went to East Grinstead for a further week's convalescence. He realised only too well that he was lucky to have got out of his burning Spitfire in the nick of time and he confided to F/Lt. Douglas Matheson afterwards that he could not have held out much longer in that rough and chilly sea, had not the Walrus arrived so opportunely.

For his meritous war service as a fighter pilot, McNair was awarded the DSO, DFC and 2 bars and was promoted to Wing Commander and later Group Captain but it was in the thick of the fighting at Malta that he proved his worth as a first-rate leader in combat and earned the respect of the pilots he commanded. He wasn't afraid to speak his mind and often did so to his senior officers. McNair served with Laddie Lucas in Malta in 1942 - they were both Flight Commanders in 249 Sqdn. and as well as the frequent combats in the sky against superior Luftwaffe numbers, life on the ground was equally hazardous in those dark days of siege when the Island was subjected to saturation bombing and hardly any supplies were able to get through. It was during one of these raids that Buck McNair narrowly missed being killed. The RAF had requisitioned a hotel in Rabat as quarters for Officers stationed at Takali and the hotel received a direct hit, killing five of their scarce resources of fighter pilots. McNair and two other pilots were returning to the hotel during the raid and along the route, they sheltered in doorways to dodge the debris that was being hurled about. He had just got inside the foyer when the hotel was hit and the blast blew him 20/30ft. up on to the first floor but miraculously he escaped unhurt, although he was engulfed in dust and his uniform was badly ripped. The carnage he encountered on returning to the ground floor was a scene that haunted him for a very long time afterwards - the desperate cries of those with lost limbs and the agonised suffering of the mortally wounded. In fact at one stage, he had even considered using his own revolver to put those about to die, out of their misery because their injuries were so horrific. The two friends who were with him, also survived unscathed.

It was on four consecutive days in July 1943 that the A/S/R service recovered three very experienced and valuable Canadian squadron commanders - two were from 'Johnnie' Johnson's Kenley Spitfire Wing. The D/F crew who were on duty on our day off would have taken part in the rescue of dark, handsome Sq./Ldr. George Keefer, who baled out 5 miles off the French coast on the 27th. His staunch and inseparable friend, Walter Conrad became extremely agitated when he heard Keefer was missing. In the RCAF they were known as the 'inseparable twins' and had recently seen combat together in North Africa. Conrad 'pulled out all the stops' in getting as many aircraft as possible to join in the search and his friend was located and picked up by Walrus late in the evening, none the worse for his dowsing.

During the first week of August 1943, Peter and I had arranged a leave to coincide and I managed to get off morning duty half an hour earlier (big deal!). We were quite busy and the time passed quickly enough. As soon as we got on duty, four Spitfires of 412 (Can.) Sqdn. became airborne at 08.40 on an A/S/R search 8 miles east of Pte. de Barfleur (Cherbourg Peninsula) for a crew of an Albacore aircraft reported down in the sea. They flew

V220 "from Selsey for 15 minutes - altered course to 210" for 4 miles and after searching up and down the coast, they eventually found a dinghy with one occupant, in position WV0900. A Walrus landed in a rough sea and picked up S/Lt. Schofield of 841 Sqdn. Fleet Air Arm, Tangmere, but on take-off an extra heavy sea hit the Walrus and buckled the hull at the pilot's seat. It got back to Shoreham alright despite the serious damage. A search was mounted for the remainder of the Albacore crew but no trace was found.

After that interesting episode, I caught a bus to Rye Station and 'phoned Peter when I got to London Bridge. Then I went home, dumped my 'clobber' changed into civvies and met him at the Duke of Wellington with two of his friends, Ron and Derek. The next day. his brother Harry joined us for lunch at Bush House - then we went back to their parents' apartment for a swim in the Dolphin Square pool, and dinner at Simpson's later on. It turned out to be a busy leave but not particularly eventful. My WAAF friend from Stafford and Cranwell, Garland Skilton was on leave also - she lived at Clapton - we met in Town and went dancing at the Lyceum a couple of evenings. My WAAF sister from Digby came home on a 48 hr. pass and Peter came out to Wembley one day. He was in Coastal Command and I knew he flew with No. 245 Beaufighter squadron, engaged in shipping strikes in the Norwegian Fjords - there was a picture on the front page in one of the daily papers of their Beaufighter Wing in action over the coast of Norway. He hardly ever spoke about his flying operations and when on leave, the best way to try and forget about the war for a while, was to refrain from talking about it.

****

The popular image of fighter pilots driving around in open-top sporty cars, wearing polka-dot cravats, with the top button of their tunics undone, was very far from reality. There was more grit than glamour in the life of a fighter pilot in No. 11 Group - in fact they led rather a nomadic existence and were constantly on the move, flying to airfields such as North Weald, Bradwell Bay, Coltishall, Manston, Hawkinge etc. to join other squadrons when undertaking a large scale operation, or flying to the most convenient 'drome to rendezvous with the bombers they were going to escort.

While I was on leave, 403 and 421 squadrons were 'put out to grass' at Lashenden in Kent, an Advanced Landing Ground (only 8/9 miles from our D/F Station but we didn't know that at the time 'cos we weren't told). They lived in tents, meals were prepared in field kitchens and all maintenance was carried out in the open - including washing and shaving - pilots and ground crew alike, shared the same hardships. The exercise was intended to prepare them for similar conditions when they would be required to occupy temporary airstrips on the Continent while giving air cover to the eventual invasion force. They only stayed there about two weeks when their 'upwardly mobile' skills were put to the test and they had to move, lock, stock and barrel to another A.L.G. at Headcorn, a few miles up the road towards Maidstone, where they stayed for a further two months.

The other Canadian Wing (No.126) comprising 401, 411 and 412 squadrons based at Redhill, were also sent on a similar toughening up course to another A.L.G. at Staplehurst, only about three miles from 127 Wing at Headcorn. During their last week, they were taken on an escape exercise to improve their chance of evading capture, if they were forced down over Occupied Europe. They were taken by truck and dropped off in pairs from various locations around Kent and told to make their way back to base, only speaking French or German and without being detected by the local Army Defence Force, who would be seeking them out as though they were the enemy.

There's nothing the Canadians enjoy more than an initiative challenge and their ingenuity during this exercise caused some embarrassment and red faces in certain quarters! Without wasting any time, some of them chose the shortest route, doing what they knew best. F/O Murchison and P/O Davenport infiltrated Ashford aerodrome and with comparative ease, managed to get into the cockpits of two Spitfires, assisted by two ground crew who apparently did not question or seem to be unduly suspicious that two mute and uncommunicative civilians, except for hand gestures, were making off with two of Ashford's aircraft! When it was realised that two Spits had 'gone missing' there was panic stations at Ashford because it was immediately assumed that German agents were responsible - one of the Spitfires was the latest and most secret Mk.XII type and orders were issued right away to shoot them down. Fortunately, for the two Canadian pilots, their return journey to Staplehurst was only a short flight of some 15 miles and they had landed, even before the truck that had dropped them off got back and before the Ack Ack received orders to fire. F/O D.P. Kelly 'lifted' a Tiger Moth from the same airfield and arrived back at Staplehurst a slightly slower third.

Fl/Lt. W.R. McRae (who I met in Toronto in 1992) was also on the same exercise and this is his personal account of what he likes to call . . . 'The Great Escape Caper' . . .

"Its purpose was to gain experience in, and test our ingenuity at, evading capture. Hopefully it would be of use to us if we ever found ourselves wandering around in France. We wore civilian clothes and were not allowed to communicate with anyone, unless we spoke in French or German. Those selected for the exercise were put into the back of a transport truck, with the canvas sides pulled down so that we couldn't see where we were going. At varying distances and different directions from the airfield, we were dropped off in two's and the objective was to get back to the Intelligence Tent at Staplehurst without being caught.

On the outward journey, I had roughly determined the direction we were going by using the compass from one of my 'escape' buttons. This was the reason for being supplied with these buttons, so I saw nothing unfair in this. I was paired with F/O Tom Kock and we decided to try walking back to our airfield. After a long hike, we found ourselves near the perimeter of the field and to avoid detection, we crawled on our bellies towards the fence but to our dismay, we saw that there were dozens of RAF Regiment types and others inside the entrance gate. Our only chance for success seemed to be to fly in, if we could find an aircraft.

We retreated down a country lane and passed a large house which appeared to be a Headquarters of some sort and there was a 3-ton truck parked in the courtyard - a Commer I believe. I turned to Koky and said "Why don't we try and pinch the truck?" I had just got the cab door open to see if I could get it started, when an Army Sergeant came out of the house. I ducked down behind the truck and held my breath - Koky had smartly disappeared too. After checking around, the Sergeant went back inside. We both got in the truck and I managed to start the engine, the sound of which, made the Sergeant come charging out again. I shoved the gears into reverse and backed out on to the road as fast as I could but in my haste, I scraped the side mirror off on the inevitable stone wall on the opposite side. I could see the Sergeant standing in the middle of the road through the rear mirror - he was waving his arms and shouting but we were well on our way.

I knew there was a back entrance to Staplehurst and thought that perhaps we stood a better chance of getting in that way. As we approached the rear entrance, the RAF Regiment type on duty saw that it was an Army truck and raised the bar but at the same time another RAF guard stepped into the middle of the road, put his hand up, *summoning us to stop. Instead, I leaned on the horn and stepped on the accelerator but in retrospect, it was a foolish thing to do because I might have hurt someone. As we charged through, he jumped aside and dived in the ditch. But we were in and from there it was an easy drive up the side of the north/south runway, across the main runway to the Intelligence Tent, home free . . .!*

When it was all over, W/Cdr. Keith Hodson came up to me and said "Mac, I am asking you to pay for the replacement of the mirror you damaged. The driver is embarrassed enough about losing his truck and I think its the least we can do for him". As I remember, it was only ten bob and needless to say, I was happy to pay up."

Equally audacious was the escapade of Sq./Ldr. Ian Ormston and F/Lt. Douglas Matheson from 412 who, at Headcorn got underneath and into the tent of Group Capt. 'Iron Bill' MacBrien, the C.O. of both Canadian Wings. Douglas Matheson recalls his part in the day's exercise from his diary notes:-

"The object was to inculcate us young fellows with the idea that just because we may have been shot down uninjured 'over there' we should make every effort to evade capture and as a trial run, the pilots of Staplehurst airfield (126 Wing) were to find a way into Headcorn airfield (127 Wing) and vice versa, without being detected. We had great fun that day. Ian and I had been dumped out of the back of the truck somewhere in Kent and we pinched a couple of bicycles, which helped us to reach the vicinity of Headcorn airfield. We were all living in tents at that time and after we sneaked through the barbed wire, we crept under Group Capt. MacBrien's tent and Ormston donned his uniform. As luck would have it, his personal Staff Car was parked outside and I acted as chauffeur. We did consider making off in his personal Spitfire but found it to be too closely guarded. His car, with Insignia was a familiar sight at both airfields and we drove out through the main gate in some style and returned in triumph to Staplehurst where the RAF guard raised the barrier and actually saluted as we drove through unchallenged and no questions asked!!

All in all, it was a welcome break in a very busy summer of operational flights and in less than two months I was able to put that seemingly 'nonsense' training to good effect when I was shot down and dropped by parachute on French soil, successfully evading capture for six months until the Gestapo caught me."

But leaving 'egg' on your G.C's face is a sure way of putting paid to any recommendation for an up-grade in rank and as far as I am aware, Ormston and Matheson 'got no promotion . . . . this side of the ocean!'.

During war-time, all unattended vehicles were supposed to be demobilised when stationary, even to the extent of removing the distributor cap and such lapses were inexcusable. These Canadian pilots ought to have been congratulated and given the highest praise for exposing the deplorable lack of security at military establishments, especially in that vulnerable south-east corner of England, where they should have been more alert!!

During their ten weeks 'In the Field', both Canadian Wings continued their routine operational sorties across the Channel and during Ramrod #249 Sq./Ldr. Ian Ormston reported that his engine had packed up due to glycol failure at 11,000ft. just off the French coast near Dieppe. He glided over the Channel for about 10 miles and baled out at 2,500ft, where he made a parachute descent into the chilly water of the English Channel. He relates the experience:-

"I was told at short notice that I was to take over 411 Sqdn. immediately, so we had a bit of a party that evening and my old friend and C.O., Jeep Neal, asked me the next morning (26 Sept.) whether I would like to lead 401 for the last time - I don't think he was feeling too well! 401, 411 and 412 RCAF Sqdns. took off early, led by W/Cdr. Dal Russel and we were acting as close escort to 18 Mitchells whose target was the marshalling yards at Rouen. As I recall, we flew on the deck until half-way across and then did a long slow climb. My Spitfire YOA developed a glycol leak at Dieppe, so I glided back across the sea and baled out 40 miles south of Dungeness, where I was found by a Walrus within 50 minutes but there was an enormous sea running which made boarding difficult. I secured a line to my waist but I was unable to release my dinghy. The Walrus had also developed a throttle-leakage problem and away we sailed across the high seas, with the aircraft towing me and the dinghy behind. I remember thinking I would drown. Eventually, the crew pulled me on board and my logbook says that we taxied for 2½ hours in heavy seas. The Walrus pilot made repeated efforts to get airborne but each time struck a wave and fell back, so he taxied on. I do recall a Spitfire over me after my own boys had to leave. I was told at the time that we were in a minefield and that an Air/Sea Rescue Launch was waiting outside to take me on board. Despite my protests, this eventually happened but it was not an easy

transfer. I was given some warm clothes and a tin of hot Mock-turtle soup which tasted good when it went down but the Skipper was not too pleased when I brought it up again over his deck! The launch took me into Dover Harbour and I was picked up at the dockside by a pretty WREN, who was the daughter of author J.B. Priestley. After a check-up at the local hospital, we were joined by an A.L.O. from No. 126 Wing and after high tea, we drove back to our airfield.

Four days later, I flew down to Hawkinge with an armful of cigarettes for the Walrus boys who had rescued me from the sea. Although I can't remember the names of those three RAF Sergeants, I will never forget their courageous efforts in snatching me from the sea. I thought at the time - what unsung heroes these guys are and how dangerous was their profession".

The Canadian squadrons returned to their more congenial winter quarters at Kenley and Biggin Hill in October.

****

Our D/F involvement with the Canadian home-based squadrons lasted for over a year and when I began to write my story, I contacted several Branches of the Aircrew Associations in Canada, following my research of squadron records at P.R.O. Kew. The response was very rewarding and I entered into correspondence with several pilots whose Mayday I'd heard and taken part in, and I learned the 'end of story' of what happened to them after they baled out.

Some time later I was sent an invitation to attend their Reunion in Toronto in September 1992, where I met many of those fighter pilots who were only 'voices in the sky' when we eavesdropped on their R/T chatter over that one-way Receiver system. I told them I had waited 50 years and had to travel some 3,000 miles to get a 'spoke-in' at last! It was a four-day gathering at the Royal York Hotel in Toronto and even though I had not met any of them before, everyone was very friendly and I was made most welcome.

I was particularly pleased to meet two of the participants of the Staplehurst 'Great Escape Caper', Bill McRae and Ian Ormston, who filled me in with some interesting details. I had also been corresponding with Ian's partner on that expedition, ex Fl./Lt. Douglas R. Matheson, who had written to me about the unfortunate day he had been shot down over France.

I was again on duty at the time and I was hoping to hear the last part of his adventure when he spent six months with the Resistance, before the Gestapo caught him . . . . but he did not attend the Reunion.

411 Sqdn. were airborne, escorting 72 Marauders to their target - Cambrai aerodrome. Buck McNair was leading the Wing with Ian Ormston as Squadron Leader and Matheson, Flight Commander. The following is an account of the day's events Douglas Matheson sent me in a letter . .

"I don't know how much conversation you would have heard over the R/T on that fateful day but it happened to be my 153rd operational flight. On crossing the coast, we met the usual rather ferocious flak which caused the Marauders to turn somewhat to the south to escape the worst flak intensity. We then headed inland about 30/40 miles and from about 18,000ft. I could see some movement on the ground which looked like enemy aircraft about to take-off. It turned out to be Chevres airfield, one of the many airstrips used by the Luftwaffe in northern France. I led my flight straight down to ground level and we destroyed two of the FW190's - then we proceeded to climb up again to resume our bomber escort duties but as we were withdrawing from the target. a double section of FW190's approached us from an 8 o'clock position. Two of them closed for the attack and I broke my section into them. We had near collision head-on firing and just as I passed the first 190, starting to complete my breaking turn, a second section of 190's came down on us and caught us on the turn. In the meleé that followed, my No. 2, Jack St. Denis from Waterloo, Quebec was shot down. My Spitfire was also badly damaged and caught fire, so I baled out. I landed near a small French village called Bailleulmont and spent a rather eventful and interesting six months with the French Underground before eventually being captured by the Gestapo on 9 April 1944. I spent several months in a PoW camp and towards the end of the war, we were marched from Poland right across the whole breadth of Germany and encountered a number of RAF raids of the heaviest kind.

It was not for many years after the war that I had any news of the fate of Jack St. Denis. In 1984 my wife and I were invited to France by the Pas de Calais Historical Society which is affiliated with the French Air Force. They had decided to honour some Allied airmen who had been shot down. They randomly picked a site where a Spitfire had crashed in the village of Saulty on 1 December 1943 and after digging out the engine from 30ft. down, began their research. It was in a good state of preservation due to its deep entombment in the earth and the serial numbers married the engine to the airframe and the airframe to the Supermarine Works, who verified that the Spitfire had been delivered to Biggin Hill and the whole story unfolded. They eventually discovered that the pilot they intended to honour was Jack St. Denis and that another pilot from the same squadron had also been shot down on the same day, and so I was invited to attend the ceremonies.

A special monument now commemorates the crash site where Jack St. Denis was killed, located in the village of Saulty, 12/15 miles south of Arras.

On several occasions since the war, I have visited the French families who cared for me during those many months and I am planning to go again next year."

****

Three weeks after Matheson and St. Denis from 411 were reported 'Missing', Sq./Ldr. Ian Ormston was also involved in a serious accident. On 21 December 1943, just after take-off on a raid to Dieppe, his engine cut out but he was unable to land on the runway because 412 Sqdn. were in the process of taking off and he was forced to land on the east side of the airfield, where he crashed and his Spitfire overturned. He was rushed to Orpington Hospital suffering from shock, fractured spine, multiple bruises and abrasions. Although seriously injured, he fully recovered.

Meeting with A.V.M. 'Johnnie' Johnson at Duxford

****

Forty years later, in September 1983, some of the veteran Canadian pilots returned to Headcorn and at a small ceremony, Air Vice Marshal 'Johnnie' Johnson unveiled a Memorial there, which reads . . . .

WORLD WAR II - 403 & 421 SQUADRONS
ROYAL CANADIAN AIR FORCE
106 GAVE THEIR ALL TO GIVE US PEACE

****

Chapter 5

PLAYING THE FIELD

The billet I shared with Joan Wedgbury and Eileen Bond was called "The Oast", in Kingsgate Lane, the entrance of which was exactly opposite the gate of the field where we worked, so we did not have far to go on duty. Past the wooden type house of our 'digs', the private lane let ultimately to Lady Cobb's residence and our landlord, Pop Packham, was one of her estate workers, a gardener-cum-general factotum. The accommodation was basic but fairly comfortable and we were treated as one of the family. Mrs. Packham had a grown up daughter and son and even with our extra rations, she had to provide daily meals for seven healthy appetites. It can't have been easy for any Mum during the war to make meals interesting and appetising on meagre rations and our diet lacked variety, although we fared better in a country environment. All the tinned produce and a lot of fruit that used to be imported had long since disappeared, as the ships cargo space was needed for more important war materials. Children born during the war years would not have tasted a banana for the first few years of their lives. We didn't have a lot of space in our bedroom with three single beds lined up against one wall but we realised we were much better off than communal living in a Camp Nissen hut.

The USAAF also had a D/F Tower like ours in the same field, attached to the 52nd Fighter Control Squadron and two more American D/F Stations were soon installed in the adjoining field belonging to the 50th and 57th F.C. squadrons.

The village of Wittersham had one main street and the size of the place hardly warranted having four pubs in pre-war days but they were well frequented when Service personnel 'invaded' the area. They were The Swan, The Queens, Ewe and Lamb and Dirty Dick's. If the latter had a 'proper' name, I never knew it as it was always referred to as Dirty Dick's. The local Church Hall was converted into a NAAFI for the duration and this was also used by the local troops, among which was a contingent of the North Staffordshire Regiment, who were more or less permanently based at Wittersham, except when they disappeared from time to time on manoeuvres. The pub we mainly favoured was The Swan as it became a regular meeting place for those off duty in the evening, where you could usually find someone you knew from the local U.S. Forces community to have a drink or a chat with. Bart, our Corporal i/c and Ambrose, one of the G.I's, were marvellous pianists, so there was often a sing-song in progress.

Thank goodness war-time emancipation freed us from the male imposed bigotry of not serving a woman a drink in a pub, unless she was accompanied by a man - our thirst and the need to quench it, could not be gratified otherwise?!! The choice pre-war was - go without or be branded a 'loose woman' if you dared to enter a pub on your own. Sometimes, after we were 'chucked out' at closing time, we would take a crate of beer to the haystacks, conveniently situated outside our billet, which invariably had a fair-sized chunk cut out of it, providing a handy platform out of the wind, where we could all sit and continue the party.

Lord Jowett had a country estate with an outdoor swimming pool on the outskirts of Wittersham and he very kindly allowed us to use the pool whenever we liked. He was an active member of the war-time coalition Government and probably spent most of his time in London because I don't remember ever seeing him. All the beaches along the south and east coast were mined and closed for the duration with barbed wire defences to deter any German invasion attempt so we certainly appreciated being allowed to swim there. The local G.I's and Army Officers also had the free use of . . . . and to begin with, the local soldiers also but they abused the privilege and were banned after they were caught stealing Lord Jowett's chickens. It was a medium-sized pool, surrounded by a high hedge of conifers which gave good shelter from any cool breeze. I used to go there often during the two summers I spent at Wittersham. I had learned to swim at an early age and was fair competition for a race the length of the pool and I certainly knew what it meant to be 'thrown in at the deep end' because the WAAF's were usually out-numbered and an easy target for a ducking. One of the G.I's took a rather flattering pin-up type photograph of me sitting on the side of the pool. The Americans were the only ones with film and cameras - another of our luxuries that were no longer available to the general public in war-time. I must have had the negative at some time because it was

Joyce Millard - in swimsuit by Lord Jowett's Pool

my standard 'hand-out' when asked for a photograph and the number in circulation probably ended up in various parts of the globe!

Off duty, we were never at a loss for something to do or somewhere to go. In that small insignificant village, barely on the map, we reckoned we worked hard and played hard. We were just 14 WAAF's (or thereabouts) with a male Corporal in charge (who was married) and apart from the local village girls and a few Land Army females working on the village farms, there was no other competition for miles in any direction and we reigned supreme for a whole year, before some A.T.S. girls were posted to a nearby Army Camp in late summer 1944. Invitations abounded and transport was provided to Army Dances in Rye, the American base at Woodchurch and to nearby RAF Stations.

When I first arrived at Witt, several of the WAAF's already had regular G.I. boyfriends from among the local American D/F personnel but I hadn't been overly impressed with the Yanks I had met in London or by their reputation! I had been treading a bit more warily since Peter and Stan had both turned up during my previous leave - in fact during the time I spent at Kenley, though the opportunities were there, I hadn't met anyone I was eager to go out with a second time and on arrival at Wittersham, the thought uppermost in my mind was that at long last, I was about to start the job I had been waiting six months to do.

It was soon very evident that there was an abundance of every kind of Armed Servicemen in the vicinity and that it could be a happy hunting ground for an unattached female with so many local 'men-of-war' within our grasp. The local Yanks weren't slow in looking over any fresh WAAF 'talent' when it arrived and Stewart Blanchard was one of three G.I's who casually (or maybe purposely) called at our billet on my first day and were invited to stay for tea. Later on, I was taken to the preferred local, The Swan and at closing time, Stew gave me a lift back to my billet on the cross-bar of his bike - I hadn't yet been issued with one I could call my own. "He's nice" was my diary comment but if space had

Sgt. Stewart Blanchard - G.I. D/F Operator

41

allowed, I could also have added that he was rather reserved and shy - not in the least bumptious or full of his own importance - in fact the exact opposite of most of the Americans I had met hitherto. The next day we met by chance (or maybe by design) in our mutual D/F field and he showed me over their Tower and introduced me to the other Yanks on duty with him. He then asked me for a date and I suppose from that second day, until I left 14 months later, I was considered to be 'Stew's girl-friend' among the local D/F crowd. Not that I was at all anxious to be dubbed as anyone's girl or get involved in any regular association but inevitably, it just seemed to happen. My partner Donnie Mayhew, who was on 'B' crew with Joan, Eileen and myself, had a G.I boyfriend, Frank Coushane, who worked on Stew's team and they were pals. We started going out together in a foursome to various places around the area and then it got to be a habit because our days off regularly coincided. I have to admit that we had some great times on these outings and they were both good fun but I told Stew at the outset that I wasn't interested in any serious involvement and he knew the score. For one thing, he couldn't dance and like many shy people, he would rather not try at all than risk making a fool of himself in

Donnie Mayhew - Wittersham WAAF

public. I loved going to dances and this led to the occasional tiff when I announced I was going to one, rather than go to a movie with him. He would have a little sulk but I was not going to deny myself that pleasure, when he wasn't even prepared to learn. But in a way, it was an added bonus because it allowed me extra boyfriend activity outside the village!

I was on my own in our Rest Hut one day, when a handsome American Captain called with an invitation for as many WAAF's as were off duty, to go to a Dance on Saturday night at their base at nearby Woodchurch. Transport would be provided both ways. His name was Mark and during our chat, I told him I would be free to go as it was my day-off on Saturday and he said a truck would arrive and collect us at a given time. As he was going out of the door, he turned and said "I'll be bringing my private Jeep for you, if that's alright?". I smiled demurely and replied "O.K. by me".

Before Saturday, a couple of WAAF's had been persuaded (or forbidden) by their local G.I. boyfriends not to go to this dance but Stew knew it was no good putting his foot down with me . . . . because I would just stamp on it! "No-one is going to run my life" I defiantly confided to my diary. As arranged, the transport for the dance duly arrived and I rode in Mark's Jeep in front, with the other WAAF's in the truck behind. Along a straight stretch of road on the way to Tenterden, came a second American truck going at a helluva pace, blasting his horn as he passed both vehicles. Mark couldn't believe his eyes - "What does that stupid bastard think he's doing?" he bawled out, as he instructed his driver to overtake and signal the truck to pull over. I had a pretty good idea who the truck driver might be and sure enough, as we pulled alongside . . . . it was! Mark gave Stew a severe ticking off while I sat silently in the back of the Jeep, giving no sign of recognition. The G.I's in Stew's truck were on their way to a movie in Tenterden and they all joined in a loud and prolonged 'B-O-O' as Stew drove off. Mark naturally thought it was because of the ticking off and might have led to further aggro: for them but I knew who it was really meant for. I was quite expecting to be given the cold shoulder by the Wittersham G.I's for 'two-timing' but to their credit, they let it pass. They may well have been scared to death going at such a break-neck speed - I thought the reprimand was well deserved for such a dangerous tantrum and I told Stew so, next time we met.

The girls and I had a marvellous evening with great entertainment provided by an American Air Force Band, who were every bit as professional as bands we heard on records. Many musicians from the Big Band names in the States were serving in U.S. dance orchestras over here, recruited to keep up the fighting troops' morale. We really indulged ourselves in all the scrumptious goodies provided in the Buffet - we had not seen such a variety of delicacies and yummy ice cream desserts for over four years and we couldn't have cared less about the number of calories, had we known about them in those days! The occasional binge was a welcome supplement to our plain war-time diet which didn't stretch to meat every day, when it was rationed to a few ounces. The G.I's were certainly well looked after and all their supplies were shipped over from the States. I had several more dates with Mark and then we parted company - I think I can remember why, but it wasn't something I would have spelled out in my diary because it would have taken too many lines to explain!

The local G.I's at Wittersham caused me to change my rather biased opinion of Yanks, though how can you generalise about a vast country like

America, which encompasses such a brotherhood of nations from every corner of the world. The D/F Yanks were a friendly lot, housed in civilian billets like us and integrated well into village community life. They were generally well-behaved, caused no trouble and seldom exceeded their drink limit. Among the mixed bunch were little Mexicans and Puerto Ricans, guys from Brooklyn we could hardly understand - a few from the deep South with that fascinating southern drawl and several first generation Americans of European origin with names like Boedekker, Caldroni, Guiseppi. There were also some of Polish ancestry with unpronounceable and unspellable surnames.

We had the occasional fracas in the village between the American and English soldiers who, often the worse for drink would wait outside the back of the pub ready to 'bash-up' a Yank when they went to the toilet. They were resentful that the G.I's had far more money to splash about than they had and assumed that the girls preferred them for that reason. On another occasion, English soldiers broke into a local shop and stole goods and money from the till, leaving behind an American service cap they had stolen, to try and incriminate one of the Yanks. They were rather trivial skirmishes but instead of fighting each other, they ought to have saved their aggression for the common enemy - the Krauts!

The WAAF's diplomatically favoured both sides - Joan Wedgbury had met and fallen in love with a North Staffs. Sgt. and they were married in Wittersham Church on 16 September 1943 - for a while Eileen went out with an Army Lieut. stationed at Rye, until she eventually learned he was married. There were several, like Donnie Mayhew and I, who had G.I boyfriends and we were often the target for some verbal abuse, which didn't bother us one iota.

At the outset, we couldn't help noticing how many _more_ Yanks were needed to man one D/F Tower than our modest 14 WAAF's, who had an additional two mobile trucks to operate and we soon discovered the reason - the G.I's had _three_ fellas to do the work that one WAAF did! One to turn the wheel and find the bearing, one to write it down and another to 'phone it through to their base in East Anglia. We teased them unmercifully about this AND for the medal they were awarded immediately they set foot on English soil - before they were ever near any action . . . . for 'Combat in a Front Line War Zone'! The Americans also had to put up with a lot of stick about 'being over-paid, over-sexed and over here' but we couldn't have won the war without their vast military might and resources. Many poems were written about them during the war - this was my favourite . . . .

THE ENGLISH GIRLS LAMENT

Dear old England is not the same
We dreaded invasion - well it came
But no . . . it's not the beastly hun
Oh yes, the goddam yanks have come

With admiration we just stare
At all the ribbon's G.I's wear
And think of the deeds so brave and daring
That won the ribbons they are wearing

Alas, they have not fought the hun
No glorious battles have they won
The pretty ribbon just denotes
They crossed the sea - brave men in boats!

They chat us up in bus and train
What can we do - except complain
We try and dodge these dreadful creeps
Then get run over by their jeeps

When Yankee officers come to town
In light coloured pants they strut around
Are they harmless - these macho men
We think they're wolves - and avoid the den

They boast that they can shoot and fight
It's true they fight - when they are tight
We do admit their shooting's fine
They sure can shoot a goddam line

They tell you - you've got teeth like pearls
They like your hair - the way it curls
Your eyes would dim the brightest star
You're competition for Hedy Lamarr

You are their love - their life - their all
And for no other would they fall
I'll love you dear till death us do part
They're so sincere - you give your heart

Then they depart - your love has gone
The camp has moved - to fight the hun
You wait for mail that doesn't come
Then they realise you've been awfully dumb

In a different town - in a different place
To a different gal with a different face
'I love you darling - please be mine'
The same old yank . . . . the same old line!

Chapter 6

TWO OF OUR AIRCRAFT ARE MISSING

During my first six months at Wittersham, instructors often came down to give us lectures and frequent tests to keep us on our toes, which we had to fit in during our off duty time. Suitability for the task could only really be assessed by this method and we were soon sorted out. Those who could not cope with the pressure of the pace or who lacked dedication, were transferred to other trades. It was a responsible job and men's lives depended on accurate 'fixes'.

The summer and autumn of 1943 were very busy periods for ditchings and rescues and when thumbing through my diary, checking on details and dates, I pondered many times on the entry I'd made on 27 August 1943 when I was on afternoon duty from 13.30 to 21.00 hours. My jargon of . . 'An Important Do' - 'Bags of panic' - 'A B-I-G Flap On' or the like, usually meant that we were engaged in something even more important than the daily routine sweeps and escorts, possibly involving a VIP. If only I'd given more of a clue as to what it was about, I might have been been able to find a connection. Again, we might not have known or have been told the full story at the time but I obviously knew it was an incident worthy of special note to have written in those terms. I had also added that the Tower and both Mobiles were on the alert - we all wanted to 'spend a penny' but there was no-one to relieve us. When a pilot was in trouble, he might only have enough time to give just the one Mayday transmission, so during an important 'Do' like this, we needed to be 'on the ball' and under no circumstances would we have left the set while there was a crisis on. I had also made a note of the crucial time - 18.30. My memory had let me down but I kept the date in mind in case something turned up and in a roundabout about way it did.

Whilst reading about the war-time activities of Biggin Hill during 1943, I became thoroughly absorbed with the excitement over the Station's 1,000th Hun, about to be shot down. Word soon got around that the score was 998 and the tension mounted as the last bets were placed and as many RAF personnel as could be packed into the Sector Ops Room, awaited the outcome. Three enemy aircraft had been shot down almost simultaneously - two by Sq./Ldr. Jack Charles, the Canadian C.O. of 611 squadron and Commandante 'Rene' Mouchotte, the C.O. of 341 (the Free French Alsace squadron) had bagged the other, making the score 1001, but which of them had actually shot down the 1,000th? Both pilots chivalrously gave the credit to the other pilot but no decisive proof was obtained, so 'Sailor' Malan, Biggin's Commanding Officer, thought the fairest way would be for both to share the honours and the sweepstake of £300. The event was celebrated by a lavish party at the Grosvenor Hotel in London, to which more than 1,000 guests were invited, including Air Chief Marshals Mallory and 'Bomber' Harris. The festive spread of delicacies, not seen since pre-war, surrounded the piece-de-resistance - three especially dressed large lobsters, labelled Hitler, Göring and Mussolini! The guests were entertained by the legendary Windmill girls from the theatre that 'never closed' during all the bombing of London. The party cost around £2,500 - a princely sum in 1943. When the new Intelligence Officer took over in September, he had to settle the Grosvenor account, which left Biggin with a deficit of over £1,000. A levy was said to have been imposed on all other stations in No. 11 Group to cover this debt, which caused a certain amount of aggravation, especially by those senior RAF officers who were expecting to get an invitation and didn't! Another version of the story says that Vickers-Armstrong, the manufacturers of the Spitfire, were said to have footed the £2,500 bill. So, like the question of who actually shot down the 1,000th enemy 'plane, there is a discrepancy over who paid for the celebrations.

The New Zealand No. 485 squadron, under the command of Sq./Ldr. Johnny Checketts was also stationed at Biggin Hill and on the 27th July 1943, with 'Rene' Mouchotte's 341 Squadron, escorted Marauders to bomb Tricqueville aerodrome, when they were attacked by three squadrons of FW190's. In spite of being heavily outnumbered, the Frenchies and Kiwis managed to shoot down nine enemy aircraft in the space of eight minutes, without loss to themselves and for this outstanding achievement, they received a personal telegram from Winston Churchill.

As I continued reading further, the report said "one month later to the day - Mouchotte was reported 'Missing - believed killed'". My interest was further aroused when I realised that would be the 27 August 1943 - a date I had been keeping in the back of my mind. The time of day was not given and I had to wait until my next visit to P.R.O. Kew to find out whether there was a possible connection. When I checked 341 squadron records, the date and time coincided with when we were on that special alert. The official account of that operation is as follows:-

27/8/43 Cdt. Mouchotte led the Biggin Wing, escorting 60 Fortresses to rendezvous with another 140 Forts on a raid to the marshalling yards at St. Omer. Cdts. Martell and Boudier took off from Biggin and made contact with the Forts at 20,000ft. The Alsace squadron was escorting the leading wave of bombers when they were attacked half-way between St. Pol and St. Omer by several formations of FW190's diving out of the sun. From then on the sky was a whirling mass of fighters - the FW's trying to reach the bombers but being thwarted by the Spitfires. It was every man for himself and a general meleé took place for the next quarter of an hour. Mouchotte got separated from the rest of the squadron, who all split up in various directions. His now famous last words over the R/T were . . "I am alone with the bombers" and nothing further was seen or heard from him again.

It was dark when the Wing landed back at Biggin and anxiously awaiting their return were 'Sailor' Malan (Biggin's C.O.), W/Cdr. Al Deere and Intelligence Officer, Spy - Sq./Ldr. de la Torre. When the last Spitfire checked in, two were still missing. Calls were made to other airfields in case either of them might have made an emergency landing elsewhere. Air/Sea Rescue and the Observer Corps were contacted - and D/F Stations, such as ours, would have been alerted to listen out for any R/T message or Mayday. But there was no hopeful news from any source. Commandante Mouchotte and F/Sgt. Pierre Magret had both failed to return.

'Rene' Gaston Octave Jean Mouchotte fought in the Battle of Britain with 245 and 615 Hurricane squadrons and was commissioned in 1941. He formed the 341 (Alsace) squadron in January 1943 and became its first C.O. For his meritous war-time service he was awarded the DFC, Croix de Guerre and Croix de la Legion d'Honneur.

Like the Canadian squadrons we could identify by their accent, we also recognised the two French fighter squadrons quite easily, as they sometimes lapsed into their native tongue when communicating with each other over the intercom. They had their own special Continental way of saying 'M'Aidez' and we would also have connected them to their call-sign 'TURBAN', although in 1943, we wouldn't have been told their squadron number.

Cdte. Mouchotte's body was later washed up on a Belgian beach and local residents buried him in a grave at Middlekerke. It was sometime after the war that the discovery was eventually made and his body was then transferred to the family vault in Paris.

In the Chapel of Remembrance on the aerodrome, 453 pilots who gave their lives while serving in various squadrons at Biggin Hill, are commemorated including the names of Cdte Mouchotte and F/Sgt. Magret.

Chapter 7

THE AIR RESCUERS

For many centuries, ever since the Norman conquest, the waters that divide Britain from the Continent of Europe have been regarded as our most valuable defence because they have undoubtedly saved us from further invasion. But for returning fighter pilots and bomber crews during WW11, the North Sea and English Channel became . . . 'that dreaded stretch of water'. Often weary and tense from the strain of a hazardous raid over enemy territory, pilots could be faced with the decision, if time allowed, whether to crash land a crippled aircraft in Occupied Europe and become a prisoner-of-war for the duration, or risk crossing that last watery hurdle before they were 'home and dry ' and had survived one more operation.

As the war progressed, so the Air/Sea Rescue Service expanded, at the same time achieving a much higher recovery rate. Many aircrew, when faced with such a decision, often chose to take their chance over those hostile waters, increasingly confident that they would be diligently searched for and picked up. The insignia of the A/S/R Service - 'The Sea Shall Not Have Them' personifies the dedicated spirit of the rescuers devoted to saving others and countless aircrew owe their lives to this vigilant force. If there was the slightest chance of finding a survivor, they would venture out in all kinds of weather and when a search had to be abandoned because of approaching darkness, they would be out again at first light, resuming the search. Their 'customer' (the term used by the Walrus squadrons for a 'ditched' airman) was often located a few miles from the enemy coast, where they might be within range of coastal flak or 'jumped' by German fighters. These daring snatch and run rescues might also entail alighting and picking up a pilot who had come down in a minefield.

The Walrus squadrons had detachments at intermittent coastal airfields along the south and east coasts, where one or two Walrus aircraft and a few of the earlier type Spitfires were based, ready to answer any emergency call. The Spitfires were equipped to carry dinghies and smoke floats and acted as spotters and escort cover to the Walrus, known affectionately as the 'Shagbat', with the appearance of an ancient amphibian. The engine was centrally situated under the upper wing, with the propeller at the rear. The circular hatch behind the cockpit could be opened in two halves for mounting a gun position and a hatch at the rear of the fuselage was used for hauling a 'customer' on board.

When our D/F Stations had taken bearings on a Mayday call and a 'fix' had been obtained on the pilot's last transmission before he baled out, the Controller would see the position from the marker on the Ops Room table and would then order the nearest available Walrus to 'Scramble'. Hawkinge and Shoreham were the units used for rescues from the English Channel, south of the Kent and Sussex coast line. Two Spitfires and a Walrus would become airborne and the Controller would give them a course to steer. The Spitfires, able to fly a lot faster than the trundling Walrus would go on ahead and locate the pilot in the 'drink'. Then one Spitfire would return to meet the Walrus and lead it to the dinghy, while the other Spitfire remained hovering over the pilot, protecting him from prowling enemy fighters and by his very presence, would give reassurance that his rescue was imminent.

As sometimes happened, a dinghy might get damaged or lost and the pilot would be found floating in the water, supported only by his Mae West life jacket. On such occasions, the hovering Spitfire would release two smoke floats to land either side of the pilot in the water, to mark the spot. Then he would drop two yellow cannisters - one would contain a dinghy which would open before it reached the water and inflate on contact with the sea. The other cannister, attached to the dinghy by a rope, would contain essential commodities for survival.

In a routine rescue, a Walrus landed on the water, picked up the 'customer' and took off again, escorted back to base by the two Spitfires. The final task when the pilot was safely on board, was to dispose of his dinghy, usually by shooting it full of holes by machine gun, so that it sank. This was done to eliminate empty dinghies roaming the seas, which might be reported as a 'ditcher' needing to be picked up.

Rescues were not all straightforward - landing on the water in rough seas could damage the undercarriage or tail plane and constant battering when afloat, could also prevent it from taking off again. In the case of a bomber crew waiting to be rescued, a Walrus pilot would not know exactly how many men were in the dinghy until he landed and the combined weight of 7/10 men might prevent the Walrus from getting airborne again. In such circumstances, the only alternative was to taxi all the way back on the crests of the waves for some 40/60 miles, which often happened, as I have related in the rescue of P/O Jimmy Fiander on page 78. On another occasion, a Walrus based on the east coast taxi-ed for seven hours in the dark, after picking up a bomber crew from the North Sea.

Fighter pilots usually crossed the sea in pairs and a far more accurate position was obtained when a companion was able to hover over a dinghy while continuing to transmit. When a pilot on his own gave a Mayday call, it did not necessarily follow that he would abandon his aircraft right away. Any number of factors could delay the ultimate jump - he may have difficulty in getting the canopy open - may have drifted or glided farther on, in the hope of finding a sea-going vessel to land near or he might need a little time to pluck up courage to make the jump, if it wasn't desperately urgent. Even for a first attempt, there was no trial run! Fighter pilots sat on their dinghy, which was folded in the form of a cushion, with the parachute underneath. Before ejector seats, baling out of high speed aircraft was no mean feat and the recognised drill was to reduce speed to ensure getting clear of the 'plane, then wait a few seconds before pulling the ripcord, otherwise the parachute might get tangled around the wings or fuselage, with fatal results. A tactic used most successfully by fighter pilots was to turn the aircraft upside down and literally fall out. By the time a pilot eventually landed in the water, his ultimate position could be some distance from the 'fix' obtained from his last transmission in the cockpit and the difference could make the search more difficult for the rescue team in a vast expanse of water.

The rescue squadrons were often required to perform Line and Square searches in pairs, looking for a 'customer' reported having been seen in a vague area of sea. It needed intense concentration and extra keen eyesight to spot a mere speck of a man or dinghy in varying degrees of visibility, sometimes in choppy seas with white caps. Some reported sightings turned out to be floating debris from sunken vessels.

****

To further my research, I contacted the Secretary of the Walrus squadrons in the summer of 1992, which was well-timed because that very week-end they were about to have a Reunion in Norfolk and I was given an invitation. I gathered some useful information and was particularly pleased to have a talk with ex-Sq/Ldr. Jack Forrest, who had travelled down from Argyle. He was one of the Spitfire spotters who helped locate quite a few of the 118 stranded Fortress crews on 6/9/43 when based at Shoreham with 277 Squadron. This detachment also carried out daily routine patrols and searches for Kenley and Tangmere and we regularly listened in on their frequency in case they found someone to rescue.

F/O Pop Ewens, a 276 Sqdn. pilot recalls an unusual sighting in the Channel in July 1944 -

"Survivors were reported having been seen in the sea about 20/25 miles south-east of Start Point and F/O Tony Lamb and I, in two Spitfires, were sent out to search. We began with a north to south square search but no joy until Bolt Head Control directed us westward and then we spied them - a long string of over 40 chaps in life jackets, waving frantically and obviously mighty pleased to see us. I got airspeed down to a minimum so that I could get the best possible view and from that height they all appeared to be clinging to a long rope, so we dropped smoke floats and dinghies for them. My first assumption was that they were troops who had survived a glider prang. We called out the Walrus and gave our position. When it landed, the crew soon discovered that they 'Nicht sprechen ze English' and were in fact, approximately 45 survivors of a U-boat. The Walrus took off with the Kapitan and returned to our base at Harrowbeer, south Devon, leaving the rest to be collected by the High Speed Launches."

The Walrus crews received many decorations for their bravery and the combined efforts of the four squadrons, 275/8 rescued more than a thousand men, mainly aircrew. Among the most remarkable survival stories must surely be the ordeal of Vic Dorman, a pilot of 276 who relates his experience;-

"I had just returned from leave and as I entered the crew room, I was immediately collared by a fellow pilot who was on stand-by duty. "I say Taffy, be a pal and do me a favour eh?" he said "Stand-in for me until sunset - I've got a date in Plymouth tonight and I would like to catch the early bus." I had nothing better to do anyway and more import: I was BROKE . . . so I agreed.

I pulled up a deckchair on to the grass of the dispersal area in full view of our two Spitfire IIc's, the Avro Anson and two Walrus Flying Boats, smugly thinking that I could settle down and enjoy the late afternoon sunshine but it was not long before I was startled by the

F/Sgt. Vic Dorman

Klaxon horn bellowing out SCRAMBLE - SCRAMBLE. I grabbed my helmet, slung my parachute over my shoulder and dashed towards the Spits but F/O Barry Hill, my Flight Leader got there first - he was over 6ft. and I am only 5ft.6". "What's on?" I yelled after him. "Get upstairs (airborne) - we'll get the gen over the R/T" he replied.

We took off in formation and headed towards the coast, by which time we had been informed we were to search for an airman in a dinghy off the French coast. Luck was with us and we soon found the bright yellow dinghy drifting in the mirror-like calm sea, and as far as we could tell, there was someone in it. Barry returned to look for the Walrus and I was to stay with the dinghy. We had already come a long way and my fuel gauge would indicate how long I could remain. I throttled back to conserve fuel and continued orbiting the dinghy when, from the direction of England, I saw six aircraft approaching - head on and line abreast. At first I did not suspect they could be Luftwaffe coming from the north but when they broke off and banked into line astern, I knew I was their target and on closer inspection, there was no mistaking the sinister black crosses on the fuselages of six FW190's. I needed to draw them away from the dinghy so I turned north-east and almost at sea level, I flew straight underneath them. They could not fire down on me, as they would risk flying directly into the water but it didn't take them long to do a complete turn as the FW190 was very manouevrable and they were soon on my tail. At first shells were buzzing past me on either side, and then more accurately, punching plate sized holes in the starboard and port wings - as I crouched down in my seat for protection by the armour plate behind (thank God I was the small one) a shell passed immediately overhead, smashing the gun sight before my eyes and carried on into the petrol tank, which caught fire. The flames started to slowly flicker towards me - I was too low to parachute out and my only option was to crash land on the water. This was something for which there was no rehearsal - it was right first time, or else! Sliding open the cockpit canopy, I throttled back - fine pitch, flaps down, wheels up and the Spit belly flopped on to the surface of the water. The Rolls Merlin engine weighs more than half a ton but on water it only has one direction to travel - straight down! It began to sink immediately and I was already down 20ft. or more before I managed to struggle out. I rose to the surface with lungs bursting as I gulped the sweet air, instinctively grabbing the dinghy pack within my reach. I pulled the press studs open on the cover and inflated it but I found my sheep-skin flying boots had filled with water, so I kicked them off. Many times during the following years, I regretted doing so, as the only footwear I had was an old pair of rope soled sandals. My flying helmet had disappeared too and the FW's were nowhere to be seen either - they probably thought I had gone down in the Spitfire.

I covered myself with the large canvas awning and rigged up the mast and sail, which subsequently proved useless. Then I took stock of my survival kit which contained a Verey Signal pistol with three cartridges, a floating dinghy knife, two half pint tins of water, and in the emergency pack - Horlicks tablets, condensed milk, concentrated chocolate, water-purifying tablets, a wound dressing and a fishing line, complete with hook. By the time I had sorted myself out, I realised it was getting too late for anyone to come searching for me, so I resigned myself to spending the night in the dinghy. So ended <u>Monday 7 June 1943</u>.

I slept quite well after my strenuous activities to survive and I awoke the next morning full of confidence that the boys of 276 would soon be out to get one of their own. What I did not know was that a thick sea mist had blanketed the south coast of England and all aircraft were grounded. It gets very uncomfortable sitting in a dinghy for any length of time because the depression in the canvas made by your backside, begins to collect water and I had nothing to bale it out with, except my hands but I suppose it helped to keep me occupied. Not a sign of anything all that day and I thought I had better eke out my rations carefully, so I only indulged a few sips of water and a small amount of condensed milk on my tongue. When I had finished the first half-pint tin of water, it provided me with an empty can to bale out the water so I knelt in the bottom of the dinghy and scooped nearly all of it out, while hanging my wet trousers on the mast to dry.

The following day, I reckoned the weather was about to change when I saw cotton wool cumulus clouds scurrying across the sky, gradually getting darker but the welcome rain did not appear until the evening. The dinghy cover caught some of the precious liquid - I collected about half a pint in my hands which I drank straight away and the rest I used to wash the salt off my face and hair. The sky eventually turned from grey to a vengeful black, with the ominous signs of a storm brewing. I quickly lowered the sail and mast and secured the cover as best I could to prevent being swamped by the buffeting waves which seemed to come from every direction. As the gale gained momentum, the dinghy began to spin round like a whirlwind in the conflicting gusts and currents, as the great troughs deepened. Loud thunder drums rolled and sheets of sulpherous lightning illuminated the scene like giant arc lights, giving me a frightening glimpse - upward one minute at a sheer wall of towering marble-green water topped by dancing white foam, which threatened to crush the helpless intruder in his yellow cocoon. Then I would be looking down some 30ft. into the bottom of the next trough. It was a terrifying experience and one I hope I never have to go through again but may I beg a prayer of thanks to all those wonderful people at the P.B. Cow factory at Stanmore in Middlesex who made this marvellous dinghy which carried me through the storm totally undamaged.

Everything was calm again but by now I was beginning to feel the effects of exposure and the hopelessness of my situation, having been adrift for four days without seeing any living thing except a puffin, who visited me periodically and sat on the water for a while nearby, eyeing me curiously. I almost decided to end it all and actually went over the side but my Mae West kept me afloat and after a swim, I thought better of it and got back in the dinghy. My drinking water was practically gone so I thought I'd try purifying my urine with the tablets provided for that purpose but when I had done it, I just didn't fancy it! By the fifth day I was becoming weak and listless and spent the day drifting in and out of bouts of drowsiness but what must have been late Saturday night or Sunday morning, I was awakened by the sound of heavy bombers overhead. Not thinking too clearly, it took me a little while to remember I had the Verey pistol, which I fired twice. The triple red flares hung in the air for a while but I hadn't been quick enough and the sound of the engines had already passed by, leaving no sign of having been seen. Further sleep blotted out my total despair.
BUT SOMEBODY HAD BEEN AWAKE AND HAD SEEN THEM.

I was awakened at first light by the sound of aircraft engines quite near and when I opened my eyes I was astonished to see what appeared to be islands of rock and land on the distant horizon. I had almost lost track of how many days I had spent all by myself drifting around this endless expanse of water and began to wonder whether I was becoming delirious and seeing a mirage. I blinked hard, almost afraid to open my eyes in case the land I thought I had seen had just been a figment of my imagination and with it my hope of deliverance dashed. The second glance confirmed that it was real and furthermore the aircraft, as they got nearer turned out to be two German fighters - ME109'S. They circled my dinghy, waved and waggled their wings before flying off to summon help, I earnestly hoped.

Before long, a Dornier 18 Flying-boat appeared and I knew, after my long test of endurance, that I was going to be saved. It landed some way off and as it taxi-ed towards me, I threw any tell-tale evidence overboard and ripped the faithful old dinghy with the knife. It gave a long complaining splutter, leaving me to swim towards the Dornier in my Mae West. It took two of them, with the aid of a boat hook, to lift and haul me on board because I was too exhausted to be of any assistance. The Dornier must have sustained some damage when it landed because after a couple of attempts, the pilot was unable to get airborne and had to radio for assistance. It was a long time coming and whilst waiting, I tried to ask in French for l'eau, the only foreign word I knew for water, and although one of the crew eventually guessed what I wanted, they did not have any on board. After a while a boat arrived, which I presumed was a tug, but I couldn't see much out of the porthole window near to me. A line was secured, while the two crews chatted to each other and then a large enamel jug of ice-cold water was handed over for me. As I was eagerly gulping the delicious liquid, one of the Dornier crew said 'langsome' or 'take it easy', which was sensible advice. The tow took some hours before we beached in a rocky cove, I now know to be Greve du Lecq on the north Jersey coast, and I was told that it was Sunday, 13 June. The land I first sighted was probably the Paternoster Rocks further out.

Some local fishermen first came to my assistance and helped carry me ashore but they were pushed aside by German soldiers who had rushed down the beach to get me. I was half-carried, half-dragged up the beach to a hotel, requisitioned by the Germans for their military, bearing the sign "Prince of Wales" - this was indeed the ultimate indignity for a Welshman! I was shoved into a small ground floor room, the door closed and the key turned in the lock. I was still in my soaking wet clothes when I curled up on the hard floor, completely exhausted and passed out. I was shaken awake on Monday morning and transported by Field Ambulance to the German Headquarters at the Merton Hotel, St. Helier, still in my sodden uniform but I can't remember much about the journey or my arrival there as I kept passing out. When I came to, I was in a nice bed between clean sheets and a lady of about 40 years of age gave me a cup of tea and two Marie biscuits. She spoke English and gave me a book to read, as well as a large towel marked St. Brelades Bay Hotel, a razor and a small piece of soap. They were my only possessions at that time, and I kept them throughout my prisoner-of-war captivity and for many years after the war.

Not surprisingly, I was suffering from exhaustion, exposure and severe sunburn to face and hands. I peeled off strips of black skin, revealing baby pink new skin underneath which was quite sore. I wasn't allowed long to recuperate, as on Wednesday I was judged well enough to travel. My clothes had been washed and pressed before being returned to me and I was given a pair of rope soled slippers. In the evening I was taken to the quay accompanied by two guards and we boarded a small steamer full of German soldiers going on leave.

We landed at St. Malo and from there I was taken to Paris, thence to Fresnes Prison, some 30 miles further south. This was THE notorious Gestapo Prison and it was a very grim place indeed. I was kept in solitary confinement in a cold bleak underground cell with a wire bed frame and one blanket. Twice a day, early morning and late evening, a very elderly Frenchman brought some very thin soup, a small piece of black bread and some acorn coffee. He would whisper "Quand la guerre fini?" amd I would reply "Six mois" At intervals, I would be taken out for interrogation by various people but I was spared the more extreme methods.

Several days later I was taken by train to Oberusel, near Frankfurt on Main to the Luftwaffe Interrogation Camp. Here the individual cells were over-heated by day and freezing at night. All sorts of tricks were tried to obtain information, including fake Red Cross questionnaires but we all knew the drill - name, rank and number only. After a few days, I was moved to the adjoining general compound, to await dispatch to a regular camp. The walls here were covered with messages written by newly captured prisoners - I suppose it was a way of letting other crew members know that they were safe and had passed this way. One day I was approached by an elderly German civilian who hearing my accent, asked if I was Welsh. He told me that he had a shop in Aberystwith before the war and had been on holiday in Germany when war was declared. He seemed to have the run of the place so I suspected he was planted there to pick up tit-bits of information.

A further week passed by and I was marched with about 50 other

RAF prisoners to Frankfurt Railway Station and on the way we were subjected to strong verbal abuse from German civilians. "Terror Fliegers" was shouted at us but nothing physical, thank goodness. At the station, we found we were going to be transported in cattle trucks - 10 HORSES OR 40 MEN - were painted on the side and the engine tender also had a large sign on it. RADER MUSSEN ROLLEN FUR DEN SIEG - Wheels must turn for Victory.

We spent about a week on that train, as it made its way through Germany, Poland and some Baltic States, until we eventually arrived at Memel in Lithuania. The sea air was quite sharp, even though it was June. The camp was some miles away and the present occupants had already spent a winter there, and dreading the next one. I was fortunate to pal up with a towny called Bill Bailey, who scrounged enough stuff for me to make life a bit more comfortable in our brick warehouse 'home'. I was just about getting into the Camp routine when at the end of the first week, I was told to gather up my belongings, as I was being sent back to Frankfurt. Apparently, I had been sent to Memel by mistake. The return journey was by passenger train with wooden slatted seats which was a bit more comfortable than the cattle truck floor.

I spent two days back in Oberursel, before being sent to STALAG IVB at Muhlberg am Elbe, Saxony. The Camp was shrouded in the morning mist and our first glimpse was of the ominous barbed wire fence surrounding it. The entrance gate was a large wooden structure, reminiscent of an American cowboy film fort and had STAMLAGER IVB in large letters above it. The brick-built camp offices were outside and as we marched through the gate covered with barbed wire, with guards at our backs, we looked up at the machine guns protruding from the Guard Towers which overlooked the compound at regular intervals around the perimeter. We were taken to the de-contamination building, where we were told to strip off and place all our gear in one of the six oven-like rooms. The cast iron doors were then closed. These were gas chambers for disinfecting our clothes but they may also have been used for another purpose. We were then taken into the bath house and lined up for our heads to be shaved with horse shears, one man turning the handle for the chap in front. Next was a cold water shower with a piece of clay soap. Before proceeding to the drying room, an old Russian dabbed each man's underarm and crotch with some brown liquid, like creosote. The hot air blowers soon activated the disinfectant and there were cries of agony as it burned into the skin. We then had to wait in the nude for an hour outside in the open air before our clothes were free of the chemicals. Finally, we had to be photographed and recorded.

Apparently, we were the first batch of British prisoners in this Camp and some 40 of us occupied one of four huts (each eventually to hold 200) in what became called 'The RAF Compound'. Our rations were collected from a central cookhouse in bulk to be divided equally, which, as time went by, soon developed into a fine art. German ersatz tea, like the coffee can best be described as hot water flavoured with herbs or ground burnt chestnuts. The so-called bread was made with black potato flour, mixed with other crops and powdered over with chaff to stop it sticking whilst baking, during which process, each of the ingredients settled into layers, with the stodgy potato flour at the bottom. Our daily ration per man was a 1" slice about 5" square and each loaf was stamped with its date of birth e.g. 20 VI 43. I mention this date because in April 1945, towards the end of the war, we were issued with brown waxpaper loaves with this date on them. They were baked for the Afrika Corps but because of Rommel's collapse, they were never sent out. When opened, the top half under the crust had turned to white powder although the potato part was O.K. The soup was always thin vegetable, occasionally with small pieces of meat in it. At first our only eating utensils were Italian army dixies but by bartering with the guards, we gradually acquired cups and cutlery. The other huts were soon filling up with a mixture of Army and Air Force captives and winter was fast approaching.

Wooden huts and brick floors do not hold much warmth but the body heat of 200 men in three-tier bunks did raise the temperatures slightly. Each hut was allocated a supply of coal brickettes but these soon ran out. The inmates of our hut made a few successful attempts at stealing coal from the brick-built store, which was securely padlocked but someone had discovered that the whole door could be lifted off its hinges, with the padlock still intact. Raids were carried out with the precision of a bombing operation . . . . with Intruders sweeping the compound after dark to make sure it was clear of Goons . . . . Pathfinders led the way and lifted off the door . . . . the Heavies followed carrying a wooden chest with handles to transport the coal and the Loaders filled it up inside the building. All this was carried out under the noses, searchlights and dogs of the guards but the raids *came to an abrupt end when one of the German Senior N.C.O's (Feldwebel) surprised the party. Everyone scattered but F/Sgt. James (Taffy) Jones was trapped inside the coal house. The Feldwebel just fired off his revolver into the darkness and Taff Jones was killed. He had only just received word through the Red Cross that he had been awarded the DFM., as well as his Pathfinder badge for completing his second tour of Ops. The war was not always over for those who became P.o.W's. (I visited his home town of Bedwas in South Wales a few years ago and found his name on the War Memorial but I did not find anyone who remembered him).*

The RAF quarters eventually became overcrowded with all the new intakes and we were moved to another separate enclosure, previously occupied by Russian prisoners. During our first night there, we were bitten alive by bed-bugs and the next morning, we all congregated in the yard outside and refused to stay within the infested huts. By kicking up a bit of a rumpus, the German guards were ordered to seal up the huts and decontaminate them with the killer gas Cyclon B. We were not allowed back inside again until midnight, when we literally shovelled up all the dead bugs that were scattered around. There might still have been pockets of lingering gas so we had to pair off for 24 hours - one to sleep and one to stay awake for any ominous signs of the effect of the toxic fumes.

Two important events happened around this time which remain etched in my memory. I receive my first letter from home but the joy at hearing from my family was turned to sadness by the news it contained - my father had passed away. He had been ill for some years but his death did not affect me as deeply as it might have done, under normal circumstances. I had changed and was now a hardened 21 year old man who had come to accept death as common-place.

The other event was the arrival of the first Red Cross parcels. One for each prisoner. There was such excitement as we checked the goodies over and over and we went a little mad, mixing milk powder and cocoa to make chocolate and various other concoctions to add a bit of variance to our bland diet. And there were cigarettes, which became the currency of P.o.W camps. One loaf - 40 fags. One tin of salmon/sardines or pilchards - 10/15 fags. A bar of chocolate - 30 fags. The Canadians and later the Yanks had so many cigarettes to barter, they ruined the market!

The Allied prison population grew and grew in Stalag IVB and the Russians, French, Belgians, Serbs, Croats and even Italians, all had to squeeze up to make room for more. The Battle of the Bulge brought in hundreds of Americans, who were not used to such cramped conditions and we were doubled up in our bunks to accommodate them. The Arnhem debacle also landed us with many captured airborne troops but they were a different class of bloke.

We had a daily barter market going and almost everything could be obtained - even the guards were willing to trade for cigarettes and chocolate when they were no longer available to German troops and once they succumbed, they were easy prey to be blackmailed for everything, even wireless parts! Our wireless system was excellent and every night, each hut would have had the BBC Six O'Clock News read out to them within half an hour. The Germans were frantic to find the receivers and to make their regular searches and raids more interesting, we would delight in burying tins with wires leading from them and when discovered, the tins had a message in them. 'Ever been had?!!'. In the latter stages of the war, the German Commandant was presented with a copy of the BBC news to keep him up to date with the Russian advance.

We were allowed to use one of the huts as a theatre and there were some excellent shows staged there - in fact German Officers used to bring their wives for what must have been the best laugh in Germany at that time. Some of the female roles performed by soldiers and airmen in drag were beyond belief. Rather surprisingly, one female did get into Stalag IVB and an English woman at that. An RAF Airgunner, whose name escapes me, was called to the Commandant's office and was astonished to find that his English mother had been granted permission to visit him. Apparently her first husband died when he was very young - she went to live in Germany and he was brought up by his grandparents. She married a German, who became a Luftwaffe pilot and was later killed in action. Somehow or other, she found out that her son had joined the RAF and was a PoW in Stalag IVB and rather audaciously, she managed to arrange a visit. Starved of much of interest to gossip about in our enclosed world, the news spread around the whole Camp and became a topic of much amusement but the Germans were unaware of the end of the story. It was arranged that she would stay somewhere around Muhlberg and when the opportunity presented itself, she was to infiltrate one of the daily working parties that were sent out to local farms. A quick switch was done - one of our chaps got away and she took his place. In the latter stages of the war, the sentry guards were not so strict about discipline and as long as the numbers in and out of the camp tallied, they didn't look too closely. She was kitted out with an RAF uniform, lived in one of the huts and nobody split. She and her son made it home. Stalag IVB was situated about 30 miles north-west of Dresden and in February 1945, the city became the target for the most severe bombing raid of the war. RAF bombers at night and USAAF Fortresses by day, wiped out the whole city and the sky above was a towering vortex of devouring flame. The camp buildings seemed to bellow in and out with the vibration of the thousands of aircraft passing overhead and the ground shuddered like an earthquake beneath our feet. We were fortunate that no stray bombs came our way.

American Mustangs and Lightning aircraft flying overhead were now becoming a common sight and one day they jettisoned some of their empty long range fuel tanks which landed in the compound. We knew what they were by the way they fluttered down but the German guards - by this time mostly old men and boys of the Volksturm (Home Guard) - thought they were being bombed and dropped flat on the ground. The explosion they expected was only a hollow clunk and caused them some embarrassment from our derision.

We were rather saddened by what happened a few days later. We had been out of coal for the past month or so and foraging parties went out two or three times a day to look for wood or anything that would burn. One such group were returning to Camp in the afternoon when a short-sighted U.S. Lightning pilot shot them up and killed three. After a protest to the Commandant, we got immediate permission to lay out a large brick P. O. W. sign in the middle of the compound, which was then white-washed. After that we received friendly waves from low flying Allied pilots as they flew over.

By the 20th April 1945, the Russian advance met the Americans at the bridge at Torgau, 16 miles north of us and a Jeep load of Yanks drove into the Camp. They told us "Wait here until our trucks arrive to take you back" but if we had, we might still be there! Three days later, the Russians arrived and took over but the Polish contingent had escaped the night before, after burning down their hut - no Russian salad for them, thank you! We stayed around for a couple of days, foraging in local farms for food. My pal and I tried to get drunk on what we thought was cherry wine but it was only cherry juice - we didn't need any Andrews for a few days, I can tell you.

The Russians then decided to move us south to a steel town about 16 miles away, called Riesa. Three of us - Goldie (an S.A.S. man/German Jew/now Palestinian), Tex Peck (an American who joined the RCAF to get into the war) and I lagged behind in Riesa, living with German families in flats on the west side of the Elbe. The rest were taken to a Luftwaffe barracks in Riesa and became prisoners of the Russians.

We heard Winston Churchill's 'Total Capitulation' speech on a small radio and with immense pleasure, we announced to the Germans present (as had been said to us) . . . "For You the War is Over . . " and also the news that Hitler was dead. Their propaganda had been very effective and they absolutely refused to believe it.

We hung about Riesa for about 10 days, then Goldie and I decided we didn't much like the look of all the brand new Russian lorries, filled with young soldiers, that were arriving in the Town. We got on our bikes and headed southwards toward Meissen. The bridge had collapsed into the water but a wooden footbridge had been rigged up for pedestrians to get to the other side. A Russian guard wanted to see our identity papers before we were allowed to cross and fortunately, we had had the foresight to pinch our official registration cards from the Camp Office before we left, so we were able to prove who we were. On reaching the other side, we saw some G.I's playing baseball in the square. They told us they were pulling out in the morning and that we could sleep in their stores and help ourselves to anything we wanted. After a slap-up meal, we kitted ourselves out with trousers, boots etc. and made up a blanket bed each. Goldie threw me a sack for my pillow from a pile in the corner but some of the contents spilled out and guess what they contained? Standard Army issue 'rubber wear' . . . G.I's, for the use of! Only a few hours earlier, Goldie and I had been told off for talking to some German girls - the Yanks said "No Fraternising" or a $20 fine. Some 'Non Frat eh?

Next day we joined the convoy to Halle, where we met a General who asked us where we had come from and on hearing Stalag IVB, he said "Hell, we've been looking for the boys from there. Do you know where they are now?". We reckoned still in Riesa and he said he would send in tanks, if necessary, to get them out.

The following day we reached Brussels but when we thought we were nearly home, we were delayed there for a further week, due to fog grounding all aircraft. During that time, the rest of the lads from IVB caught up with us

and we were eventually flown back to Blighty in Lancasters.
****

During his two years as a P.o.W, Vic Dorman often wondered whether the pilot he and F/O Barry Hill were sent out to search for, had been rescued but after the war he learned that one of 276's Walruses had already landed and picked up F/0 Dick Thatcher, a Canadian Spitfire pilot from 412 Squadron and they were on their way back to Harrowbeer, when Hill and Dorman were sent out to join in the search at 18.00 hours. In the event of a rescue not being achieved before darkness fell, they were to drop survival supplies for him but had Vic had time to make a closer investigation before the ME109's shot him down, he would have realised that the dinghy was empty. Fate had indeed dealt Vic Dorman a cruel hand that unlucky day. If toothache hadn't made him return from leave a day early, he wouldn't have been asked by his mate who had a date in Plymouth to stand-in for him until sundown. And if he and Barry Hill had known that the pilot they had been sent out to search for, had been picked up, he might have been on his way back to Harrowbeer and not encountered the 190's. Hill had returned to meet the Walrus and landed back at 19.35 but had lost radio contact with Dorman.

When I told Vic I had been invited to attend the Canadian Fighter Pilot's Reunion in Toronto in 1992, he asked if I would enquire whether Thatcher had survived the war, as he'd heard that he had been shot down over France in 1944. Among the pilots I met in Toronto was Don Dewan from 412 squadron, and I learned that nine months after his rescue from the sea, Dick Thatcher collided in mid-air with another Canadian pilot from 412 when they were dive-bombing a V-1 target in France during March 1944. The other pilot, F/0 Joe Hamilton managed to get part-way over the Channel with his damaged Spit before he was forced to bale out and almost immediately, was picked up by Air/Sea Rescue. It was reported at the time that 'Thatcher was missing and never heard of again' and had been listed as KIA (Killed in Action). Don Dewan told me he had seen Dick Thatcher in London shortly after the war, very much alive and in good health. Don later heard that he went to live in America and had started his own airline there - the last information he'd had was from a mutual acquaintance when Dick Thatcher was living in Indiana. Joe Hamilton did not attend the Toronto Reunion. I passed this 'gen' on to Vic when I returned and he was pleased to learn that D.T. had definitely survived the war and may well have evaded capture or been a PoW for the last year of it.

****

It was over 30 years before Vic returned to Jersey with his wife for a holiday and retraced his steps during the few days he spent there at the end of his six-day ordeal in his dinghy. One lady he met had kept a diary during the German occupation and this was what she recorded the day Vic was brought ashore . . .

14 June 1943 - *Yesterday afternoon an RAF Sgt. was picked up at Greve du Lecq in his rubber dinghy by German seaplane. Two fighters were patrolling and must have seen him (seaplane could not rise again so was towed but several lorry loads of troops came down and a few guns were placed on beach to guard it). Mr. Renouf saw airman who could hardly stand through weakness. He looked exhausted and was very wet and cold. He said he had been seven days adrift in the Channel and that he had been machine-gunned. Mr. Renouf could not hear any more as the Germans cleared people away. The airman was taken to hospital in an ambulance. We are very thankful that this one is still alive and hope that he will recover completely. It is a wonder he still lived after seven days at sea in a little rubber dinghy.*

16 June 1943 - *The British airman who was rescued the other day and was in hospital here, was taken away yesterday to France. He was only about 21. His name is Dorman. Short with fair curly hair.*

She added that she kept her diaries hidden, in case the house was searched and was careful not to put anything incriminating in them. "To know the RAF was about cheered us up tremendously but not to hear any had been shot down - then we were very distressed. A week previously two British airmen had been buried in Jersey. We love our little Island and owe a lot to the British that we were saved from destruction. It could have been a very different story."

Another Jersey man wrote to Vic saying . . . "You will never know the excitement and hope that men like you gave to Occupied Countries, by even just flying over". Vic must have been very touched by those last few words.

Vic's wife Megan informed me that he died in June 1994, aged 72 - sadly without seeing his story in print but the deeds of courageous men like Albert Victor Dorman need to be recorded so that . . . .

We will remember them.

Chapter 8

THE DAY I REMEMBER - THE SIXTH OF SEPTEMBER

The High Speed Launches formed the Marine Section Unit of the Air/Sea Rescue Service and the crew were sailors in Air Force Blue uniforms with RAF ranks. They figured prominently in this day's rescue operations because the sea was too rough for the Walrus aircraft to alight on the water. The Skipper of an HSL was a commissioned RAF Officer and among his crew were 2 Coxswains, 2 Engineers, a Wireless Operator, a Medical Orderly and 2 deck-hands. Around the shores of Kent and Sussex, small contingents operated out of Dover, Ramsgate, Herne Bay, Sheerness, Folkestone, Winchelsea and Newhaven. The 68ft. Hants and Dorsets joined the A/S/R Fleet in 1943 - they were built with more living accommodation below decks, so could stay at sea for longer periods. Their duties ranged from 'Crash-calls', square searches and regular patrols, co-ordinated with other craft, so the nearest launch could be directed to a pilot/crew needing assistance, far quicker than one starting out from their land base. These stream-lined buoyant speed-boats were an impressive sight travelling at a high rate of knots and with their shallow draught, they rode high on the water and almost leapt out of the sea from wave to wave, crashing into and cutting through the crests with tremendous power. These small craft were often at the mercy of the worst weather on the North Sea and English Channel - high winds could reach gale force at times and movement on deck for the crew was extremely hazardous. They needed to hang on to rails and ropes to prevent being thrown off their feet or overboard and with limited head-room below decks, they could also be butted on to the ceiling in rough weather. Dover-based boats sometimes had to return because of the risk of being capsized by mountainous seas outside the harbour wall.

During large scale bombing operations, the launches would set out several hours before the RAF/USAAF squadrons were airborne and would take up rendezvous positions at intervals across the sea beneath the air routes. On the outward flight to targets, the bombers might develop engine problems, be harassed by enemy fighters trying to infiltrate the group, or the occasional collision between formating bombers en masse in a congested air space. These large scale day and night raids, involving several hundred to a thousand bombers, entailed long and tedious vigils for the HSL crews, which could stretch from hours into days, until the returning 'planes had passed over and all reported 'ditchers' had been found. Nursing orderlies in the Sick-bay had to be prepared to deal with any form of injury sustained by the survivors they picked up - from minor abrasions, exposure, broken limbs, to the extreme cases of the dying, with wounds beyond their medical qualifications, when they could only administer drugs to ease the pain. One of their more unpleasant tasks - along with other crew members - was the recovery of bodies from the sea in varying stages of mutilation or decomposition. After a long time in the water, bodies became bloated with exposed flesh often bearing signs of being attacked by fish and corpses were sometime found minus eyes - pecked out of their sockets by sea birds.

Apart from VE and D-Day, Monday the 6th September is probably the day that stands out most vividly during 'my war' because it was one of our busiest and the vibrating hum of engines all day long indicated the tremendous amount of air traffic that was going to and from the Continent. When we arrived on duty, the Kenley Canadian Wing led by W/Cdr. 'Johnnie' Johnson had been airborne since 07.00 hours - they had escorted 72 Marauders on a bombing raid to Rouen and they also indulged in some 'train bashing' of half a dozen locomotives and rolling stock on the track into Amiens before they re-crossed the Channel.

Sq./Ldr. Buck McNair led the Wing on the next Ramrod, escorting Fortresses to Cobourg at 11.25. Then No. 122 Wing took over - the Spitfire Wing returned, refuelled and then escorted another beehive of 30 more Forts across to Europe. We were fully occupied taking bearings on our three units. 421 had a very successful day - they had destroyed three enemy aircraft and damaged two more, without loss to themselves, although on the return flight a Mitchell bomber crashed in flames on the Dungeness foreland, between Lydd and New Romney.

The 6th September 1943 was also the day when 118 Fortress aircrew ditched in the Channel and were picked up by Air/Sea Rescue (mentioned briefly in my Introduction). The American Air Force were inexperienced in matters of A/S/R when they arrived in the U.K. and had neither the equipment nor training for recovering aircrew from the sea. They were totally dependant on the RAF's facilities and increasingly called on them. Grateful U.S. Commanders awarded decorations to A/S/R personnel who had recovered American service men from the sea. 65 were picked up on 26 July 1943 but the 118 rescued on the 6/7th September must have been an all-time record for the highest number saved on one day during WWII, although recorded facts are hard to find. Details of daily events at sea and names of individuals rescued by A/S/R boats are not well documented by the Marine Section. After a long and tiring sojourn at sea, a Skipper was often too fatigued to concentrate on writing out a lengthy report of who they rescued etc., especially if there was no senior officer ashore insisting that he do so!

All these years, I had wrongly assumed these Fort crews had needed to 'ditch' because they had either been hit by flak or shot down by enemy fighters but I have discovered a lot more facts about the events of that day, than I was allowed to know way back in 1943.

A large beehive of some 400 Fortresses from various bases in England became airborne just before 10 a.m. and rendezvoused prior to setting off for their primary target - the VK Ball Bearing Works at Stuttgart. After assembling they circled, expecting the signal to proceed but this was delayed because the weather reconnaissance aircraft reported that the target was frequently obscured by cloud. The Forts were eventually given the green light by the USAAF High Command but by this time a lot of gas had been consumed while they were orbiting. From here on, it became a mission beset by one disaster after another. While trying to locate the target, in weather that had further deteriorated, they were attacked by more than 100 enemy fighters who drove in as close as 50/60 yards before rolling over and diving through the formation and 31 Fortresses were shot down. The 388th Bomb Group lost half of the Fortresses they dispatched and the 563rd squadron was wiped out in that air battle. The Groups circled the target several times before catching a glimpse of Stuttgart through a momentary break, but visibility was further reduced by a smoke screen put up by about 30 smoke pots. They descended to salvo their bombs into the centre of the city but missed the instrument factory. Formations became separated and the secondary targets - Offenburg and Strasbourg were attacked with more success when bad weather conditions prevented the greater part of the force from bombing the primary target. Intelligence later reported that railway sidings in Offenburg were severely damaged and all rail traffic between Basle and the Rhineland had to be diverted over the Colmar/Strasbourg line for the next four days. In addition, all telephone and telegraph communications north of Basle, between Offenburg, Karlsruhe, Mannheim and Stuttgart were severed until the day after the attack.

On the return flight towards the coast, the Forts again met with enemy fighters but they were not harassed for long because the fighters were getting low on fuel and had to turn back. By the time the B-17's were crossing the English Channel, many found their fuel tanks almost empty and the crews were jettisoning anything surplus to requirements and removable, in an effort to lighten the aircraft and gain a bit more mileage. Guns and ammo: were thrown overboard and in their panic, some parachute packs went out too. Of those that managed to reach the Kent coast, two Forts of 303 Group crashed about 15 miles from West Malling, two from 306 Group crash landed at New Romney and Deanland, one at Winchelsea, one at Penhurst, two near New Romney and 1 from 381st Bomb Group near Ashford. Another landed at Gatwick and taxied into a Halifax. Four B.17's decided to fly on to Switzerland and one other crashed into Lake Constanz but the 9 crew were rescued and interned along with the other four crews.

Twelve Fortresses completely out of fuel didn't reach the English coast and crashed into the Channel. The Spitfire spotter aircraft of 277 squadron from Hawkinge and Shoreham were 'scrambled', taking with them dinghy packs under the wings to drop to survivors. The wind was West S.W. force 6 and the sea was too rough for the Walrus Flying Boats to land on the water but the spotter aircraft were a tremendous help in locating the dinghies and directing the nearest launches to pick them up. A Shoreham Spitfire met one of the Forts, obviously in difficulties and stayed with it until it finally ditched and then gave a transmission over the R/T for the D/F Stations to get a fix. HSL 177 arrived soon after and picked up the 11 crew. Another Spitfire was searching in the Pevensey Bay area and found a Fortress in the water with 10 of the crew on the wing - High Speed Launches were already in the vicinity and they too were soon rescued. Eight miles south-east of Beachy Head, two more Spitfires were orbiting Forts in the water, with two dinghies alongside each, containing five of the crew. One of the Spits increased height to transmit for a fix to mark their location and he could then see two more dinghies a few miles south-east of the first two. The pilot, F/Sgt. Jack Forrest went to investigate and found four men in one dinghy and five in the other but he had to fly on a further 8 miles to contact HSL 177. Before the launch reached the dinghies, Forrest saw a man in the water only in his Mae West. floating beside wreckage, so he diverted 177 to pick him up first. Meantime, the other two dinghies were picked up by HSL 156 and they also assisted 177 in picking up the second pair.

Shoreham Spitfires were then directed to search an area 25 miles south of Beachy Head and they found two dinghies tied together with ten men on board - they were picked up by HSL 156. The Kenley Ops Room Controller master-minding the rescues, then asked them to continue on a south-westerly course to search for other Fort crews much nearer the French coast about 10 miles west of Le Havre but they found nothing. They later learned that the crew had been picked up by a destroyer. Other survivors were picked up by Royal Navy Minesweepers who transferred them to RAF launches from Dover and they were landed ashore at 15.00 hours. The searches extended from Cowes to Dover and went on all through the afternoon and early evening.

We came on night duty early to repay the afternoon crew for a previous favour and they told us what a hectic time they'd had taking bearings to locate the Fortress survivors waiting to be picked up and I think they were quite glad to hand over. When we did, we heard a pilot say that he had just sighted two bomber dinghies tied together. Black 2 remained orbiting the dinghies while Black 1 flew off to find the nearest launch, which happened to be 16 miles away. Meanwhile, Black 2 called on the R/T - "Poor visibility is making it difficult for me to keep the dinghies in view, so I am dropping two smoke floats to mark their position for the launches to find them, as daylight is fading". The Controller gave him a vector back to Hawkinge from our bearings and the last two Spitfires landed by flarepath at 20.30 hours. According to 277 squadron records, the Ops Room rang Hawkinge about an hour later to say that due to their efforts, ten more USAAF aircrew had been picked up before nightfall by Motor Launch 115. The report for 6/9/43 ended . . . . 'This was a big day for Air/Sea Rescue and even though Walrus aircraft were non-operational, 118 aircrew were saved'.

We must have been given similar information from Kenley Ops Room on night duty, because I had noted in my diary at the end of that eventful day that 119 (a discrepancy of 1) Fort aircrew had been picked up from early afternoon and that Kenley had been involved in 85 of those rescues. My final sentence was 'Listened to the evening news and was astonished to hear the announcer say - <u>ONLY 2</u> of our aircraft were missing'. Even though we would not have been told about the 30 plus Forts shot down over Stuttgart, I did know 11/12 had come down in the Channel, though not the reason why. The BBC often reported on the news that so many hundreds of <u>Allied</u> bombers had dropped so many thousand tons of bombs on such and such a target . . . . American Fortresses were obviously included in the numbers quoted that went over but it seems their losses on the way back were conveniently ignored!

I made no further diary comment about that night duty but I reckon we were again listening on the dawn patrol frequency, when 277 Squadron Spitfires went out to search for any more stragglers, as soon as it was light. Ten more B-17 crew members who had spent the night in their dinghies were soon located and picked up by MCU Launch 2548 at 07.00 hours. They had drifted 38 miles during the night. Searches continued all through the day and at twilight flares were spotted and three more dinghies were found. The last Fortress crew to be picked up belonged to the 388th Bomb Group and they were taken ashore at Dover in the early hours of the 8th September, having spent over 24 hours in their dinghies.

This mission to Stuttgart was one of the most costly and ill-fated raids in the history of the 8th Air Force during WWII and but for the combined co-operation of the Air and Sea Rescue units, it might have been even more disastrous in respect of lives lost. I found no evidence that any men were lost among those who 'ditched' in the Channel and to have recovered 118 aircrew within hours during one operation, was an outstanding achievement and should have received more recorded merit than it did.

The Spitfire squadrons from Biggin Hill had also been involved in escorting and providing withdrawal cover for the Fortresses and had an equally eventful day on the 6th September with some tense moments. They were afraid they had lost the revered New Zealand C.O. of 485 N.Z Sqd. Sq/Ldr. Johnny Checketts, who did not return. He had been the other recipient, with Rene Mouchotte of 341, of Winston Churchill's congratulatory telegram for their success rate on 27th July. "Nine for nought is an excellent score" the Prime Minister said.

On their third operation of the 6th, 485 squadron escorted Marauders to bomb the ammunition dumps in the marshalling yards at Serquex, when they were attacked and outnumbered by some twenty ME109's. Checketts was hit and had to bale out south of the Somme Estuary, in the area of Abbeville. He recalls the experience:-

"There was a terrific explosion under my feet and the cockpit caught fire. As I dragged the hood open and released my harness, the flames were engulfing me. I stood out on the slipstream and as I parachuted down, my Mae West was still smouldering and my trousers were burned almost to my waist. In the intense heat, the skin of my forehead was falling over my eyes, but I was just able to see vehicles moving in the direction of where I was expected to land, so I knew I had been seen. I landed in a field where French farm workers were harvesting and on landing I realised I also had shrapnel embedded in my knees and foot. I quickly tried to hide my parachute and Mae West among the corn sheaves and then an elderly French woman told a youth with a bicycle to get me away before the Germans arrived. The bike had a flat back tyre and it was a most uncomfortable ride on the carrier with my injuries becoming extremely painful. The youth left me in a copse about half a mile from where I landed and as I lay hidden in the

undergrowth, a German on a motor cycle drove past on a nearby road with my parachute laying on the petrol tank. I was later taken to a farm, where my wounds were tended to and during the night I was transferred to a 'safe' house, several miles away. I was now in the hands of the Resistance and joined an escape route which was the start of a seven week journey across France to get back to England."

Biggin Hill Station records for 6/9/43 reported 'Two ME109's shot down - one by Sq/Ldr. J.M. Checketts DFC and one by F/Lt. K.G. Lee. A bad day - lost Checketts who was shot down when 20 ME109's attacked 485 (RNZAF) Sqdn. 341 (French Alsace) Sqdn. also jumped'. The following day, the Station Log recorded . . . . 'German broadcast stated that Checketts is a prisoner and badly wounded. He was seen to bale out'. This inaccurate information probably came from one of Lord Haw-Haw's propaganda broadcasts, which were mainly a 'pack of lies', tinged with a whisper of truth here and there to make them plausible. How did they know it was Johnny Checketts who baled out when he was never captured?? William Joyce, known as Lord Haw-Haw because of his upper-crust manner of speech broadcast regularly from Hamburg and his opening words were always - 'Germany calling, Germany calling'. He had a supercilious taunting voice which seemed to compel people to tune in to hear him. I did quite often and the reception was as clear as a bell. He was Irish born, educated in England and became the English-speaking mouthpiece of the Third Reich, considered by many to be the most hated traitor of the war.

I wrote to W/Cdr. Checketts who lives in Christchurch, New Zealand. mainly to enquire (because again we were never told) how far away from Biggin Hill could the Controllers and D/F Stations still hear fighter pilots' voice transmission. I received a most helpful reply to my several queries and to quote from his letter :

" Reception of VHF from Biggin or other fighter stations varied with altitude and in this respect were affected by the curvature of the earth. At low level, the distance was fairly short but we could receive and send from Paris and beyond at altitudes of 20/30,000ft. On the odd weather conditions (fhon winds), I have spoken to Biggin from Duisberg in Germany at 30,000ft. but these were freak conditions. Generally, the R/T was very good, especially for Homing and Mayday fixing. We had great confidence in the D/F operators in England and the fixing stations saved many lives, mine among them. I was also shot

down in May 1942, halfway between Boulogne and Dungeness at 20.30 hours. Reg Baker of No. 485 gave a fix on my position and I was rescued by the Navy an hour later, just as night was falling. I was lucky. I was still in R/T contact with Biggin at 10,000ft. when I was shot down on 6th September 1943 at about 15 miles inland from the Somme Estuary.

We weren't told anything, other than what was necessary either. The Intelligence people were scared what aircrew might disclose to the Germans in the event of us being captured. We never knew where our own D/F Stations were for instance, so we were both in the same boat in this way . . "

W/Cdr. Checketts also sent me copies of the call signs and corresponding squadron numbers in use on D-Day and just after. This was most helpful as I was only just finding out how often squadrons were given new call-signs and I certainly didn't know before that they had all been changed for operation 'Overlord' on D-Day. No doubt to confuse the enemy during the invasion . . . . and nearly fifty years on, me too, in trying to match call-signs with squadron numbers!

I learned from another source that W/Cdr. Checketts had been the subject of a 'This is Your Life' programme on New Zealand TV in 1990 and had been reunited with Marie van Belle, one of the Resistance members on whose farm he had hidden for a month. It was 45 years since they last met. He also has among his prized possessions, one of a set of three pewter tankards which were specially made and presented to the Officers Mess at Biggin Hill, suitably inscribed to commemorate the 900th enemy aircraft shot down by squadrons while based there. Successful pilots had the privilege of using these tankards to celebrate a confirmed 'kill', the second tankard was for 'probables' and the third one for enemy aircraft 'damaged'. Group Capt. North, a former Fighter Command Controller acquired the 'damaged' one and on his death, bequeathed it to his son, who became a Master aboard the vessel 'Cumberland'. On a voyage to Dunedin, South Island in 1972, John North invited W/Cdr. Checketts on board and presented the tankard to him.

From all accounts, Johnny Checketts was a valuable pilot and skillful leader - one of our modest war heroes, liked and admired by all who knew him. In squadron records he was referred to as . . . . 'that very popular C.O of No. 485 Squadron' and later Wing Leader of the Horne Wing.

Wing Commander Johnny Checketts, of Christchurch, with Mrs Marie van Belle, a member of the French resistance who helped save his life after he was shot down over France in 1943. The two were reunited for the first time in 45 years for a "This is Your Life" television programme.

Pair remember French escape

NZPA   Christchurch

It was an emotional moment for the former New Zealand fighter pilot Wing Commander Johnny Checketts when in Christchurch this week he met again the woman who helped him to escape from German-occupied France 47 years ago.

Marie Van Belle, aged 73, was one of the French Resistance fighters who risked her life to smuggle foreign servicemen out of France during the Second World War.

The pair were brought together by Television New Zealand for the *This Is Your Life* programme on Tuesday evening honouring Mr Checketts.

Mr Checketts, aged 79, last saw Mrs Van Belle in 1945 when he returned to France to thank her and her family for aiding him in his escape.

Two years earlier, on September 6, 1943, he was in a Spitfire aircraft acting as escort on a bombing raid over France.

While heading for England he was shot down near Abbeville in central France.

Mr Checketts bailed out of the aircraft before it crashed, but suffered burns to his face and body.

He was found by a French boy and hidden in a house used by the French Resistance.

For the next month he was moved continuously to avoid detection by Germans who were looking for him.

In October he arrived by train at Vannes, in Brittany, and was met by a young Resistance agent, Marie Lavenant, who was later to become Marie Van Belle.

Mr Checketts and two other pilots were hidden at the Lavenant farm for a month before being moved to another safe house.

A few weeks later the trio were hidden on a fishing boat and returned to England.

Mrs Van Belle joined the French Resistance in 1940 at the age of 23.

During the war the family's farm was local headquarters for the movement and was a safe house for about 24 pilots shot down over France.

Mr Checketts said his reunion with Mrs Van Belle after 45 years had been a very emotional moment for both of them.

In due course, the following letter arrived at Wittersham D/F Station and I am glad now that I had the presence of mind to write out a copy because, apart from being tangible proof that we did exist, it is the only piece of official appreciation that ever came our way, during the war or since, although the credit goes entirely to the afternoon crew on that busiest of busy days.

To: N.C.O's i/c WATERHALL and WITTERSHAM
Dated : 18 October 1943
From: Sector Signals Officer, Kenley   Ref :KEN/S/150/Sigs
AIR   SEA   RESCUE
Enclosed copies of two letters dated 12th and 17th October to be brought to the notice of all personnel . . . Good Show!
(Signed) G. Howard, S/Ldr.   Sector Signals Officer, RAF Kenley

****

Enclosed is a copy of a letter received from H.Q. No. 11 Group and doubtless you will wish to relay the information contained therein to the crews of the D/F Stations, whose efficiency in fixing played a prominent part in the success of the operation.   (Signed) ? Air/Sea Rescue Officer, Kenley

****

A letter has been received from the Commanding Officer of the 92nd Bombardment Group USAAF, referring to the rescue of several of the crews of that Group on the 6th and 7th September 1943. The letter expresses the very deep gratitude and keen admiration of all American crews and their relatives for the work of all connected with Air/Sea Rescue. The letter continues . . . . 'Your courageous and highly successful service has not only become a strong factor in the very high state of morale of our combat crews but today enjoys the mounting appreciation of the entire Allied world and I may add, even of the enemy itself'.
It is requested that you will convey this extremely generous tribute to all who were concerned in the magnificent results on the 6th and 7th September.
(Signed) Air Vice Marshal Hugh W.L. Saunders - Commanding Officer No.
11 Group, RAF.

****

After our busy night duty on the 6th, Eileen Bond and I were so tired we spent most of our day off in bed. There was so much noise going on downstairs and outside that sleep was impossible, so we got up for lunch and then tried again in the afternoon with a little more success. Our day's off were very frequently spent catching up on lost sleep and it often seemed like 'all work and no play' 'cos we were back on duty again the next afternoon. One of the Fortresses had 'pranged' close by to us at Reading Street and the next morning Donnie and I cycled over to see it. There were no bomber stations in Kent and we had never seen one close to on the ground before - we were staggered at its size. I had written in my diary "Had a look over it. Donnie and I managed to nick a souvenir although if we'd had a screwdriver, we would have pinched something worth while. We both had our eye on the knob of the joystick!"

Chapter 9

PRESSING ON REGARDLESS

Still only half-way through September '43 and not many dull moments in our corner of Kent. Donnie and I were on night duty on the 15th and the WAAF in the Kenley Ops Room, with whom we were always in touch, saw from a plot on the Ops Room table that there was a raid in progress and hostile aircraft were in our vicinity. She asked if we could hear anything - "Can we hell?" I replied from under the table "there's bombs and 'planes whizzing about like nobody's business around here" (an exact quote from my diary that night). The Advanced Landing Ground at Lydd was a few miles south of Wittersham, towards Dungeness and was obviously the main target that night. A.L.G's had sprung up like mushrooms at suitable sights in Kent and during the summer months they were occupied by mobile fighter squadrons for pre-invasion training under conditions they were likely to encounter on the other side. Three squadrons Nos. 174, 175 and 245 (121 Wing) were based at Lydd during the summer/autumn of '43, equipped with Typhoons - called Tiffie's when acting solely as fighters . . and Bomphoons when converted to a fighter/bomber. The personnel lived in tents and the ground staff performed maintenance work in the open. The runways were laid with Sommerfeld track, a heavy steel mesh netting which caused excessive wear and tear on the tyres of aircraft wheels when landing and the track did not stand up well to the constant pounding by the heavier fighter/bombers. This night's raid could well have been a retaliatory attack because 121 Wing had recently been engaged in dive-bombing targets in France and Holland.

Of all the nights to do it, I had left my supper-cum-midnight snack in my billet and knowing that I wouldn't survive the night without it, I had to venture out on my bike to get it, before everyone in my billet went to bed. Somehow or other I must have met Stew and he cycled down the lane with me. We nearly always carried our steel helmets around and we certainly needed them that night for protection against shrapnel from the Ack Ack guns and whatever else might fall out of the skies. The searchlights were scouring the skies for the Jerry bombers we could hear circling around - Stew was far more interested in what was going on above, instead of looking where he was going and promptly fell off his bike, into the ditch. At that precise moment, the whistle of a bomb made me dive for the ditch too, just as it landed nearby. This was no night for wandering about in the dark, so I quickly fetched my sandwiches and went back on duty with Donnie.

Our Canadian pilots at Headcorn, 8 miles up the road, were also on the receiving end of hostile aircraft activity that evening. Padre Carlson was living with them under canvas and recorded the raid in his journal. On the 15th September, a service commemorating the third anniversary of the Battle of Britain had been held earlier in the day but their movie in the Blister hangar in the evening was interrupted by an air raid warning. "Bags of individual Jerries and pairs around. Coloured chandelier flares and bomb explosions nearby. Watched the proceedings from the Mess with W/Cdr. Brown and pilots. Got under cover several times. Pilots hit shelters just as fast as groundcrew! Raid continued until midnight."

Our next morning duty was on the 18th and after a rushed breakfast through not getting up early enough, the first thing Donnie and I usually did was to put the kettle on for a cup of tea as soon as we got to the Rest Hut. That welcome cuppa and first cigarette were the perfect combination to put us in the right mood for whatever the early shift might have in store and that morning, we didn't have to wait long for the action to start. We knew from the accent that it was a Canadian squadron on our frequency (although at the time we wouldn't have known or been told that it was 401 at Staplehurst). They hadn't been airborne long before one pilot said he was returning to base with engine problems but it wasn't an emergency and he got back alright. Then sometime later, Donnie was on the wheel and dealt with a Mayday on an aircraft almost due south of our D/F Tower - the bearing she passed through was 175° and the resultant 'fix' from the other D/F Stations would have placed the pilot about 10 miles off the French coast.

A Walrus aircraft from No. 277 Sqdn. was 'scrambled' from Hawkinge but the sea became very choppy the farther they got out into the Channel and it was almost too rough for the Walrus to land. The Spitfire spotters had already located the dinghy and the Walrus arrived at 11.16 a.m. and picked up the 'customer', who was P/O J.W. Fiander. The following personal recollection written by Jimmy Fiander shows the courage and determination of the Walrus pilot to get them all back safely during a particularly long and arduous return journey, which Walrus pilots would modestly say . . . . "Was all in a day's work" . . . .'

The 18th was rather an unusually eventful day for me. 401 became airborne at 09.25 as part of Wing providing close escort to 12 Mitchells whose target was the Rouen/Sotteville Marshalling Yards. I was Blue 3 and on the way over, Blue 2 turned back in mid-Channel with engine trouble and the spare, F/Lt. W.S. Johnson took his place.

We crossed the French edge 14,000ft. up just before 10.00hrs. The Mitchells dropped their load on the target and from the air, a large red explosion was seen west of wagon shops and hits were scored on railway tracks and rolling stock. It was 2 minutes flying from Rouen that the engine in my Spitfire YO-T gave way with a sudden cough, losing all power but not quitting completely. The very unpleasant thought of a glycol leak that far from home shook me but that's what it was. I turned back and headed north but was unable to say anything over the blower to 'Lin' (Flight Commander Ozzie M. Linton) because my R/T had also packed up a few minutes before. My No. 2 told 'Lin' and turned back to take me home (as far as I got!). I glided over Dieppe at 11,000ft. at 132 m.p.h with everything back (boost and rev.) so I wouldn't seize up or catch fire. A few miles off the French coast I pulled back the hood and disconnected the oxygen, wireless tubes and wires. F/Sgt. D.M. Wilson was still circling and watching, evidently giving my Mayday on Channel 'D' for a fix. It was about 10.15 and at 1,500ft. I was forced to abandon old YO-T (the second one). Speed was 100 indicated and when I let go of the controls 'T' went into a dive. I climbed on to the seat and jumped out but it took me a few seconds to find the ripcord. I hit the Channel and untangled myself from the shroud lines and inflated my Mae West. It took me about five minutes to get safely in my dinghy, by which time I was quite exhausted.

    I noticed Wilson was still hovering above and then he dived down over me, we both waved and he flew off. In less than five minutes after Willie left, two A/S/R Spits came to patrol me. Meantime, I kept busy baling out water from the dinghy, pulling the rubber cover over me as protection from the rough seas, which were making me feel sick. When the Walrus arrived about an hour and a quarter later, it landed with difficulty a few yards away and I was dragged in the back gun hatch. The crew were all N.C.O's - W/0 Butler, F/Sgt. Brodie and the WOP/AG, Sgt. Humphreys. The sea was far too choppy with a 10ft. swell for the pilot to take-off again so he decided to taxi to calmer sea ahead but found none and two more attempts at getting airborne failed. I was given a sleeping suit to put on which warmed me up. One of the crew punched holes in a tin and to my surprise it contained cold water. An escape kit was opened and we all had some barley sugar and Horlicks tablets. For four hours we taxied on the crests of the waves, covering some 40 miles, and then two Rescue Launches came to provide escort for us when we were a few miles off the English *coast. The pilot tried another take-off but this was also unsuccessful. Daylight was fading when we approached Hastings and then HSL 149 towed us for the last part of the journey along the coast - it took from dusk until 12.30 a.m. to get to Dover, where we tied up to a large buoy. I was transferred from Walrus to launch and given warm rum and warm clothing. I had been on the Walrus for 13 hours altogether. I was interrogated at H.Q. and at 3 a.m. started off for Hawkinge, where I was given a room in the Officers Mess."*

Jimmy Fiander survived the war and resided in Ottowa until he died in 1990. His widow sent me this excerpt from his war-time diary.

****

In mid-September, a Farewell Party was held for W/Cdr. 'Johnnie' Johnson who had led the Kenley Canadian Wing for the last six months on many sorties over Occupied Europe and frequent clashes with the Luftwaffe. He was presented with a gold watch and after a spell of leave, joined the staff of No. 11 Group Headquarters at Uxbridge, engaged in planning and co-ordinating forthcoming operations within the Group.

The new Wing Leader of No. 127 Canadian Wing was Sq/Ldr. Hugh C. Godefroy, the C.O. of No. 403 Sqdn., who chose 'Darkwood' as his personal call-sign.

Sometimes on duty, the Ops Room did not want us to take any bearings - we would just be tuned into a certain frequency in case someone had to bale out and we could sit back and listen to what was being said. That was all I had to do on morning duty on 24th September when W/Cdr. Godefroy was leading his squadrons while escorting 72 Marauders to bomb Beauvais/Lille aerodrome. It was a German fighter base and the FW 190's quickly got airborne to attack the Spits. A scrap soon developed and the Canadians managed to shoot three of them down without loss to themselves. Nearing the coast, the now familiar voice of 'Cookie' (one of the pilots of 421) called out "I've just spied a goods train a few miles south of St. Valery. Am going down to attack". Some time later, Red 3 enquired "How did you make out Cookie?". "O.K." answered Cookie excitedly - "That train won't be going anywhere no more! I scored a direct hit and the train lurched to a halt - you should have seen the smoke and steam from the engine. It rose up like a cloud." His elation was short-lived because soon after, he called out that he'd been hit by flak from the shore batteries - "The bastards have damaged my port wing and aileron" he shouted. I swung my D/F wheel into action, expecting a possible Mayday call and found him at 143°. I continued to track him, in case it was needed but Cookie was able to make it back to Headcorn alright. It was an interesting duty for me but thankfully no-one had to make a hasty exit on my frequency.

403 and 421 squadrons flew a diversionary operation on October 3rd in the Roye area to entice any Luftwaffe away from the Mitchells of 320 (Dutch) squadron, who were heading for Grand Quevilly Power Station laden with 1,000lb. bombs. The Mitchells rendezvoused over Rye with their escort of four other Spitfire squadrons and although they encountered heavy flak crossing the French coast, they did not meet any enemy fighters, as the Canadians had lured them away and were already in combat with them. 421 squadron shot down seven for the loss of only one Spitfire and 403 added two more. Buck McNair claimed his 16th Hun. These two squadrons had carried out three operations during that day and the 421 Spitfire that was lost was that of Cookie (F/0 Wm. Francis Cook). He failed to return and was posted as 'Missing'. "A cheerful and efficient pilot who will be greatly missed on this unit and all hope is that he is safe" was written in 421 squadron records. There was no further update about his fate and it wasn't until I saw his name and address in the Canadian Fighter Pilots Association Membership List in 1991, that I knew he had survived the war.

In a brief exchange of letters, I learned that he had spent his 21st birthday in Paris with the Resistance who were helping to get him back to England. When I met him and his wife, Esther at the C.F.P.A's Reunion in Toronto in 1992, he told me the rest of the story, and I persuaded him to write it all down for the benefit of his children and grandchildren who, in later years would treasure a full account of his exciting trek across France. He sent me a copy too and the following is a slightly abridged version . . . .

I had not been scheduled for the two earlier operations on October 3rd 1943 but was laying around the tent lines at Headcorn as there might be a third . . and there was. 421 squadron took off with me flying ass-end Charlie on the port side, as we headed for France. We were to engage any German fighters who might want to have a go at the Mitchell bombers of the Dutch boys who were on their way to a target elsewhere. My engine was running a bit rough so I toyed with the idea of aborting but pride over common sense made me continue. We ran into some FW190's who were looking for a scrap and the Red Indians were more than willing to oblige. It developed into a fierce dogfight and I was soon in some difficulty. My Spitty was not the fastest kite in the world and I was forced to press the 'tit' (an expression used by fighter pilots to get extra speed from the engine). I was having a problem keeping up with my No. 1 Karl Linton from Plaster Rock, N.B., who was a very good friend. Suddenly I lost all power. The engine was spewing oil and beginning to stream glycol and with very little power to manoeuvre in this dogfight, I was a sitting duck, so I called my C.O. Sq./Ldr McNair on the R/T and said "I'm having to pull out and head for the Channel". He asked if I needed an escort but I replied "If I can reach the sea, I'll leave my fate in the hands of those dedicated girls who listen in on the Mayday Channel for downed airmen and the Air/Sea Rescue will come looking for me!". Then I began to lose altitude and I was also being shot at from below by German Ack Ack, so I made up my mind to hit the silk but wouldn't you know, I couldn't get the coop top to jettison. There was no crowbar and I didn't relish the idea of drowning or roasting inside, so the only alternative was to head inland and find a suitable place to crash land. Once again I called the C.O. and informed him of my intention. He wished me luck and I signed off.

  I chose a field and set old AU-V down as gently as I could but it wasn't as level as it looked from above but I managed to make a reasonably good wheels up landing although I clipped my head on the gunsight as I was unable to lock my safety harness. Somehow I managed to get the perspex open and dropped the side door - stepped out on the wing and then on to the ground. I looked in the cockpit for a fire bomb to set the Spitfire alight but I couldn't find one. On the edge of the field was a small grove of trees so I headed in that direction as fast as I could but at the speed I was going, I wouldn't have beaten a tortoise, let alone a hare. Little wonder, I was being weighed down with my Mae West, parachute pack, helmet and goggles. I returned and left them in the cockpit but I was very reluctant to part with the American flying goggles, as I had only gotten them from a Yank pilot at Friston a few weeks before and I had become quite attached to them. When I got back to the grove, I hid in a bush and it wasn't long before I heard some people calling out 'Camarade' or was it 'Kamarad' - I wasn't sure. As they came closer, I thought it best to surrender before someone poked me in the ass with a bayonet or worse - shoot me! I stood up with my arms raised and I was soon surrounded by a jabbering crowd of French villagers who also walked all around the

Spitfire as well. This was done for a specific purpose - if a crowd of people trampled the ground around an Allied aircraft, there would be such a confusion of human scents that a German tracker dog would not know which one belonged to the airman and would be unable to trail him. I was motioned by a young madamoiselle to follow her and she took off across the field with me in hot pursuit - could that young lady ever run? I was taken to a small cave divided into two sections which appeared to have chalk sides. This was to be my temporary hiding place and the lady said she and some others would return when the Germans had departed. I was sure glad I had remembered a little of my school French.

During the evening, I heard a commotion outside the cave entrance and I was relieved to find that it was the villagers, as good as their word, returning with some food. I was given some beer, bread and two raw eggs and they told me the Germans were still searching for me but they had been sent in the opposite direction. It wasn't safe for the Frenchies to hang about, so they left saying they would be back again in the morning.

When I awoke, I was expecting them to come but as the hours went by, no-one did, and I was alone all that day, not quite knowing what to do for the best. I felt that something had gone badly wrong. I was afraid they might have been picked up and taken to German Headquarters for questioning without being able to tell anyone else where I was, or was it too risky for them to come back? Even if I ventured out, I wouldn't have got very far before nightfall, so I decided to spend another night in the cave and then if no-one came, I would make a break for it in the morning - besides, I was getting hungry. I set out the next morning and without meeting a soul. I eventually came to a road and then I saw a man with a cart coming in my direction. I hid in the ditch until he passed and then I ran out and jumped on the cart. He was naturally surprised at my sudden appearance but did not seem unduly alarmed. Using my best French I asked "Ou est l'Allemand?" to which he replied "Non l'Allemand ici". When we came within sight of a small village, I jumped off the cart and headed towards it, walking along the edge of a field.

I was hoping I might meet a local person who would know where I could get something to eat. The first person I saw was a man and in reply to my "Je desire pour mange et pour bouche" he conveyed to me that he was a Belgian and I think he said there was a small cafe in the *village and pointed in that direction but I could not find it when I got there. Its difficult enough to find the right words in a foreign tongue with a limited vocabulary and the next person I approached, replied with such a diatribe of gabbled French without pausing for breath, that I was unable to understand a word of it! I was beginning to feel a bit conspicuous out in the street, so I ducked into a nearby door-way which happened to be a blacksmith's shop. The smithy did not see or hear me enter and I hid behind some vertical pieces of steel sheeting for a spell before plucking up enough courage to try out my pidgin French on him. I had my escape map of France in my hand and explained that I was 'L'aviateur Canadien' and asked him, more by sign language than French, to show me on the map where I was and his finger pointed between Poix and Conty (s.w. of Amiens). I also asked where I could get food and that I wanted to contact the French Underground. He went outside and spoke to a farmer coming down the street with a team of horses pulling a cart and after conversing*

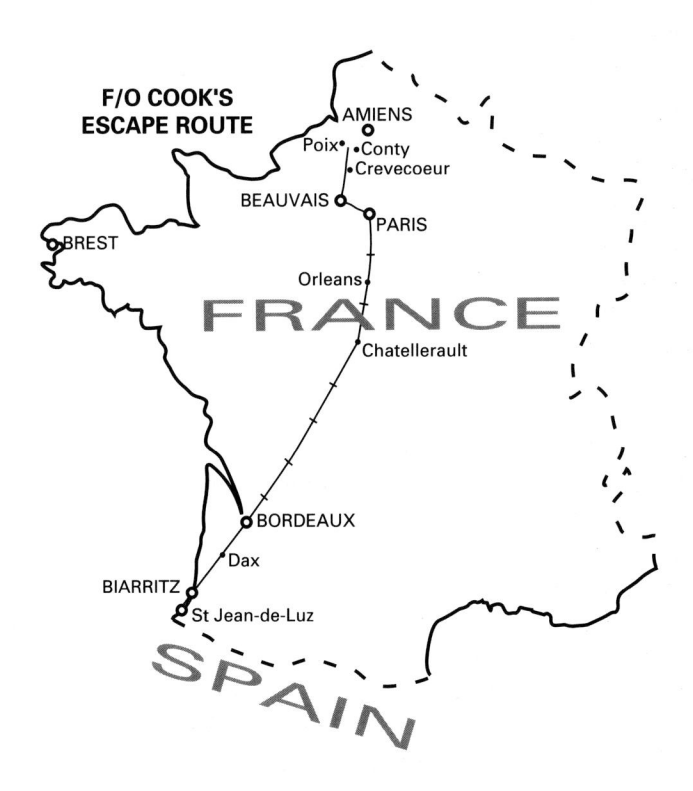

F/O COOK'S ESCAPE ROUTE

with him, he beckoned me to follow behind the cart. The farmer took me to his house and hid me in the hayloft but I had great difficulty in communicating with him. He suddenly departed and I was left with the uncertainty of what he was going to do. Was he to be trusted or should I make a run for it? He soon returned with a small boy, his son - who was supposed to be able to speak l'Anglais but in truth he only knew two words - Yes and No!

We had been told that if we ever came down in Occupied France, to seek the help of the local priest who, more often than not, was willing to assist evaders. I tried to convey as much to the farmer, who must have understood, because some time later he returned with the village 'pretre'. In his absence, I busied myself with the shaving gear and hot water the farmer had provided. The razor had a serrated edge and the soap was like pumice stone but I managed. I guess they just had to make do in war-time. I had also been given a slab of bread and some dry cheese, which staved off the pangs of hunger. The elderly priest spoke no English either but I was given to understand that I could not stay at the farm and must leave immediately. I also tried to convey that it was not safe for me to wander around in daylight and that I would not leave until nightfall. They left, perhaps hoping that I would leave of my own accord but later I heard voices and besides the farmer and the priest, I was visited by a doctor from a neighbouring village. He also tried to persuade me to leave but I was equally adamant that I wasn't going to budge until I could be passed on to another 'safe' house or when it got dark. After a further short discussion between them, the doctor told me to follow him. We had to cross some fields to reach his car, which he had parked under some trees, well away from the farm. As we drove off, I had no idea where we were going but on the way, I caught my first sight of a German soldier and if he was a typical specimen of that superior master race, I wasn't impressed!

We came to the small village of Crevecouer and I was taken to a small cafe where I was to stay with a family named Bonnevaine, who had one little boy named Regis. There I was interrogated at length and told in no uncertain terms that if I wasn't telling the truth, they would have no hesitation in shooting me. German agents often tried to infiltrate the escape lines so they needed to be extremely cautious, as a careless mistake could put every helper along the route in danger of their lives. The next morning I was told that they had contacted

England who confirmed that I was who I claimed to be and I was immensely relieved to now be in the hands of the Resistance, who would help me to get back. I remained at this cafe for a few days and passed the time listening to the BBC at certain hours, drinking wine, eating and reading French magazines. Germans frequented the cafe every night to eat and drink at the bar, so everyone had to be careful not to arouse suspicion. (I was able to visit the Bonnevaines after the invasion, when I was on my second tour and I still have the photograph of Regis and myself taken in October 1943.)

One morning, the doctor and another man came to the cafe and said that I would be moving on. We stopped briefly at the doctor's house en route and I met his lovely Brazilian wife, who could speak a little English. We continued on our way and I was taken to a farmhouse in a little village near Beauvais - the name escapes me but perhaps I was never told what it was. I do remember it was near an aerodrome and it seemed strange being on the enemy side of the fighting, watching the German 'planes take off, knowing they were scrambling to engage our fighters and bombers. The farmers were a young married couple but I never knew their name, nor did I ask. What you didn't know, you couldn't tell if you were ever captured and interrogated. The brother of the farmer's wife was in hiding from the Germans because he did not want to be sent away to a forced labour camp somewhere.   It was here that I was joined by a Polish fighter pilot, Anje Cherwinski from Kracow, who was to be my constant companion for the rest of our journey - I called him Andy. He had just been released from an Underground hospital, where he had been convalescing after suffering from burns to his face when he crash landed.

We were visited by a French school teacher who brought us a tooth brush, a tube of toothpaste and best of all, some cigarettes. I paid for these items out of the monies in our escape kit. Perhaps that is why I was asked to repay the cost of these kits after the war! (I just had to get that in my story). The teacher also gave me some lessons in French. Andy could speak French fluently so had no need to join in these sessions but I thought he was real mean when he wouldn't interpret for me unless I was really stuck but looking back, I guess he was doing me a favour.

Local German troops sometimes arrived unexpectedly at the farm on the scrounge for poultry or eggs, so we only visited the outhouse toilet when it was dark. The barns, outbuildings and farmhouse formed a rectangle and in the centre of the yard was a huge pile of manure. To reach the shanty, you passed through a gate which led into their orchard but on this particular night, I didn't close it on my way through. When I came out the moon was hidden behind a cloud and I couldn't see a thing. Like a sleep-walker, with my arms extended in front of me, I began to walk down the slight incline, expecting to feel the gate with my outstretched hands but I kept on going and ended up in the prone position on the pile of manure. I dare not repeat the words that went through my mind as I would never make it through purgatory but I do remember saying 'Shit' and I was covered with it!

After five days, we were taken by car to a village outside Paris. I felt quite at home on the roads in France, as they drive on the same side as we do in North America. We were lodged for one night at the home of a French Army Captain, who had served in the Near East. We tried out his rowing machine, which provided good exercise for us as we spent a lot of time in hiding. The Captain was later taken into custody by the Germans and I heard that he had been put to death. The next morning, we left again by car for the great metropolis . . .
P A R I S and I was about to take my first ride on the Metro.

As my French was not very fluent, I remained some yards behind the others when we went through the checkpoint. I was told to board the last car of the train which was for Jews only. The Germans would not associate with Jews, so it was thought I would be safer there and my companions travelled in the preceding carriage. At every stop on the Metro, I had to keep a watchful eye to see when my companions got off. I had been provided with a French novel which I was supposed to be reading to make me less conspicuous but the French lady next to me kept staring at the book and I realised that I had not turned over any pages! She smiled when I did and maybe she suspected what I was. I had placed myself near the door so I was able to get out promptly when I saw the others alight. I had been kitted out with a really sharp brown check suit, tie and shoes and of course, I was carrying false papers. My fellow travellers passed through a swinging glass door and up a flight of stairs to the street. I followed some distance behind and when I reached the door, I could see a German Officer immediately behind me, reflected in the glass of the door, so I did what I thought most Frenchmen would do - I opened the door and let him go past first. He looked at me and said "Merci" in a gutteral German voice, to which I replied in my best French "Ca va". That gave my confidence a boost because he did not realise I was a Canadian evader but I knew he was a damn German!

We strolled along the streets of Paris in the direction of a small Roman Catholic Cathedral where our Paris contact was supposed to meet us but someone goofed and we were in the wrong Cathedral - shades of the Air Force! Our guide was at a loss to know what to do then and had we not had Andy with us, we might have been in serious trouble. He had been in Paris before, when he fled from Poland at the beginning of the war. He had his cousin with him then and they had stayed with a French gentleman. He remembered his name, looked him up in the 'phone book and he was still at the same address. We were invited to lunch but we could not stay the night there, so Andy got in touch with someone he had met in 1940 and the three of us made our way to their apartment. I was intrigued at my first sight of the French urinals - they only hid the bare essentials! Andy also rang his cousin and told him details of our predicament and what we were doing, which I thought was a risky thing to do over the 'phone. To be quite truthful, I was getting a bit nervous by this time at the unnecessary chances he was taking but I was in no position to say anything.

When we arrived at the apartment, which was to be our refuge for the night, a middle-aged woman met us at the door and invited us in. She greeted Andy in the usual French fashion - a kiss on each cheek and I was really surprised when she spoke to him with an American accent. She came from Boston, had married a French doctor and came to live in Paris many years ago. This happened to be a memorable day in my life - it was my 21st Birthday but I never thought I would be spending it in 'gay Paris'. Despite the shortages Parisians suffered during the German occupation, we had quite a party that night, and Andy's cousin joined us. We celebrated with champagne, sardines in tomato sauce, Peak Frean biscuits and English tea. Not exactly the menu I would have chosen for such a celebration, had I been elsewhere but I counted my blessings - I was still free and had I been caught, I would have been in a P.o.W camp with even less to eat. This apartment had a bidet in the bathroom which was a new one on me but Andy explained its proper function - otherwise I might have made a serious faux pas!

The next day we were taken to a magnificent Cathedral - it had to be Notre Dame. The interior was very ornate and as we entered, we dipped our hands in the Holy Water and crossed ourselves. Although I was a Protestant, I knew what to do as I had Roman Catholic friends in Canada and had been in their church. We had to repeat the performance several times on the way to the pew, where we knelt down to pray. We were to look for a woman in a large floppy black hat and when she left, we were to follow, which we did. We caught up with her a way down the street and wandered around for a little while until she was satisfied we had not been followed. She took us to an apartment building, climbed a couple of flights of stairs and knocked at a door. The person who answered, turned out to be the young priest who was conducting the service in the Cathedral. His mother and sister were inside but they were only visiting and did not stay the night. Later, an older gentleman put in appearance - he had a noticeable limp, genuine or otherwise I couldn't tell but he began asking a lot of questions, to me in particular - about baseball and what was a Texas leaguer etc.? Testing my credibility I reckoned but I was able to provide the right answers as I had played quite a lot of sport before I enlisted. Apparently, he was the top man in the Paris area of the Resistance and Andy thought he was probably of Russian origin. He spoke perfect French to the priest, fluent Polish to Andy and the most articulate English I had ever heard.

    We spent four days in the Father's apartment and then the man with the limp returned. He informed us that we were being moved on in stages towards the south of France. He took us to the stalls that line the Seine and then left, after which a young woman made contact and she was to stay with us for the remainder of the day. To while away the time, she took us on a tour of the Botanical Gardens - maybe it was a place the Germans did not frequent, as we did not see any there. Afterwards we were taken to a small cafe and we sat down at a table away from the rest of the patrons. She ordered food and wine for us all. I wanted the Men's Room and Andy thought it must be outside but when I opened the door, there was no window in the passage and I couldn't see where to go. Someone called out "L'allume etat sur la gauche". Oh heck, was that left or right? I had to think quickly and then I remembered the coat of arms of Canada - le droit was the right and I found the light! The toilet was just a stall with two porcelain shoe imprints for your feet and a hole dead centre - why hadn't I trained as a bomb-aimer, instead of a pilot? I returned to the table and enjoyed my meal. British invaders sometimes risk being exposed in *restaurants because of the way they use their knives and forks but for once I was doing the right thing - the Canadian way was the same as the Continentals. I was quite relieved to get out of that cafe, because I began to feel uncomfortable that we were attracting the attention of other patrons.*

To pass the rest of the time before our train departure, we were taken to a cinema where we saw a German propaganda film on the great retreat of the Allied armies in North Africa. When we eventually arrived at the railway station, our lady companion gave us our next instructions before she departed. I was now supposed to be a deaf and dumb engineer, collaborating with the Germans and I was on my way to the south of France to inspect some of the newly established fortifications on the coast, where an Allied invasion from the Mediterranean might be launched. Our new guide and Andy went through the check-point first without any problem and I hoped I would be as fortunate. I followed a little way behind and not surprisingly, I felt a little tense at this supreme test of nerves, having to 'bluff if out' in front of, who I presumed were the Gestapo. I tried to appear casual as I knew one false move . . . . After my papers were checked they were handed back to me, and as I began to walk down the platform, one of the Germans shouted something after me. I couldn't understand the lingo so I did not know whether it was directed at me or someone else and was I supposed to stop? Had I done so, or even looked round, they would have known for sure that I was not deaf, so I just had to keep on walking and I was so relieved that no-one came after me. I followed the other two into one of the carriages and took a seat opposite, showing them no sign of recognition. A rather beautiful mademoiselle entered the carriage and sat down beside me - she was accompanied by an older man who I thought was probably her father. She tried to engage me in conversation but I had to pretend I didn't hear and continued to stare ahead. Our guide eventually leaned across and suggested that I might be a deaf mute. "What a shame" she replied "such a nice young man". As we journeyed towards Bordeaux, she slept with her head on my shoulder throughout most of the night and I had to sit there like a bump on a log, imagining how different things might have been!

We arrived at Bordeaux in the early morning and we followed our guide through a tunnel to another platform. We had already been briefed to hold our tickets in our right hand and they would be replaced by another. Sure enough, while in the tunnel I was jostled by a man and when I emerged at the other end, I had a new ticket from Bordeaux to Dax. Standing on the platform, waiting for the same train as we were, I noticed two young men standing together and it crossed my mind that they might also be evaders. We all boarded a much smaller branch line train and this journey took about four hours. We were now a little inland from the Biarritz coast and Andy, our guide and myself hung back to let the other two possible evaders go through first. Having got this far travelling right through France, and now getting nearer to the Spanish border we didn't want anything to spoil our chance of freedom. We all got through the barrier and that was our last train ride. I had guessed right - the two men were 'on the run' too. One was an American bomb aimer and the other a British pilot. We nonchalantly walked down the street and picked up our next mode of transport .... bicycles. Of course most everyone in the States drove about in cars, so the Yank had probably never ridden a bike before and he had great difficulty in balancing on two wheels. We started off through the village, up and down quite a few hills and on one downhill gradient, which ended in a sharp turn, our American friend went straight on and tumbled over the handlebars. His face suffered the worst of the damage but the guides cleaned him up and we proceeded on our way. The terrain was all up hill and down dale and after many hours of cycling, we eventually saw our destination - the village of St. Jean de-Luz. From here on, it was a downward slope - not so tough on our tired legs and sore bottoms. This was the last village before crossing into Spain and the increased German presence indicated a tightening of security here. It was now beginning to get dark and coming towards us was a detail of Kraut soldiers who looked either over fifty or under sixteen - they had to be Wermacht. Still on our bicycles but well spaced from each other, we pulled over to the curb until the squad passed. Suddenly, a man yelled out "L'allume". The Yank did not have his bicycle light on and not understanding what had been shouted, he did nothing. We were afraid he was going to be questioned but he was saved by a man who ran out from the pavement and switched on the Yank's light. We would not be needing our bicycles any more and deposited them in a store, as the final and most hazardous part of our journey would be on foot. In front of us was a river which could only be crossed by a long bridge which had German guards at both ends. Luck plays a very large part in a venture like this and so far Lady Luck had been with us all the way - "Don't desert us now", I was pleading under my breath. We crossed the bridge in pairs, produced our credentials and miraculously, no questions were asked. What a relief! We were taken to a house in a back street belonging to a small wirey woman who, although I never knew her name in 1943, was probably Kattalin Aguirre. (After she died, I was sent a photostat picture of a Basque woman who had helped get escapees into Spain and the description certainly fitted her to a 'T'.) We were given some food and allowed to rest there for a few hours until it was time to leave and head for the Pyrenean foothills during the night.

  This time our guides were 3 Basque women - I got the best of the deal as I was chosen and taken in tow by the prettiest one. It was very dark and raining as we climbed the winding slippery path, which eventually led to a farmhouse in the hills, where we were given bread, cheese and goat's milk to sustain us over the next strenuous part of our cross country hike. We were asked to leave behind any monies that we had on us and then we were introduced to our next guide. He was a tough looking individual - I am quite a big fella myself but I wouldn't want to have tangled with him! The rest of the group included a few other dubious characters, who were smuggling radios and other merchandise into Spain. Refreshed once more, we set off again.

  Our guides cut saplings and fashioned them in the form of staves. To each stave, we tied a white handkerchief so that we could see the man in front of us in the dark and they proved most useful to dig into the ground when the way was steep and slippery. The special shoes we were given had canvas uppers and rope soles which were very comfortable and quiet but unfortunately, not waterproof. We had been walking in constant drizzle by the time we reached the summit on the French side and then it was downhill towards the border. Our guide told us to squat down while he went on ahead to see who was coming into France by the back door. They were some of his compatriots who were smuggling coffee and other goods in short supply into France, so it seemed these guys had it going for them in both directions! It was pitch dark - the guide had a white disc on his back-pack for the person behind him to follow and the rest of us kept an eye on the white handkerchief on the stave in front. Later we halted for some refreshment of cheese and wine and our guide explained that there was a German outpost down stream from the river, which we would come to, at the bottom of our descent. From now on, we had to move as quietly as possible, feeling our way by using our sticks like blind men prodding the ground in front. It was just as well it was dark and we couldn't see how narrow a path we were treading or how steep was the drop to our right to the river below. Several times I put my stave out about a foot from where I was standing and it touched nothing! We had been in a constant deluge of rain and we were all soaked to the skin. At the bottom, we had to negotiate a swiftly flowing stream across stepping stones, which we managed to do by holding on to the stick of the man in front. Once again, the Yank nearly came to grief - he slipped on one of the stones, narrowly saving himself from falling in by holding on to the staves before and aft, until he regained his balance. As we were about to cross on to Spanish soil, we were again cautioned to make no sound, as our guide told us that the Spanish guards had a nasty habit of turning anyone they caught crossing the border illegally, over to the German garrison based down stream. The last hurdle we had to cross was a road, with a shelter of trees on the opposite side. When we were given the all clear, we scurried across in single file, thankfully unseen and then continued up the Spanish side of the Pyrenees. Not far from the summit, our guide said we could halt for a rest and we were treated to American cigarettes. We could also now talk freely.

Our feet were now firmly on Spanish land and after weeks in the hands of those wonderful French Resistance people, we had finally made it across the border. Through the early morning mist we could see a railway line which we followed into a village and there we were taken to a house to rest up for the day. Three smiling rather plump Spanish senoras greeted us and the guide said they wanted us to strip off our wet clothes - yes, everything! We were given a good rub down to restore the circulation and then told to put on a pair of itchy woollen Longjohn underwear, before being put to bed. We were then given a large tumbler full of brandy - the largest dose I've ever drunk in one go and coupled with exhaustion it was a knock-out potion to complete oblivion!

We were awakened in the early evening and told to get dressed. Our clothes had been dried and pressed while we slept and dinner was about to be served. After days of meagre rations, it was a sumptuous meal of about seven courses to celebrate reaching freedom once again - on the menu was soup, fish, meat, dessert and fresh fruit, ending with coffee and liquers.

Around midnight, we left the house and outside we were introduced to an official from the British Embassy in Madrid, who was standing beside a 1940 Buick. I could have kissed the Union Jack flying from the front fender! As we got into the car, we were told that if we were stopped, to hide under the blanket in the back seat and not to make a sound, even if we were poked by the end of a bayonet! The Spanish chauffeur drove like a madman, doing at least 70 mph through the narrow streets of the villages along the way. It began to get light as we approached the outskirts of Madrid and the car stopped on top of a hill, where we viewed the awakening city, which still showed the scars of destruction from the Spanish revolution. We were taken to a large villa, which I believe was the Ambassador's residence. We revelled in the luxury of a nice hot bath and a decent shave which we hadn't been able to have for a while. This was followed by a hearty breakfast of bacon and eggs in the Dining Room. We were then driven to the British Embassy and once inside those iron gates, we felt we were really safe at last. At this stage our Yank friend left us, as Americans were able to buy their way out of Spain, while we had to wait to be deported, as undesirable aliens. We spent four days at the Embassy, recuperating, watching movies in the evening, drinking lots of beer and generally enjoying the relaxation of our new found freedom, no longer afeared of a tap on the shoulder or being woken in the night by a visit from the Gestapo. In one of the recreation rooms was an upright piano with one sheet of music on it, which I could just about play with one finger. It was called 'Memories of You' and whenever it is played I always associate it with the time I spent at the British Embassy in Madrid. It was the signature tune of Sonny Durham and I bought his record the first chance I got.

    Four days later a man from the Embassy informed us that arrangements had been made for us to leave late that night, as deportees. Apparently, subterfuge was still needed and I was to be an escaped prisoner-of-war in the disguise of Captain Miles Standish of the Canadian Army. We were trucked down to the Station under guard, although I don't know why we needed one, because no-one wanted to stay in Spain! On the train journey, our Spanish guard kept telling us jokes that no-one could understand and then he would kill himself laughing at the end. He became a bit of a bore but we found a way of shutting him up. It seemed that every time someone wanted to go to the toilet he felt it his duty to keep an eye on them. We were a mixed bunch of deportees, including a number of Frenchmen just out of Spanish prisons, who looked as though they'd had a pretty rough time. So when *one man came back from the John, someone else would put up their hand to go - the guard was kept on the run, up and down the corridor and we were spared his rotten jokes!*

When we arrived at the disembarkation station, we were taken by truck to the border at Gibraltar. Here we were interrogated once more. We were asked our name, nationality, name of parents, where they lived, what branch of the Service we were in and from where had we made our escape? As Captain Miles Standish of the Canadian Army, my parents were Mary and Joseph Standish and were supposed to reside at 234 Jarvis Street in Toronto (in those days a street of ill repute!). I was instructed to say that I had escaped from a train while being transported to a PoW Camp in Germany. I often wondered where all this 'duff gen' went!

We were then allowed to cross into Gibraltar and we were issued with a wedge hat and battledress. Some kind English woman donated £10 to every successful escapee who reached Gibraltar and in those days it was a very generous gift. We spent our time in the Officers Mess or shopping in the local stores. One evening Andy wanted to visit the Polish contingent on the Rock and I went with him, wishing afterwards that I hadn't. Not one of them would speak English and I had to use sign language to get a drink of Scotch.

We left Gib in a Liberator with an Australian crew and we touched down at Reading. As we went through Customs, the English pilot and Andy had to pay duty on their cigarettes, cigars and fresh fruit but when they heard my Canadian accent, they just waved me through. I had been 'on the run' for six weeks but it seemed a lot longer with all that had happened to me during that time.

The guys in my squadron (421) were sure surprised to see me and I got ribbed ' F/O William Francis Cook has turned up again like the proverbial 'bad penny'. I was given an extended leave in Canada but returned for a second tour with my old Red Indian squadron - 421 at Kenley. We were moved to Tangmere in the Spring of 1944 when Kenley closed down and ten days after the Normandy invasion, the squadron took up occupation of an airstrip in France - B2/Bazenville. As the Germans retreated, we gradually moved eastwards into Holland and I stayed with 421 until late October 1944, by which time I had completed my second tour. I was awarded the DFC and gained my discharge in March 1945, with the rank of Flight Lieutenant.

Andy returned to operational flying in Fighter Command and was later killed in action.

Chapter 10

LISTENING IN AND OUT

Listening to the intercom of fighter pilots, as I did for two years during periods of intense air activity, many combat encounters and Mayday dramas, we were full of admiration for the outwardly calm and courageous way pilots faced the daily task of patrolling and ridding the skies of Göring's Luftwaffe and defending to the death the Allied bombers they frequently escorted on missions over enemy territory, often having to pay the ultimate sacrifice that all-out war demands. They knew only too well from the recurring absence of 'missing' fellow pilots and meeting their replacements, that their chance of getting through the war unscathed, were statistically only slim.

As far as numbers of personnel were concerned, a fighter squadron was a comparatively smaller and closer knit community than a bomber squadron and the Canadian fighter pilots at Kenley and Biggin Hill had probably joined up and trained together, many eventually serving in the same squadron, establishing a closer bond of fellowship than any peace-time friendship could. Apart from coping with their own daily survival, they also had to come to terms with frequently losing a close and valued friend - one minute flying alongside in the air and the next, hit by flak or shot down - in a flash, gone forever. There was barely time to grieve and it is perhaps true to say that in war-time, men guarded their emotions more closely, spoke of them less easily but felt them just as deeply.

During less tense moments over the intercom, we especially liked the Canadians free and easy R/T chatter - not quite so staid and formal as the English squadrons and when airborne, their casual style and wit frequently made us smile or sometimes even laugh out loud. We often joined in with a snappy reply, momentarily forgetting it was a one-way system and we could not be heard. At times their boyish exuberance at being 'free as a bird', roaming the heavens in such a manoeuvrable airplane as the Spitfire, could not be subdued. Sometimes you would think they did not take anything seriously but we knew that personal fears were contained and camouflaged behind that joviality. It was no joke 'up there' trying to cheat death and an outward show of high spirits was the best way to keep up morale between themselves. When one of the Canadians baled out over enemy territory, his pals knew he would probably become a prisoner-of-war and those who saw him take to the skies, would vie over his possessions. One might say . . . "I bags his typewriter" and another would chirp up "O.K. but I'm staking a claim to his radio". Then someone else would chime in . . . "Well, you're not having his car. We made a deal that if he was ever shot down, I would look after it until he came back". On another occasion, when I was dealing with a Mayday and the pilot was about to bale out, someone called out "Where d'ya think you're off to, Hank? What about that fiver you owe me - I knew you'd pull a stunt like this, just to get out of paying me back!".

Unlike the United States, who were eventually provoked into joining the conflict after being attacked by Japan, Canada did not hesitate in coming to our aid right at the start and has proved a staunch friend in both wars this century against German aggression. We have a close bond with the English speaking Canadians as many of their ancestors came from this country and that affinity continues through later generations. But let us not forget that 38,000 young Canadians gave their lives in all three Services for this country's freedom in our hour of need. They suffered 80% casualties in the ill-fated Dieppe raid. Canadian pilots fought in the Battle of Britain and there were soon enough volunteers in the early stages of the war, to form RCAF squadrons in Fighter and Bomber Command. Our gratitude has not been expressed often enough.

I had hoped to be able to quote some of the genuine rapport we heard over the intercom between the Controller and fighter pilots, which the WAAF's at Kenley took down in abbreviated long-hand but I have been unable to trace these Intercom Log Books. I had been banking on being able to quote what was actually said at the time, to enhance all the episodes I wanted to relate and my dejection was such that I nearly abandoned the project altogether, thinking that I would be unable to convey a genuine sense of realism without them. Enquiries at all the obvious places where such records might be kept, have been negative. In fact, I have been told that most probably they did not survive the post-war purge, when a team of reviewers were given the unenviable task of sorting out the mountain of documentation accumulated during WWII and deciding what should be kept and what discarded. Inevitably, there was indecision over some documents and these were put aside for further review in 5, 7 or 10 years time - long since dealt with. A lot of criticism has since been levelled at the inadequate qualifications and lack of expertise of the civil servants who made these crucial decisions. A heap of mundane material, such as Forward Planning (which never came to fruition), who won Inter-Group or Station sports events, training facilities and syllabuses or how many gas masks were issued etc. etc. has been carefully stored for posterity but it seems a lamentable loss to future historians if more valuable documentation which ought to have been saved, has been lost forever. Intercom evidence was often used in crash enquiries, especially when it contained the last messages spoken by the pilot and comments/observations of other squadron members; also whether correct directions had been given - essential data in ascertaining the cause of a crash. They were also confirmation by a reliable witness, of an enemy aircraft shot down, when recorded having been seen by another pilot at the time. My hopes were raised when I found a small file at Public Record Office, Kew - 'R/T logs and Correspondence' which contained some pages of intercom when fighter pilots were tackling the V-1's in 1944 but what had become of the rest, I wondered? I fully appreciate that the sum total of these Intercom Log Books over the war years amounted to a formidable pile and space to store must have been a criteria, but surely a carefully selected portion of combat intercom, would have been preferable to discarding the whole lot? As a civilian, I can now justifiably . . . . reason why?

The official Station Records of Kenley and Biggin Hill contain the operations of their home-based squadrons and the arrival/departure movements of Station personnel etc. A host of other activities unrelated to the parent base, took place in the Sector Operations Room, involving squadrons and rescues from elsewhere but unfortunately, neither Ops Room kept a separate daily record of these events.

The invaluable work of the Controllers in Fighter Command has received very little recognition in the written word and they are rarely named individually. They were the key men in Group, Sector and other Operation Rooms and carried an immense burden of responsibility dealing with the many lives in their hands. They had to cope with an amalgam of information at their finger-tips and the spur-of-the-moment decisions they were regularly called on to make, required an uncanny sense of perception in deciding which squadrons should be airborne to confront a hostile raid and positioning them to intercept - keeping some squadrons in reserve in case of attacks elsewhere - diversionary raids and unconfirmed information had to be evaluated - fighter squadrons needed to be recalled at the appropriate time for refuelling and re-arming and pilot endurance also had to be taken into account. Day after day, during the Doodlebug period, Controllers were engaged in manoeuvring several fighters at once, to intercept the hordes of V-1's being launched from ramps across the Channel. And through it all, they had to remain unflappable. Many ex-pilots who had completed tours of ops and others who were considered a little too old for active combat duty became Controllers and their mature knowledge of flying techniques was a valuable asset for the job. They were regarded as 'father figures' and their calm, friendly voices and reassuring words saved many a young pilot from panicking when he thought he was in a near death situation. He might be wounded or in a crippled aircraft and a Controller would gently coax the pilot every step of the way with directions and encouragement that he would make it to the nearest airfield, which invariably happened. D/F operators listened to many such dramas and Controllers had our well-deserved respect and admiration.

The need for R/T silence when in the air - 'Stick to the Code' or 'Be brief' was instilled into our pilots and Controllers and we who also listened, were vaguely conscious that somewhere Jerry might be eaves-dropping on our frequencies but at the time, my imagination wasn't fired to the extent that I can ever remember visualising a lot of Fritz's on the other side of the Channel listening to exactly the same intercom we heard! But they were and our 'Y' Service was monitoring theirs.

One of the best kept secrets of the war was probably the covert existence and activities of our 'Y' service, which from its humble beginnings in 1940, with just a handful of German speaking staff, gradually expanded as the war progressed and developed into a comprehensive network of receiving equipment which monitored the airwaves across the Channel. The Germans used their complicated coding system extensively all through the war years because they were confident that it could not be broken. Messages were conveyed on a machine which resembled a portable typewriter but they were further transposed inside the machine by several rotating drums, also displaying the letters of the alphabet but the key to the sequence of letters was frequently changed. Our boffins were able to break the code with intelligence from France and Poland early in the war and in 1941 an Enigma cypher machine was recovered intact from a captured U-boat, before it sank while the Royal Navy were towing it back to port. (The U-boat's skipper, Lt. Cdr. Fritz-Julius Lemp was responsible for the sinking of the British liner Athenia on the first day of the war, with the loss of 112 lives.) This valuable break-through of classified German intelligence, code-named 'Ultra', kept the Allies informed in advance of plans for every major strategic move they intended to make - for example, a signal from Hitler to Rommel was passed on to Montgomery, before Rommel had even received it. Only the top-ranking Chiefs of Staff, besides the code-breakers at Bletchley Park, were privy to the source of this classified information. The 'Ultra' secret was shared with the Americans but the knowledge was never imparted to the Russians, although they were given 'Ultra' source information that concerned them. Alternative subterfuge explanations were invented to provide a credible source as to how such information had been obtained and the Germans never realised their system had been 'cracked'.

The Nazis had of course, been preparing their evil intent in Europe long before we became involved in war and they knew the value of being one jump ahead of the enemy. They were well advanced in monitoring technology and they rescued quite a lot of Air Force pilots during the early years of the war from listening to RAF frequencies.

In Fighter Command squadrons were often 'scrambled' at the first notification of an attack and they would be airborne and on their way to intercept, while further information as to numbers of bandits, height and probable target was being obtained, which the Controller would then relay over the R/T to the Wing or Squadron Leader. In times of crisis, they would not have in the forefront of their mind that Fritz might be hanging on their every word. Seeing a friend being attacked, it was instinctive to call 'Look out Doyle, there's one on your tail', instead of using his section number. Little lapses revealing a surname could, over a period enable the listening Hun to recognise accents and gradually work out which squadron was airborne. A classic example was when Sq/Ldr. Johnny Checketts baled out - the Resistance got to him first and he was never in German hands but they knew his name and had claimed in a broadcast the following day that he was badly wounded and a prisoner. Biggin would not have been able to confirm or deny this only 24 hours after. When I wrote to W/Cdr. Checketts I asked him about the German's false claim that he was a PoW and he replied - 'Your Ops Room log for that day is very interesting. I did not know they had ever made such a claim or how they knew me by name. Perhaps they deduced it from the R/T chatter received by their 'Y' service. Thank you for the information.' Had I managed to uncover those elusive intercom log books, I would have been able to discover exactly what had been said when he baled out.

We soon managed to twig what the frequently used code words implied, although we wouldn't have been told - but most were so elementary, they wouldn't have baffled Fritz for long either! Whether 'oranges were sweet or sour' was a devious way of conveying if the weather was good or bad. For instance, a pilot wanting to land might ask the Controller - "Are the oranges sweet at my base?" and he would reply "Yes, Yellow 3, the oranges are sweet". Another time a pilot might enquire - "How are the oranges at Coachride base?" and be told "The oranges are sour at Coachride base". So far, so good - but sooner or later some unthinking clot would say "Oranges very sour. . . " and blow the gaff by adding "visibility down to 300yds"!! The code word 'gravy' as substitute for fuel and 'thirsty' as being short of . . . were easily 'crackable', when we heard a pilot say "Very little gravy left - doubt if I can make it all the way to base", and a Controller might reply "If you are really thirsty you had better re-fuel at Manston first!" Our monitoring 'Y' Service operators must have positively squirmed when they heard a code word used and then elaborated on in plain language in the same breath. Thankfully, such rather farcical lapses in R/T procedure had no detrimental affect on the final outcome of the war!!

From time to time at Wittersham, Kent Constabulary sent us and other local military establishments, frightening little memos warning us about suspected enemy agent activity in our area. Realising there were far more important places to be targeted, we didn't bat an eyelid. After all, weren't we chosen for our unflappability in a crisis - 'Don't panic' - 'Carry on D/Effing' and all that! But the memos that did nearly scare the pants off us were those that said footprints in the sand from the sea, were reported having been found on a local beach (Camber Sands) and all military personnel should be extra vigilant. When our Mobile II truck went out of action one night, it was discovered that the cables leading to the Tower had come adrift and the most plausible explanation was that those wretched cows were the culprits. It was duly reported to the authorities by the morning crew and when I came on duty with Joan, Eileen and Donnie, some men from the Air Ministry arrived to investigate, along with two mechanics to repair the faulty wires. The cause was not a loose connection after all but a definite <u>cut</u> which had severed the cable underneath Mobile II and could not have been due to any animal, we were told. This certainly increased our unease at having to cross that field alone at night in the dark, when we were needed to man one of the Mobiles. There weren't enough of us on duty for a spare bod to accompany you and anyway, she would have had to return to the Tower or Rest Hut on <u>her</u> own. We just had to put a brave face on it - or as our Scottish lass, Curly Dunsmuir recalls . . . "We were frit to death"! The Air Ministry never informed us of their conclusions, so the cause was never satisfactorily explained.

We did feel somewhat peeved that the Yanks, besides having three operators to our one to do the D/F work, also had an extra armed man on duty to guard their Tower, whereas all the protection we girls had, was a bayoneted rifle hung on the wall by brackets. If there was any ammunition for it, I doubt if we knew where it was kept.

A few nights later, when Donnie and I were on night duty in the Tower, we heard strange noises outside, so we decided to investigate with 'our weapon'. Between us we could hardly lift the thing off the wall. Donnie took the barrel end and I carried the heavier butt end and before venturing outside, we turned off the light because of the black-out and waited silently in the doorway for a few seconds to determine the direction of any more noises. We couldn't see or hear anything but to satisfy ourselves there was noone about, we bravely circled right round the Tower and gradually our eyes became more accustomed to the dark but we could see no shadowy figures in the open field. We got back inside, quickly locked the door, heaving a sigh of relief but when we were returning the rifle to its place on the wall, we realised what a couple of twerps we'd been and burst out laughing 'cos we wouldn't have done much harm to any prowler, as the leather sheath was still over the end of the bayonet!!

****

I was able to keep tabs on my correspondence during the war, by noting in my diary from whom I had received letters and the date I replied, which has been most helpful to me now. Although I had not seen Stan Atkinson for a month or so - the Canadian Wellington pilot stationed in Yorkshire - we had written to each other quite regularly and I met him at short notice at the end of August, when he came to London for a few days. It now sounds like one of my 'spur of the moment' take-off's! I left morning duty at noon, went back to the billet and threw a few things in a bag. Caught a bus to Ashford and a non-stop express train at 2.30 to London Bridge. Got home to Wembley about 5, 'phoned Stan - changed into civvies and met him in London at 7 o'clock - W H E W1 We had dinner at the Queens and saw the film "Coney Island". The next day I met him at noon with his RAF WOP/Air Gunner, Pat Chubb - we had a few drinks, lunch and then went for a stroll in

P/O Stan Atkinson

St. James' Park, where they took some photographs of us all. Stan gave me two pairs of silk stockings - a rare luxury, as most of our silk went into making parachutes etc. Canadians and Yanks were the chief source of getting any silk stockings and contrary to the general belief, they were often given generously, without any strings attached! That was my experience anyway!. Parachutes were being made of nylon in England but nylon stockings were still a thing of the future on this side of the Atlantic.

    Next morning, I had to get up early to get back to Witt for afternoon duty - my young brother Derrick cooked my breakfast (dear boy!) and Stan was at Charing Cross when I got there. We had a little time together before he saw me off on the Ashford train. A week later, he wrote saying that he and Chubby had both received their commissions and with the additional tremendous news - that Chubb's wife, Hilda, was expecting twins. A good excuse for a double celebration. In a later letter received on 29th September, he enclosed the photographs they had taken in St. James' Park (which I still have) and he said he would be getting leave shortly to have that celebration with me. After a week or so, I was becoming concerned that I had heard nothing further, as without his firm dates, I could not arrange my leave to coincide and it was unlike him not to have replied right away. I certainly didn't expect to have my last letter returned, with 'MISSING' stamped across the envelope. He only had four more ops to do to complete his tour but there was always the hope that the crew had managed to make a forced landing or baled out over enemy territory and had become prisoners-of-war. 'Missing' was not quite as final as 'Killed in Action'. In such circumstances, it was only the next- of- kin who would be notified if and when any further news was received and the only source of getting information for non-relatives was through the Red Cross. I wrote to them, as very often through their network they hear first if an Allied airman is in a PoW Camp and in due course they replied that nothing further had been known of his fate. I also hoped that if any of his Wellington crew had survived, I might hear something but no news came.

    Even in war-time, tragedies like this were always a shock. I had heard of quite a few lost loved ones amongst brothers of girl-friends and people I knew but this was the first time it had touched me so personally and little did I know that when Stan kissed me 'Goodbye' on Charing Cross Station, I would never see him again. At only 19 years of age, he was a skipper of a Wellington bomber, and had already flown 25 missions, with the added responsibility of his 6 crew members. I often thought about poor Hilda Chubb, about to give birth to twins, who would never know their father -

deprived of his loving care and guidance as they were growing up. Some time later I wrote to the Red Cross again but there had been no further news, so I came to accept that he had been killed.

Every once in a while, I had to discard a lot of correspondence because it was necessary to restrict one's clobber to the amount that would fit into a kit-bag, but in an old address book, I had his address at Skipton-on-Swale and Eastmoor and his squadron number.

During my recent research at Public Record Office at Kew, tidying up all my war-time loose ends, I thought I would look up No. 432 squadron records, hoping that I might find out what had happened to that Wellington crew. I had actually received Stan's last letter on the 29th September and I found that they were reported 'Missing' on the night of 27/28 September 1943, so he wrote and posted that letter before their Hanover op. Official details from records:-

A mixed force of 678 aircraft comprising Halifaxes, Lancasters, Stirlings and 24 Wellingtons attacked Hanover. No 432 Squadron dispatched 9 Wellingtons from Eastmoor and P/O Atkinson and crew were third in order of take-off at 19.38hrs. on 27 September 1943.

Wellington X HE817 coded QC-K   Crew
P/O Stanley Kyle Atkinson J18229   RCAF   Pilot 25 Ops
Sgt. L. Cook   RCAF Navigator
Sgt. W. Grant   RCAF B/Aimer
P/O A. Chubb   RAF Wop/AG
M/S S. Bybee   USAAF A/G
Sgt. I. Bowden   RCAF 2nd/Pilot

Nothing was heard from them after take-off and this aircraft was reported 'Missing'. The glow of fires raging at Hanover could be seen for 150 miles. A total of 38 bombers failed to return from this raid -
17 Halifaxes   10 Lancasters   10 Stirlings   1 Wellington

This was one of the last operations by 432 Squadron flying Wellingtons as early in October 432 Squadron began converting to Lancasters and they were stood down for the remainder of the month while the crews underwent re-training.

It seems that two of the crew did survive, becoming prisoners-of-war for nearly 1½ years before the fate of that missing Wellington could be told. The following excerpt is from a letter to the Atkinson family dated 22 June 1946, -

"On Sept. 27 1943, we took off from England for Hanover, Germany. We reached the target in good condition, a little ahead of time. We

were the only plane over the target at the time. The Jerry's picked us up in the searchlights. A fighter came up from the front and underneath hitting my turret. I was wounded at the time but did not know it. My communication was cut from the rest of the plane, therefore, I did not know what happened in the front . . . who was wounded. Another plane (fighter) came in on me from the tail. I shot him, he ran into us, hitting us in the mid-section. It turned the plane upside down, threw the turret with me inside away from the plane, that was about 18,000 feet. I bailed out about 2,000 feet. The two planes were stuck together and came down in flames. Bill Grant who was the Bombardier, was thrown clear of the plane, came down unconscious, landing on a building, fell off and broke his leg. Bill and I landed about two blocks apart. There were six of us on the plane. To the best of my knowledge we two are the only ones that survived. I could have found out the details from the German authorities at the time, if there were any survivors but I would not give out any information concerning our plane, that is, what plane I was on, etc.

After my liberation, I went to the RCAF Headquarters in London, England. I checked all reports stating Bill Grant and I were the only survivors. I saw these photostatic copies, and to my belief they are correct. I am very sorry to give you this report but I do not want to tell you something I do not actually believe myself. This is the truth as far as I know. I have written to Mrs. Chubb in England, stating the same thing. Her husband was our Wireless Operator.

I have not held back any information at all. I'd like to tell you that the Canadian boys were some of the best I was ever with, and the Canadian people treated me like a King.

(signed) Shelton C. Bybee.

Stanley had four sisters and their father was the rector of the Anglican Church in Kapuskasing, Ontario. I have recently been in touch with one of his sisters and sent her copies of the photographs I have.

Chapter 11

'SCREWBALL' BEURLING

It must have been a good few years after the war before I again heard the name of 'Screwball' Beurling. Hey, I immediately recalled, we used to hear that guy over the intercom and took bearings on his Spitfire. His nickname is probably why I remembered him - I had been intrigued but had never found out at the time, how he came by the handle of 'Screwball' - he was also known as 'Buzz' Beurling because of the joy he got from tree-top flying, often in defiance of authority on this side of the Channel. His fame then, as one of the top scoring fighter pilots had not reached us at our remote D/F outpost - to us he was just one of the boys in 403 squadron, part of W/Cdr. 'Johnnie' Johnson's Canadian Wing operating from Kenley during the autumn of 1943. I was eager to find out more of the background to this voice from the sky we had heard so often. Before Kenley, he had been out in Malta in Laddie Lucas's 249 squadron and had shot down 27 enemy aircraft there and earned himself a considerable reputation as an excellent pilot and a deadly shot. By the time he was 21 he had been awarded the DFM and bar, DFC and DSO and had been officially credited by the Air Ministry with shooting down the 1,000th enemy aircraft over Malta. He was also among the privileged few who were invited to sign their names on that now famous black-out screen at the White Hart, Brasted along with other legendary fighter pilots such as 'Sailor' Malan, Al Deere, 'Johnnie' Johnson, Brian Kingcome, Jamie Rankin, Grubby Grice, Johnny Checketts and many more. The White Hart was a favourite haunt of fighter pilots from Biggin and nearby airfields where they could relax and try to forget about daily encounters with the Luftwaffe and narrow escapes from being hit by enemy flak - they would 'Eat, drink and be merry . . . ' as the final words often became a reality.

George Frederick Beurling had many setbacks at the start of his career. He left school at the age of 15 so that he could get a job and earn enough money to pay for flying lessons. Very soon he had clocked up sufficient flying hours and passed all the necessary examinations to be eligible for a commercial pilot's licence but was still under age to be given one. At the outbreak of war in September 1939 he applied to join the RCAF but was told his educational qualifications were not up to the required standard for pilot training. This was a bitter blow, as he left school prematurely for the express purpose of gaining flying experience. Undeterred, he worked his passage over to England on a cargo ship to join the RAF, only to find when

'Screwball' Beurling

he got here that he was required to produce his birth certificate, along with his parents' written consent, as he was under age. This entailed a return trip to Canada to get them and to make sure he wouldn't be rejected a second time, he also increased his academic qualifications by extra studying. He was accepted by the RAF and after flying training, he flew with two squadrons in England and then applied for a transfer to Malta. He much preferred the more relaxed atmosphere and working conditions in war-torn besieged Malta, than the stricter, more disciplined Wing operations in England. Fighter squadrons operated as a team but Beurling often broke formation to attack an enemy plane, leaving other members of his flight at some risk without cover. For this reason, he was considered unreliable in the air by fellow pilots and unpopular in the Mess because he seldom joined in social activities, as he neither smoked nor drank. He was of Scandinavian descent and both parents were deeply religious members of the Exclusive Plymouth Brethren, whose teaching disapproved of worldly pleasures and shunned social activities. George led a rather sheltered childhood as friendship was not encouraged and as an adult he much preferred his own company and spent many evenings reading books to improve his flying and marksmanship skills. This dual talent, combined with keen eyesight was soon noted by Ginger Lacey (of Battle of Britain 'Few' fame) when he was an instructor at the Operational Training Unit at Hawarden, Scotland while resting from Ops and G.F.B. became one of his most outstanding pupils. In combat, this extraordinary eyesight enabled him to see an enemy aircraft long before it spotted him and with his precise judgment of distance, he could forecast which vital part of the enemy aircraft he was aiming for, such as the starboard or port engine, glycol tank. The pilot himself was often his target and an otherwise undamaged aircraft would spiral to the ground with a dead man in the cockpit. With such accuracy, he was very economical with his ammunition and could remain airborne a lot longer than pilots who needed to re-arm.

It was in Malta that he acquired the name of 'Screwball' because he had a peculiar habit of calling everything and everybody by that name - even hundreds of flies trying to do nasty things on an unsavoury piece of meat on the ground. By carefully lifting his flying boot and waiting for the precise moment to pounce, he found he could kill off a few dozen flies each time, without disturbing the rest, and after every success, he would murmur 'Of all the Goddam screwballs'. He quite liked the handle himself - it was distinctive and suited his highly individual personality and anti-establishment behaviour.

In one of his first encounters with the enemy over the Mediterranean, Beurling sent four of them spiralling down for their last dive to the bottom of the sea. He was in his element and his score soon mounted but his solo activities brought a severe reprimand from his squadron commander, with the threat of being sent back to England if he didn't toe the team spirit line. He suffered a severe attack of 'Malta Dog' - a nasty type of dysentery prevalent among service personnel due to poor diet and lack of fresh vegetables. Up until then, he had been reluctant to accept a commission in the RAF but changed his mind and became a Pilot/Officer in the summer of 1942 and later transferred to the RCAF. During his last engagement in Malta, he shot down three enemy aircraft and then became a victim himself. Even though severely wounded in the chest and foot, he successfully baled out at low altitude and managed to get into his dinghy and was soon picked up by a rescue launch. He lost a portion of his heel and spent the next two weeks in hospital with his left foot in a cast. While recuperating, he was told he was being sent back to England and then on to Canada at the request of the Canadian Government for a recruiting campaign and War Bond drive. His flight back to England was as a passenger in a Liberator with 19 other passengers. A war-time bomber had no seats or safety harness straps in the fuselage so they sat on whatever was available. The pilot overshot the runway when trying to land at Gibraltar and in an attempt to get airborne again, the aircraft stalled and plunged into the sea just off the end of the runway and sank almost immediately. Many men on the quay side who saw the crash, dived into the sea to help rescue the occupants but only George Beurling and another pilot managed to get out in time.

After a few days in England, George was on his way back to Canada with mixed feelings. He had been carrying a 'chip on his shoulder' about his early rejection by the Canadian Air Force and now he was going to be their prize exhibit on a political and recruitment drive across Canada, which away from combat, would also deprive him of the chance of becoming the highest scoring Air Ace of WWII, which he was well on the way to achieving.

It was six months before George returned to England, when he was first posted to the Central Gunnery School, Sutton Bridge as an instructor and then he joined the Kenley Wing, when 403 Squadron was at Headcorn, and for the next six months, he was often on our frequency. I must have known his call-sign to have been able to recognise it whenever he was airborne but my main recollection of that time was on 18 October 1943 when I was on duty and he very nearly came to grief. He had been chasing some Huns and called out over the intercom - "I've had it - I'm in a dive" which he was unable to pull out of, apparently. A chilling silence followed, while the Controller, the rest of 403 squadron and we on D/F Stations, were fearful that he was out of control and plunging earthwards. He must have momentarily blacked out for a few seconds, but recovered sufficiently to level out in the nick of time. It seemed an interminable interval to us before he regained his composure and was able to speak again, saying that he was alright. War-time movie dramas often portrayed a Fighter Operations Room personnel attentively listening to the tannoy relay of the R/T with the sound of aircraft firing at each other and the noise of 'planes crashing - this was not so. We could only hear the pilot's voice over the intercom - there was no background sound of crossfire or engine noise and the pilots could not hear the additional hubbub in the background of the Ops Room when the Controller spoke to him. 'Clear' was the operative word in 'Receiving you loud and clear'! Bomber Command had a different system in their Control Towers.

It was afterwards learned that during Beurling's steep dive from 20,000ft. on the track of an FW190 far below, his elevators had frozen up but before blacking out, he had turned back the elevator trim and his Spitfire had fortunately righted itself. The centrifugal force had driven the blood away from the vessels behind his eyes and when he landed, about half an hour after the rest of the Wing, the whites of his eyes were all bloodshot. The underbelly rivets of his Spitfire had come adrift under the tremendous air pressure and his Spitfire was a complete write-off. This was only one of the many occasions when he broke formation while flying with 403 to fight his own private war, and was often unwilling to conform to the squadron rule to work as a team. W/Cdr. Hugh Godefroy, who had recently taken over the Wing when 'Johnnie' Johnson left, had cause to reprimand Beurling for continuing to perform aerobatics over Kenley airfield in the Wing's Tiger Moth under 1,000ft. and sometimes in bad weather, after he had been warned several times not to do so. It was rightly considered that he was setting a bad example to junior, less experienced pilots who might try and do likewise and running the risk of killing themselves in the process. He narrowly missed being court-martialed for this open defiance of authority.

'Screwball' Beurling was a complex character whose unpredictability and attention-seeking behaviour, can only be described as 'rather odd'. An ex-WAAF friend of mine, Elsie Dickinson, nursed him when she was a Medical Orderly at Rednall in Shropshire. He was 'difficult' about conforming to hospital routine, Elsie recalls and they had great difficulty in keeping him in his hospital bed. He 'escaped' from the Ward one night and managed to acquire a rifle from somewhere, which fired a type of pellet. Next morning he was found at an open window, firing at the legs of WAAF passers-by on their way to work and scaring the living daylights out of them, which no doubt was the object of the exercise. Once again he proved his marksmanship skills because there were no crippled WAAF's limping around Rednall Camp! The nurses thought he was a bit of a 'nut-case'.

He was undoubtedly Canada's most famous fighter ace of WWII but there was no niche for individualists within the team tactics of a modern fighter squadron and eventually his senior commanders decided they had put up with his idiosyncrasies for long enough and he was unceremoniously sent back to Canada in May 1944. For short while, he became a ferry pilot with the RCAF Training Command but non-combat flying held no thrills for young Beurling and he resigned his commission. Later on, he applied for flying duties in the American services but his past record of misdemeanours and non-conformist attitude were known and his application was refused. He was also turned down by the Chinese Air Force. He tried his hand at several occupations after the war - selling insurance, commercial flying and he had a brief spell as a stunt pilot but he never really settled down to civilian life. He returned to Europe in 1948 and agreed to become a mercenary for the newly created Israeli state. In May, that same year, when flying a Norseland from Rome with a co-pilot, the aircraft stalled and plunged to the ground, killing both men. The Italian investigation into the crash was far from thorough and the cause was never satisfactorily established but sabotage was not ruled out either. This was 'Screwball' Beurling's tenth and final crash - at the age of 26 his luck had finally run out.

Chapter 12

CHRISTMAS IN HOSPITAL 1943

I was on morning duty on 23rd December and nearly froze to death in Mobile I, where I sat for hours on end. I faced a bitterly cold wind as I cycled back to the billet and I felt absolutely lousey with a helluva sore throat. I was cursing my luck as I thought I was developing 'flu two days before Christmas - I didn't feel like any mid-day dinner, so I took myself off to bed, hoping that I might feel better later on, as it happened to be Stew's birthday and there would be a party up at the Swan. I stayed put as I felt I was running a temperature and the next day I developed chronic ear-ache, which gradually got worse and Christmas Eve, I howled most of the night with excruciating pain and I don't suppose Joan and Eileen got much sleep because of my moans and groans. The following morning - Christmas Day - Eileen went down to Lady Cobb's house, to ask if she could use her 'phone to contact our nearest Medical Officer at Rye, an Army Captain called Jones, who responded promptly to the call. After examining my ears, he said I must go to hospital at once and I was duly transported by two Army Lieutenants in a Field Ambulance to the Buchanan Hospital in Hastings. What a nuisance I was being, messing up everyone's Christmas. I don't suppose the two Lieuts. were very pleased at having to turn out on Christmas morning but it was obvious I was in a lot of pain and I must say they were very kind and sympathetic. I was thankful that Eileen had taken such positive action after realising that I was in need of medical assistance. I had reached 19 years of age without ever having to go into hospital before but what a day to choose for a first visit! On admission to the Buchanan, a doctor examined my ear and then a nurse wrapped a huge bandage around my head and put me to bed. I couldn't face any Christmas turkey - in fact I couldn't keep any food down for the first few days and I had a terrible thirst. As soon as I was admitted to hospital, my parents were notified - I was under age and if an operation was necessary, their consent would be needed. They came down from Wembley by train to see me on Boxing Day. I was diagnosed as having Otitis Media, which is inflammation of the middle ear - I believe it was lanced and the fluid drained off but I am a bit squeamish about such matters and I preferred not to delve into the gory details! I was just thankful to be in expert hands and they soon relieved the pain. I was confined to bed for four days and I did not take too kindly at having to suffer the indignities of a bed pan for the first time in my life. When I began to feel better, I started eating again and managed to keep it down.

People were so generous giving me their precious oranges and eggs which were scarce commodities and a rare treat during the war. Four cargoes of oranges had recently arrived from South Africa, 2lb. per head to be distributed to all children under 16 and as the oranges were not able to be stored, any surplus could be sold free of restriction.

During my first five days in the main ward, three 'old dears' had died which was a bit depressing and then I was moved to a side ward - a good indication that you were 'on the mend' and no longer needing the nursing staff's constant watchful eye on you. The side ward had six beds but only three were occupied and thankfully not a snorer amongst us! I could not believe how weak I was when I was allowed to get up for the first time - I was very unstable and felt as though I was 'tight' and wrote in my diary "Wish I jolly well was!" because it was New Year's Eve and Sister had packed us all off to bed at 8 o'clock. All I could do was lay on my bed and think about the good time I was missing with all the gang at Wittersham and my New Year's resolution was to make sure I made up for it next New Year's Eve! This was the fourth New Year of the war and each one was greeted with renewed optimism that this was the one that was going to bring peace to the world.

I met a girl called Pam in the Buchanan, who was also in the Forces but I can't remember which service because we were always in night attire and dressing gowns. She was in a different side ward to me but we spent most of the day together, either around her bed or mine and quite often by an open window in the toilet having a crafty smoke - strictly forbidden in the ward and not allowed in the loo either, had we been caught. We were never where we should have been when wanted and Nurse West and Nurse Ellis often had to chase round to find us. We used to help them out by taking round the early morning tea and refilling patient's jugs with water, having a laugh and a joke as we went round. I was even entrusted with supervising the bathing of a few of the young girls in the ward. It all helped to pass the long day which began at that unearthly hour - dawn - which in January was still pitch dark. Goodness knows how the conversation between Pam and I eventually got around to Michael O'Brien Tippett, even before he came to see her. Amid shrieks of astonishment, she couldn't believe that I had been out with him three years before, when I was sweet sixteen and he was with the Irish Fusiliers billeted in the G.E.C. Sports Pavilion, only a stone's throw from my home at Wembley and I was equally surprised that he was her current boyfriend. What a hoot and talk about a small world - quite incredible given the unusual circumstances and the odds against our meeting at all. We had no doubt it was the same fella 'cos there couldn't be two with a name like that! When he did come to visit her, she teased him that his past was catching up with him but she wouldn't let on who, and made him go and see for himself. That might have been a bit unnerving for the lad because of what he might have been up to in the intervening three years! He was an Irish charmer alright and not in the least non-plussed at seeing me again . . . with good reason!

On January 1st 1944, I started the new Five Year Diary Joan and Eileen had given me for Christmas - this was my first entry "Saturday. I'm afraid I will have to start this diary in hospital. Not a very good beginning - wonder where I'll be at the end. Ate one of my oranges and read 'That Wild Lie' by Naomi Jacobs. Sister says I can now get up and spend my own penny - oh joy!" Like a new broom, I started off with my best and neatest handwriting but it didn't last long and gradually reverted back to my hurried scrawl. Its hard now to visualise life before Biro's but seeing the splodge of ink on the front cover of my diary has reminded me that in those days we used a fountain pen filled with liquid ink.

The Buchanan was quite lenient about visitors - the Yanks and WAAF's from Witt, when working shifts, could not always manage to come during the proper visiting hours but whenever they were in Hastings, they were allowed to see me. Stew was a frequent visitor and he brought me boxes of American chocolates and candy from their PX - our confectionery was strictly rationed and only a limited selection. One afternoon, another G.I. from Witt called to see me - Mac was standing by my bed holding my hand when, without any warning, he just slid to the floor in a faint. A couple of nurses came to his aid and lifted him on to the unoccupied bed next to mine - whatever was wrong with him he'd certainly passed out in the right place. When he came round he was more than a little embarrassed to confess that he couldn't stand the smell of anaesthetic in hospitals and that he was a bit of a coward when he looked round the ward and thought about people's injuries and what they were suffering. He never lived that down and it didn't do much for my ego either!

I normally wear my hair so that it covers my ears because they are rather large, and sort of stick out in the middle. Hidden from view, no-one would guess but of course there are no secrets between sisters. No. 2 WAAF sister wrote me a letter in which she said "I was surprised to hear that you've got ear trouble - I thought they were big enough to look after themselves!"

On the 5th January, I recorded "Hastings had an air-raid last night but I didn't hear a thing. Mr. Ligat, one of the doctors had his arm blown off". Those two lines did not recall a lot to mind - probably because I wasn't awake at the time to know what had actually happened. The next morning, I do remember that the nursing staff and other patients were amazed that I had slept through the deafening noise of the Ack Ack guns positioned along Hasting's sea-front, bombs dropping and all the commotion inside and outside the hospital, which rocked on its foundations from the near miss in the immediate vicinity. I believe I was the only patient who did sleep through it all, which must have been solely due to the insulation of the huge thick bandage covering my ears - I too was surprised because normally I am a light sleeper.

To refresh my fading memory of that raid, I wrote to the Hastings and St. Leonard's Observer recently and the enclosed cutting 'SURGEON BADLY INJURED BY BOMB' was on the front page of their weekly edition. Because of war-time publishing restrictions, the hospital was not mentioned and neither was Mr. Ligat by name. It did not say that the bombed house was his either, but it was. Hospitals are generally marked on maps and if one was mentioned by name after a raid on a town, an enemy agent would know exactly where the bomb had fallen, with a good indication of where the rest had landed. A town in south-east England was the only reference allowed, as to location. We obviously didn't find out and were probably purposely not told many facts about that night's raid. I never knew at the time that Mr. Ligat was on his way home after performing an emergency operation at the hospital or that he had been brought back to the Buchanan as a patient to have his right arm amputated. Had I known that he was in a side ward or that other bomb casualties had been admitted, I'm sure I would have related all I knew because there wasn't much of interest to fill my daily diary entry in the day to day routine of a hospital.

In the autumn of that year a Tablet was unveiled in the Frank Shaw Ward commemorating the dedicated service rendered to the Buchanan Hospital during Mr. David Ligat's 22 years as surgeon. The tribute was reported in the local Observer - "His kindliness, his skill and quiet smile had helped many a worried patient and endeared him to everyone in the Hospital from the chairman to the maid. It was a sad stroke of fate which deprived him of his right arm. Within a week of his loss, he asked the nurse for a pencil and paper, saying that he might as well start practising writing with his left hand. He had carried on his skillful work for 22 years at the

Damaged By Night Raider

Price THREEPENCE

SURGEON BADLY INJURED BY BOMB

Arm Blown Off As He Returned From Hospital

DAUGHTER'S ESCAPE IN WRECKED BEDROOM

A bomb which fell near the house of a well-known surgeon at a South-East Coast town during enemy activity early on Wednesday morning blew off the surgeon's right arm.

He was about to enter the front door of his house, after garaging his car on returning from performing an emergency operation on a woman patient at a hospital, when a bomb dropped in open ground at the side of the house.

The house was partly wrecked, the surgeon's daughter, a member of the A.T.S., who was asleep, was slightly injured, and his wife and an elderly woman servant, who were on a landing, suffered from shock.

A man fire watching on a roof opposite the surgeon's house was killed by a splinter believed to be from the bomb, and another man on the same premises was injured.

The roof of a house adjoining the surgeon's house was badly damaged and windows were blown out.

Other houses in the neighbourhood received lesser damage, chiefly to windows and roofs. A block of flats on the other side of the open ground where the bomb fell was among property most affected by this damage.

SURGEON'S COURAGE

The surgeon's wife found her husband lying injured, outside the front door of their house, and he was rushed back as a patient to the hospital which he had left only a short time before.

He calmly gave directions for his own treatment, and cheerfully making light of his serious injury, said to a colleague: "Well, that's finished my golf."

The surgeon's daughter, who received a cut on her right eye, had a narrow escape from more serious injury. She told the "Observer" on Wednesday that she had only reached home on short leave from the A.T.S. during the previous evening.

"I was tired after travelling," she said, "and was fast asleep. The first thing I knew was the ceiling of my room falling on me.

BRICKS ON PILLOW

"My bed was blown into the middle of the room and the wall was blown in. Two bricks fell on my pillow and I don't know how they missed me; fortunately I had covered up my head.

"My mother and our old 'nanny' were not hurt. We were all taken to the hospital for the rest of the night."

Civil Defence services went into immediate action, to deal with the incident, and operated very efficiently, and as soon as it was daylight a start was made on clearance and repair work.

The injured surgeon is in his 72nd year. A colleague told the "Observer": "He was filling a most essential post with two other colleagues."

When war came the surgeon was about to retire. But, despite his age, he continued to carry out his life-saving work at both of the town's hospitals and at two others in the surrounding district.

YESTERDAY'S BULLETIN

The latest report on the surgeon's condition, issued yesterday (Friday) afternoon, stated: "He has been seen by a consultant to-day and is progressing satisfactorily."

Some of the damage on the South Coast

115

hospital, for he joined the staff in 1922. In 1938 he reached the age of retirement from active service but the Board altered their regulations to allow him to continue his work until the end of the war but it was not to be. We regret the cause of David Ligat's retirement but we are thankful he was not killed."

When I was taken to the Buchanan, I was in no fit state to take much notice of the outside of the hospital or its grounds and I don't suppose I gave it much of a backward glance when I left but I believe it was designated a 'Front Line Hospital' and had to comply with certain precautions. I believe only the ground floor wards were in use and as far as I can remember, all the windows had shutters over them to prevent injury from flying glass. From my initial enquiry in the local paper, I have since heard from a gentleman who was in the Men's Ward during that January raid and he remembers one of the night nurses diving under his bed as the bomb dropped.

When Dr. Daunt said I was well enough to go home, I was surprised and overjoyed to be given fourteen days sick leave. I quite expected to return to duty right away but in the Forces, you 'never looked a gift horse in the mouth'! I had to go to the RAF Camp at Fairlight, just outside Hastings, to get my leave pass and railway warrant, before returning to Wittersham for the night to collect my belongings. I'd had very little exercise during the three weeks I spent in hospital and rather stupidly, I went dancing that first evening and suffered the consequences but I managed to make it home the next morning. Then three days of thick pea soup fog engulfed Wembley and surrounding Counties which enforced my convalescence and curtailed any chance of gallivanting.

I was due for my normal leave a month later but we had a lot of disturbed nights due to air-raids. I went dancing at the Red Cross Club at Watford on 20 February with two of my local girl-friends and we were very lucky to get back to Wembley that night. There were no trains running in either direction and we thought the railway line must have been bombed but after a long wait, one eventually came. Two nights later, we were woken by a siren alert, bombs dropping and explosions, so we all got up and stayed downstairs. Harrow School was hit that night and the Ack Ack got one of the bombers. Four German aircrew baled out and landed round about. One was captured in Wembley Park Drive, another in Alperton (an adjoining suburb) where firewatchers saw a parachutist land on the roof of a house. When they arrived on the scene, the German had got off the roof and was wandering about the street in a daze, not knowing where he was. They relieved him of his belt and revolver and handed him over to the Police. Another was captured 5 miles away at Uxbridge.

Chapter 13

THE END OF AN ERA - KENLEY TO GO

In the early Spring of 1944, rumours were rife that Kenley was going to be closed down. We were reluctant to believe that Fighter Command could dispense with it yet, as there was not a glimmer of hope at that time, that the end of the war was anywhere in sight and fighter activities on the other side of the Channel, besides escorting bombers, were on the increase, rather than diminishing. We were not likely to be given an explanation but I have often wondered the reason for the decision. In the Forces, we had to accept change as inevitable and the demise of Kenley was imminent but it invariably posed the question "Will things ever be the same again?" We were a happy team at Wittersham and had our work and play well organised. Bart, our Cpl. i/c was fairly easy going and treated us like responsible adults who did not need constant supervision and in my book, that is the way to get the best results from your work force. If we wanted to change a shift or leave early, then we arranged it amongst ourselves - as long as there was the required number of girls on each duty, then Bart gave us a free rein and I don't think we ever let him down. He was quite popular with the WAAF's - more than friendly with one in particular . . . . unbeknown to his wife!!

Our routine rural existence was occasionally ruffled by the unexpected visit of WAAF Admin. Officers from our parent aerodrome and sometimes a 'big-wig' from Group H.Q. would descend on us without prior notice. Diary says I was frequently ticked off for something or other - hair being too long (it must not touch your collar) - having red-painted finger nails (nail varnish was hard to come by and if you were lucky enough to be given some, you flaunted it!). It was against regulations to wear battledress tops with WAAF skirt but it was more comfortable than the tunic top and had no brass buttons that needed polishing! But one thing we were nearly all guilty of and reprimanded for if caught - not wearing a collar and tie when on duty. The soft detached shirt collars we were issued with, needed to be heavily starched, otherwise they would curl at the points and these stiff collars often made our delicate necks uncomfortably sore, so we invariably took them off as soon as we got on duty. Queen B'. . . s insisted that we should be properly dressed at all times and sitting in a little Tower in the middle of nowhere, spied on only by the cows or sheep, was no excuse for sloppy standards of dress! It was a good thing they were never around when we were going on night duty, with the top of our striped issue pyjamas, worn as a blouse under our battledress, which we changed into beforehand to save getting undressed when we got there - in winter that could be a shivering experience.

I was caught good and proper when on duty by one of these sneaky 'out of the blue' visits, when I was wearing <u>navy</u> slacks and a <u>white</u> blouse. I explained to Ma'am that we had been waiting six months and had still not been issued with battledress or Wellingtons and that it was rather draughty cycling in the winter in a WAAF skirt. She said no more on that score and overlooked the white blouse too. I reckon Joycie had not kept pace with the ironing of blue WAAF shirts! Even on out-stations, we were subjected to the occasional F.F.I (Free from Infection) - a regular medical inspection suffered by all RAF personnel. Visiting Queen B. . . .'s were not Medical Officers and about all they could inflict on us, was to look through our hair to see if we were lousey. On one such occasion, I was actually in the middle of taking a bearing on an aircraft, complete with headphones arched over my head, when from behind, this Queen B . . . . started looking through my hair. I had both hands on the D/F wheel, so I could only shake my head in annoyance. When I had a free moment, I told her that IF I had nits in my hair, I would do something about it, long before waiting for a WAAF Officer to tell me I had. No matter that I might have been dealing with a life and death Mayday situation - nothing must interfere with blinkered adherence to her rule book.

On Camp, these minor offences would have resulted in being 'Put on a Charge' but fortunately in civilian billets, we were almost untouchable for any enforcement of minor punishments, like being Confined to Camp or having Privileges Stopped, so we didn't worry too much about these petty rules. My encounters with Queen B. . . 's were rarely compatible and thankfully, infrequent! First impressions are usually the ones that stay with you and since Cranwell, later meetings with Admin. Officers did not alter my first formed opinion. I hasten to add that my comments exclude specialist WAAF Officer trades, such as Code and Cypher, Intelligence Officers etc. with whom I had no dealings at all.

Biggin Hill and Kenley, being the two most famous fighter aerodromes in England, often indulged in friendly rivalry and from time to time, our units were often connected to Biggin Ops Room. This I recorded as working for . . . or working on . . . the other side and judging from the comments I made, the D/F operators at Wittersham were rather 'anti' working for Biggin at the various times we were required to do so. We felt the Biggin plotters were rather 'snooty' and it certainly sounded as though they had bigger plums in their mouths with exaggerated posh accents, which were very much in vogue, as heard in old war-time movies. Sometimes we would toss for which of the crew would operate the Kenley Channel and the loser would be left with the Biggin frequency. One day, when 'muggins' lost the toss, I complained it wasn't fair and that I had been framed.

Early in February, our Signals Officer, Sq/Ldr. Howard, who sat on the right hand side of the Kenley Controller in the Ops. Room, came down to Wittersham on a visit with W/O Littler. I was taking bearings in one of the Mobile trucks so didn't see them but I was told that they had come to discuss with Bart, the merger of our D/F units with Biggin. A few days later, Bart, Curly and Jay, all long-serving Kenleyites went back to attend a Farewell Dance.

We had often been linked to Biggin Sector Ops Room in the past, without any fuss or palaver but in true Air Force style, we were told the take-over was going to be performed officially. At precisely 19.00 hours on 4th March 1944, our D/F units were going to be connected to Biggin Ops Room so at the appointed time, we were poised, ready and waiting to hear from them. Perhaps we were going to get a "Welcome on board" speech from the Sector Controller! We waited . . . and waited . . . but not a dicky bird. "Where R U Biggin?" - still no response. "R U receiving us, Biggin?" but the line was as dead as a dodo. "Ah well" Donnie smirked - so much for Biggin earlier boasting that we were now joining the elite 'first eleven' team! Just when we thought we might get a 'no work' night duty, they made contact and covered up the faux pas by not referring to it at all! From then on, Donnie and I worked for the 'other side' permanently.

The last operation from Kenley was performed by 403, 416 and 421 Canadian squadrons, escorting bombers to Namur in Belgium and during its active service in WWII, Kenley based squadrons claimed 603 enemy aircraft destroyed and 231 probables. The last remaining squadrons were soon due to move to Tangmere and for their Farewell Party in the Mess, the Canadians thought they would like to leave a mark of their presence during the prolonged period they had spent at Kenley. The best suggestion which was enthusiastically accepted, was to place ink-imprinted footsteps up one side of the wall, across the ceiling and down the other side. They built human pyramids which often collapsed through boisterous behaviour or being top heavy and of course, the soles of the barefooted volunteer they were manouevring across the course, had to be re-inked from time to time. The footsteps showed up very well against the pastel cream walls and they felt the mission was a resounding success. Well pleased with their efforts they crawled to bed, secure in the knowledge that by the time their artistic resourcefulness was discovered in the morning, they'd be long gone and beyond the reach of any reproachment.

But they had not reckoned with the unpredictable English weather and when they awoke, they were shocked to find the 'drome engulfed in a pea-soup fog - nothing was able to fly, not even the birds! The weather cleared later in the morning for take-off but not before they were required to make amends for their night's fun. The damage was assessed at £100 and they were made to pay up before they left. Even so, everyone felt their combined efforts made it a party to remember and if the truth was known, maybe the Station Commander was secretly amused at the escapade too. It was typical of the pranks fighter pilots indulged in to 'let off steam'.

Donnie and I were nearly always on night duty together every third night (Eileen Bond and partner were the other pair) and we generally stuck to the routine of one of us working the first half one night and the second half on the next night duty. This seemed to be the fairest way because we never knew for how long during the night we might have to work and if the Tower and a Mobile were needed, we both worked anyway. It really amounted to the luck of the draw - for instance, if you worked first half and were then stood down for a few hours, your partner got the best of the deal that night but it usually evened itself out in the long run, like so -

Relieved Donnie at 10.30. I worked until 2 a.m. and Donnie worked to 5.30 a.m..
I was on the wheel from 9 until 3.50 a.m. D. took over and packed up at 5.
D. and I both worked till 04.30 (Me in Tower, D. in Mobile) and again at 6 a.m.
Worked in Green Tender till 23.45 and then we were connected to Dover.
I took over from Donnie at 03.00. Closed down at 05.30. Bags of activity.
D. relieved me at 10.30 to 1.30. I packed up at 2.
I froze in Mobile 1 from 4 a.m. to 6.30 - sat with a blanket around me, shivering and numb.
Quiet night - dat's how I like it!
Bad weather - no flying - yippee!

There we were, every third night - except for leave - for more than a year in our Tower or one of the Mobiles, taking bearings through the night on aircraft who were no doubt engaged in interesting and often dangerous operations but after scrutinising my night duty entries, I gave very few clues as to call-signs or squadrons that I can connect any incident with, except for two Maydays I recorded I had dealt with during the month before D-Day. There were special squadrons who flew night operations but in the absence of a separate record of Kenley and Biggin Hill's Ops Room activities, I have no means of finding out what squadrons were being plotted or where they were stationed. The home-based Canadian squadrons used to start at first light doing early morning sweeps but they weren't night flyers.

Countless times, I have blessed my diaries for the information they have revealed about my war-time duties and for being far more dependable than my memory. Little snippets of just a few words I maybe dismissed as 'useless gen', often turned out to be like pieces of a jigsaw puzzle, waiting for the rest to fit together. In the previous paragraph, I mentioned being connected to Dover from 23.45 until we closed down at 05.30. Browsing through, I realised this happened on other occasions and I then began to question "Why Dover?" because I was not aware of any RAF establishment or airfield there during the war. In No. 11 Group, operations in each Sector were controlled by the parent Ops Room H.Q. i.e. Kenley, Biggin and Hornchurch, whose Sector in Essex encompassed a narrow strip of the extreme eastern part of Kent. I frequently pose more questions than I find answers and began to wonder whether our D/F land line was linked to any other Ops Rooms. The significance of the Dover connection gradually evolved when I heard about Controller Sq./Ldr. Hunter, who was highly praised by two Wing Leaders for his excellent ground control interception. Later I discovered that there was a Combined Forces Operations Room (part of the Navy complex) deep in the bowels of Dover Castle, linked directly to No. 27 Marine Craft Unit based at Dover/Ramsgate (High Speed Launches) and No. 277 A/S/R Sqdn. with a detachment of Walrus and Spitfire aircraft at Hawkinge. Adjoining the Ops Room under Dover Castle was an RAF Chain Home Low Station and the advantage of having plots from both Radar and D/F Stations under one roof, enabled Sq./Ldr. Hunter and his specially selected team of Radar and Ops Room staff to produce a degree of accuracy in ground control interception, unmatched by any other unit. His expertise and that of subsequent Controllers in manouevring fighter squadrons and rescue craft, quickly and efficiently to the exact location, imbued squadron commanders under his control with immense confidence. On various occasions then, our D/F unit at Wittersham became part of the Dover team.

On afternoon duty on 11 May 1944, I was given the task of listening for Maydays on 10 squadrons. At dusk 12 Tempests of No. 3 Squadron from Newchurch went on a low level Ranger looking for Luftwaffe activity around Evraux and Mondidier airfields but they only encountered ground flak from both places. One of their aircraft was hit but the pilot managed to make it back to Newchurch. The marshalling yards at Amiens were empty of trains and trucks but the Tempests successfully silenced some very active

AIR SEA RESCUE DOVER 1944
WING COMMDR E G GOUGH
WING COMMDR A D GRACE DFC
LIEUT. A.B. EDGAR
S/LDR. R.W. WALLENS DFC
WING COMMDR G. Le BLOUNT KIDD MBE
LT COMMDR D. McKINNON
S/O M.E. AUBREY
F/LT. H. EVANS
S/LDR. A.P. PEARSON
GROUP CAPT H.L. MAXWELL DSO
'CHUM'
F/LT. J. MANNING
S/O G.G. POLLOCK
S/LDR. E.A. HAINES
P/O G.M. PEACOCK
'VAGABOND'

guns. I guess the other nine squadrons were engaged in activities elsewhereon the Continent but I had no Mayday calls to deal with, so all 10 squadrons returned to their bases without loss.

During night duty on 12/13 May, I only managed an hour's sleep because Donnie and I were working almost continuously from 22.20 until we went off duty at 08.30. Between those times, I took bearings on WAGTAIL ONE-NINER, who had given an urgent Mayday call and having actually made a note of his call-sign and number in my diary, I quite thought he would be easier to identify than some of my more obscure jottings but in fact he has proved more elusive. I also noted that 'he got back O.K.' The Goldfish Club, exclusively for members who baled out and were rescued from the sea, seemed a likely first place to enquire and the Hon. Sec. John French wrote on my behalf in their quarterly magazine. . . .

> *"Come in WAGTAIL ONE-NINER - your time is up! LACW Joyce Millard is searching for you once again - as a WAAF in WWII, Joyce sat in her D/F Tower in Kent picking up hundreds of Mayday calls on aircraft heading for a splash-down in the English Channel. She is writing her story and wonders who was this WAGTAIL ONE-NINER who transmitted a Mayday during the night of 12/13 May 1944. Was it a fighter pilot based in the south of England perhaps? Now then lads - rake through memories and log books. Do we also know of any literature recording the work of D/F Stations, to which many of us owe so much?*

The membership of the Goldfish Club at the end of the war was around 10,000 but over the years has dropped considerably and in spite of the Hon. Sec's splendid effort, I did not find out the information I was seeking. A similar enquiry in the Aircrew Magazine Intercom also met with negative response.

The Air Historical Branch in London have details of RAF 'pranged' aircraft but it seems their present filing system is not yet computerised and lacks any cross reference by date. To be able to trace a crashed RAF 'plane, they need to know the type of aircraft and serial number, information which I never have, so they have seldom been able to help with any of my enquiries, including Wagtail.

Relating call-signs to squadrons was more difficult than I realised because they were not mentioned in squadron records and they were not entered in pilot's log books. Only those in the 'NEED TO KNOW' category would have been privy to this secret information, such as Controllers, pilots, Ops Room staff and D/F Stations. Ground staff personnel, not involved in R/T matters would probably not have known the frequently changed call-signs of their squadron. So, in frustration, I have given up on solving the mystery of who the pilot was of WAGTAIL ONE-NINER.

Chapter 14

EUROPE TO BE LIBERATED

In the run up to D-Day, 6 June 1944, more and more troops were assembling along the south coast and at times our small village was invaded and occupied. There were soldiers everywhere and it was impossible to find a seat in the NAAFI or get inside any of the pubs, let alone reach the bar. Then as quickly as they appeared, next day they would be gone but after these exercises, we knew they had passed through because of churned up fields and roads strewn with chunks of mud dropped from tanks and the wheels of trucks. Avoiding these obstacles on a bicycle was a bit hazardous at times and caused a few 'prangs', especially in the dark. Bicycle lamps had to be covered with paper or cardboard under the glass, only allowing small slits of light through and one night I collided with a rabbit, which broke several spokes but I didn't record the damage sustained by the bunny.

On one such Army exercise at Wittersham, 3,000 troops bivouced overnight in the village and when we arrived on night duty, we found our large field was surrounded with soldiers, just about to bed down for the night under the hedges. Four Army officers were in our Rest Hut chatting to the afternoon crew and I think they were ever hopeful of getting a shake-down for the night on the floor of our Rest Hut, rather than out in the open, but it hardly seemed fair when their men were sleeping under the stars. Apart from which, innocent though it would have been had we allowed them to stay, it wouldn't have done our reputation much good as the gossip would have flown around that small village. The next morning, our landlady provided buckets of hot water for washing and she made gallons of tea for the troops. Tony and Drew, two of the Army Officers, called in at the Rest Hut and we gave them tea and toast before we went off duty at 08.30.

Our night duties came round with habitual regularity every third evening and we much preferred to be kept busy on that long shift and more often than not, we were. On the night of 2/3 June, I worked on the D/F wheel from 22.30 to 1 a.m.. Then I was 'Stood Down'. That usually meant we could relax for the time being and although there might be other intercom patter on the frequency, Biggin Ops Room were not wanting any bearings. In the early hours of the morning on that 12-hour shift, I was often on the verge of having a cat-nap but there was no more sobering return from that twilight world than to hear the voice of the Ops Room WAAF through the earphones, telling me to switch to a particular frequency and listen out for a crippled bomber in distress - Call-sign LESSON ONE-FOUR.

Instinctively, I swung the wheel round to a southerly point because any aircraft limping home would more than likely be over the English Channel heading towards the Kent or Sussex coast. A calculated guess through practice and I wasn't far out - the first bearing was from a south-westerly direction. I found him at 187°, then moved off the dead space about 10°, pressed down the sensing plate to establish it was a true bearing and not a reciprocal. I relayed that bearing to the WAAF at the other end of my line and Waterhall and Kingsdown D/F Stations would be doing likewise, so that a 'fix' of the pilot's position could be displayed by a marker on the Ops Room Table. When the bearings differ quite drastically, it means that the aircraft is quite near and I deduced that it was west of Wittersham and travelling northwards. Meanwhile the first intercom message from the pilot was:-

HELLO CONTROL - this is LESSON ONE-FOUR. Position unclear. Request homing vector. Aircraft damaged due to flak.

LESSON ONE-FOUR - KINGSLEY CONTROL answering. Will help if we can. What is the extent of your damage?

KINGSLEY from ONE-FOUR - Hit over target and encountered coastal flak. One engine u/s and some controls not responding. Suspect quite serious damage.

K. to ONE-FOUR - I have your position - steer 349 and transmit again.

O.K. KINGSLEY - will keep on course for as long as I can but a/c becoming difficult to control.

The intercom continued spasmodically along these lines until ONE-FOUR admitted that his aircraft was becoming very unstable and he knew he would not be able to land it. Biggin Controller had no hesitation in telling him to bale out but there was no answer, only an anxious pause before Biggin repeated the message with more emphasis "Can U hear me ONE-FOUR. Bale out - I repeat BALE OUT while there is still time." Another eerie silence while we 'eavesdroppers' listened and waited - thoughts dwelling on the desperate situation of the poor pilot, battling with the controls before his emergency plunge into the limitless sky. Then came the final message "MAYDAY - this is LESSON ONE-FOUR calling MAYDAY. Abandoning a/c now on fire. Baling out."

I suppose it was about 03.15 when I was told to 'Stand Down' and I asked my WAAF Oppo: whether she would let me know if there was any further news of the pilot. Sometimes the WAAF's in Biggin's Ops Room would up-date info: - other times they didn't - but to be fair, they might not have been told anything either to pass on! Now fully wide awake, I reflected on the all too frequent night duty mid-air emergencies on our radio frequencies and wondered whether the pilot did manage to escape from his burning 'plane. What must it be like hurtling helplessly into the darkness and as the parachute descended, unable to control where or on what you might land in the black-out, until the final impact of feet making contact, fervently hoping no doubt, that it wouldn't be tall trees, greenhouses, roofs or any expanse of water?

Sometime later, the WAAF rang through and I was very relieved to hear that the pilot of the bomber had successfully baled out and was uninjured. She also mentioned that the 'plane had crashed at Coulsdon, which I noted in my diary entry for that night. . . ."On night duty. Worked from 10.30 to 1. Manned up again at 2.45. A bomber was in trouble but he didn't make it. He baled out and the 'plane came down at Coulsdon."

****

When some 48 years later, I came to assess how much factual information I knew about that war-time incident, it didn't seem to amount to a great deal. I didn't know the type of bomber and as far as I could recall, there had been no mention of the rest of the crew, who might have baled out at an earlier stage. Coulsdon was the only firm clue I had but the place, date and approximate time were too vague for Air Historical Branch to trace this particular crash.

On a later visit to the Newspaper Library at Colindale, I wasn't unduly disappointed when I found they held no war-time publications for Coulsdon or Croydon - an RAF 'plane crash might not have been reported in the press anyway during the war period but it was worth a try while I was there, I thought. The main purpose of my visit to the Library was to check on London afternoon newspapers, to find out how much we were told about the events of the dawn landings in Normandy on D-Day, 6 June - my next night duty. 'The Star' newspapers were stored in yearly volumes and I opened 1944 at the beginning of June and as I was carefully turning over each afternoon edition to reach the 6th, my eye caught a headline on the front page of the 3rd - 'BABY KILLED BY CRASHING PLANE' which landed on a house in Ridgemount Avenue, Coulsdon.

It was pure chance I spotted it because had it been on an inside page, I would have missed it altogether! A very lucky break indeed as it gave me a clue to work on by narrowing the type of bomber down to a two-man crew - possibly a Mosquito heading for an airfield north of London, maybe? The Controller would see from the plots on the Ops Room table that the aircraft was flying towards the more congested residential areas of London, where a crashing 'plane might cause far more damage and greater loss of civilian life. This would tie in with his insistence that the pilot baled out.

Step by step, over a period of two years I have gradually pieced together details of their perilous return flight from a raid over Cologne. Each new discovery produced one more clue to act on - a report in the Croydon Advertiser (not held in Colindale) revealed that one of the crew had baled out at Caterham, Surrey. Until then I had no knowledge of whereabouts in Kent or Surrey either of the crew had landed and speculating that the local Police Station was probably the only place open in the middle of the night for this crew member to seek assistance, I wrote to Caterham Police. My enquiry was passed on to Surrey County Records and from there I received the break-through I had been hoping for - their names and RAF base. I now had sufficient information to check RAF squadron records at Kew for an official report of that night's operation.

109 PATHFINDER SQUADRON - LITTLE STAUGHTON, HUNTINGDON. 2/3 June 1944

LONDON 'STAR' Afternoon 3 June 1944

BABY KILLED BY CRASHING PLANE

AN 18-months-old baby boy was killed and his parents injured when a blazing plane crashed into the front garden of their house in Ridgemount avenue, Coulsdon, early today.

The baby was Alan Roote, son of Mr. and Mrs. L. W. Roote. They were taken to Purley Hospital. Four other children who were in a back bedroom were unhurt.

The blazing petrol tank of the plane came adrift, and fell through the roof of a house in Woodlands grove, adjoining Ridgemount-avenue. The crew —two Canadians—baled out.

Several other houses were damaged, but the NFS kept the fire from spreading.

The plane was splintered to pieces, and fragments were scattered over a wide area. There is a hole where it hit the ground about 20 feet across and 10 feet deep.

A fire guard on his way home had a narrow escape. He was just going in at his front gate when he heard a roar and saw something like a flaming torch coming straight for him. "I thought at first it must be a German rocket arrived at last from the Pas de Calais," he said. "Then I realised it was a falling plane. I threw myself down behind a low brick wall. It was lucky I did so as debris flew all around."

19 Mosquitos to attack Leverkusen (Synthetic Oil Plant north of Cologne) and targets in N. France.
4 a/c detailed to attack Primary, dropping Green T.I's (Target Indicators).
Weather 10/10ths thin cloud. Defences - moderate H/F. Accurate for height.
<u>MOSQUITO XV1 - ML962</u>   Up 23.28. F/Lt. A.C. Carter (Capt.) F/0 E.W. Garrett (Nav.)
Marked and bombed from 32,000ft. by A.R.5513. A/c badly hit over target. One engine u/s and controls damaged. Hit again at French coast. Crew baled out over Kent. Both safe.

    Their names did not appear again on Ops until 21 June (after leave?) and they were both awarded the D.F.C on that day. I also established that both had survived the war - Carter's christian name was Arthur (RAF) and Ernie Garrett was Canadian. Progress was slow for a while as neither men were members of any of the Air Force Associations I wrote to, but from war-time colleagues I contacted through the Little Staughton Pathfinders Association, I was told that Arthur Carter (known as Chum on the squadron) died over six years ago but one of them gave me his widow's address. I wrote to her. I could hardly believe my good fortune when she sent me an account he had written after he retired of his recollections of that night's operation and their perilous flight back to England.
    Meantime I was in the process of making enquiries about Ernest W. Garrett to Aircrew/Bomber Command/Legion/National Archives of Canada but these met with negative response and there was not even the hint of a scent as to his recent or past whereabouts during the last 50 years. Pre-war Ernest Garrett had lived in Toronto and a 'kind friend' (who also lives there and helps trace RCAF personnel) sent me a page out of the Toronto telephone directory which contained <u>70</u> people by the name of Garrett in that one Town! There were no E.W's and at that point I was willing to concede defeat because it was too formidable a task to tackle from this side of the Pond and by this time I had received F/Lt. Carter's account of their ordeal. However, 'kind friend' said that in his next letter he would send telephone directory pages of the whole of Canada and the U.S.A. He highlighted two of the many Garrett's listed - one was E.W. in Manitoba and the other Ernest W. in America, and although my enthusiasm for finding this Navigator had waned, I felt that as 'kind friend' had gone to such trouble to help me, I thought I ought to make the effort. I intended just to write to those two but due to other demands on my time, I only managed to post the one to E.W. in Manitoba. I explained the reason for writing, with a few

details and ended . . "If you are the Ernest W. Garrett I am trying to trace, it will be a miracle - if not, please ignore this letter". In due course, a reply came and he said "Yes, I am the person you are looking for and I will be pleased to provide any information . . . . . ". I thought it quite incredible that I had struck lucky with just that one letter and I derived some satisfaction that dogged perseverance to find out the whole story, even after 50 years, does sometimes have its rewards!

2/3 JUNE 1944 - BALE OUT

My navigator, Ernie Garrett and I were due to go on leave right after this night's Op so my wife knew I would be late home. We took off on a lovely June night and I climbed the Mosquito to 35,000ft. We were trying out a new magnetron valve in conjunction with our Oboe equipment on a target we had not hit before. We turned on to the beam which gave us a straight and level course towards Germany but as we approached the border, we were hit by heavy flak. The Germans were now using radar controlled 155mm. stuff. We were expecting to find that the first Mosquitos had lit up the target but it seemed their markers had failed, so now it was up to us to illuminate the Oil Plant with our green target indicators, for the following Light Night Force to drop their bombs. I soon realised the port engine was not functioning properly and I was experiencing some control difficulty but I still hoped ML692 would get us to the target in about five minutes time. Soon after, there was a huge bang and we had been hit again, but we managed to release our T.I's before the Mosquito was rocked by another enormous jolt. Then almost simultaneously, all the searchlights in the vicinity were switched on and their beams criss-crossed the night sky trying to find us. This was a sure sign that we had succeeded in marking the target, which could remain hidden no longer. By this time, I was in real trouble - the port engine was on fire and the last hit had severed the aileron and elevator controls. We were doing a sort of spiral spin in the searchlights, diving earthwards but somehow I managed to establish enough control to level out and fly away from the range of their beams. The engine on fire had burned itself out but not before it had spread to part of the wing. The side of the cockpit was too hot to touch but Ernie managed to get the fire under control.

Above a thick layer of low cloud, it was a beautiful moonlit night as we slowly headed towards Belgium but the cloud below us obscured the coast-line. We guessed we had reached Calais from the coastal flak that was coming our way but we continued on towards Dieppe before turning north (so as not to miss the eastern tip of Kent) and there we again encountered heavy coastal flak with near misses but no further damage. Thankfully, our radio equipment was still working and after crossing the Sussex coast, we called on our emergency channel to ask for confirmation of our exact position and we were given a course to steer. The cloud began to clear as we approached the Surrey boundary but by this time, I was having great difficulty in keeping the Mossie stable and I knew I would not be able to land it, especially as fire had broken out again. It was time to abandon ship through the floor hatch. Ernie was a big chap and appeared to have got stuck, so I put my foot on the top of his head and he popped out like a cork from a bottle! I knew that once I let go of the controls it would go into a dive but I got free in time and the impact of the parachute opening felt as though I was being thrown against a brick wall at great speed and temporarily knocked the wind out of me.

    I landed in a field and before long I was approached by a soldier on guard duty who, with the point of his rifle in my back, marched me to his Headquarters. I soon discovered that it was a sealed military unit, awaiting instructions to leave at short notice for France for the invasion assault to liberate Occupied Europe. I duly explained what I was doing roaming the Surrey countryside at 3 o'clock in the morning and they contacted my squadron at Little Staughton, to inform them I was safe and well. At first, it seemed that I might have to go with them because no-one was allowed to leave but after much deliberation between the Air Ministry and the War Office, I was told that I need no longer be detained there.

    I'd had more than enough excitement for one night and reflecting on the problems I had encountered leaving France, I was relieved not to be going there again quite so soon!

****

The improved navigational aids of the Oboe equipment in conjunction with the magnetron valve revolutionised the tactics of night bombing. Two RDF ground stations in England were able to direct a Mosquito aircraft flying at 30,000ft. to a target as far away as Germany, and regardless of weather conditions, to accurately release its bombs with precision over the selected spot.

The following are combined excerpts from Ernest Garrett's letters:-

"I was most interested to receive your letter outlining your research and perseverance in gathering background data for your book. I first met Nick Carter at the Mosquito Training Unit at Marham, Norfolk in October 1943 and we crewed together during our two months training course. We commenced operations with 109 Pathfinder Sqdn. in December 1943 and the Leverkusen target was our 44th operation. I located my Flying Log Book and the notes I made at the time confirm that we took off at 23.20 hours, carrying a bomb load of 2 x 500lb bombs and 2 x Target Indicators. We sustained two damaging flak hits on the bomb run and a more serious hit after bombing release. It soon became obvious that it was unlikely we would be able to make it back to Little Staughton but rather than risk having to bail out over the North Sea in the dark, we opted to stay over land as long as possible by going over the Low Countries and Northern France and if we made it that far, it would be worth risking the shorter sea crossing over the Channel. We encountered some close bursts of anti-aircraft fire before leaving the French coast and one very near miss from our own Ack Ack shortly after crossing the English coast. We were able to carry on for a short period of time before the aircraft situation became really serious and we had no alternative but to bail out. There is no doubt that we only got back to England because of Nick's flying expertise and determined effort. I bailed out first and landed on the roof of the Town Hall at Caterham. Fortunately, my 'chute snagged a chimney which saved me from a dangerous fall to the ground. I called out, hoping that someone might be around but at 3 o'clock in the morning, whoever heard me must have thought I was a rowdy reveller returning home with the milk and I was told in no uncertain terms to "Shut up". I had no idea what sort of building I had landed on and having failed to summon any assistance, I broke in through a window and made my way down to the ground floor, where I could see a chink of light under one of the doors. Inside were some Fire Watchers on night duty, playing cards and with their help I was able to 'phone the squadron to advise them of the situation, although I didn't know at the time whether Nick had landed safely. Transport was provided to take me to nearby RAF Kenley and during the late afternoon of June 3rd, we were picked up by a Lancaster and flown back to Little Staughton. We went on leave

immediately following this event and so missed an active participation in the D-Day operations.

Nick and I flew another 19 trips together and completed our tour of Ops in mid-August 1944. It was my second tour - the first one was on Hampdens and Wellingtons with 420 (RCAF) Squadron and a 10 months' stint at 19 O.T.U at Kinloss and Forres in Scotland. Nick and I flew together for nearly a year but off duty we did not socialise very much - our friendship was that of amiable flying partners. He was married and lived off the base with his family and we did not keep in touch after I was repatriated to Canada in September 1944. I remained in the RCAF after the war, finally retiring in 1964.

Incidentally, you might be amused to hear that I have had a 'phone call from a friend in Calgary who saw the note in the Legion's newspaper, about your search for me and wanted to know if the female advertising for my present whereabouts, was the offspring of a liaison or affair I had during the war while overseas!!".

****

In the early hours of 6th June 1944, we had no inkling that the invasion of France was about to begin. Donnie and I were on night duty again and we had a very disturbed night - we manned up at 12.30, 01.15, 03.30 and again at 04.45 until we went off duty at 08.30. I don't know at what stage we were eventually told, but the massive build-up of troops in southern England signalled that the invasion was imminent and we had heard aircraft passing overhead most of the night. The fighter pilots on our frequency would have kept strict R/T silence about what they could see in the sea below.

Prior to the invasion, Allied fighters and fighter/bombers had been concentrating on attacking military and Gestapo Headquarters, and Radar Stations. The Luftwaffe had been coaxed into air combat whenever possible to reduce their numbers and German airfields had been repeatedly strafed, destroying many of their aircraft on the ground. The proof of the Allies having achieved air supremacy was evident on D-Day because the Luftwaffe were conspicuous by their absence and large stretches of the French coast were without Radar cover.

So, that immensely important day in the history of Europe had at last begun and the biggest Armada ever assembled was crossing the English Channel - a force of some 5,000 ships, supported by a massive umbrella of aircraft providing air cover, were embarking on the first stages of gaining a foothold in occupied France with the ultimate goal of freeing all those enslaved nations under Nazi domination. We were not aware at the time the full extent of the misery suffered by the conquered population but we knew enough to realise only too well that this attempt had to succeed. Our own freedom and survival depended on it, but also it was the only chance of ousting the Krauts from the countries they had ruthlessly terrorised and ravaged.

Instead of going straight to bed for some much needed sleep after night duty, we sat glued to the wireless all morning - the first announcement was read by John Snagge about 09.30 . . 'Allied naval forces, supported by strong air forces, began landing Allied armies this morning on the northern coast of France' - it was exciting and tense listening to the non-stop reports from the beach-heads in Normandy, where British, Canadian and American troops had landed. The appalling June weather had delayed the invasion go-ahead for several days and the Channel seas were still very blustery but the forecast seemed more promising. All travelling of a non-military nature in the south had been curtailed and all Forces passes had been stopped, so we would not have been allowed outside the village area.

The biggest threat to the Task Force crossing the Channel was attack by German U-boats from their bases in the Bay of Biscay but the Royal Navy and Coastal Command aircraft closely guarded the most vulnerable flanks. It was later reported that every square mile of the western approaches to the Channel were patrolled every half-hour and the 16 German U-boats ordered to attack the fleet, lost six of their submarines during the first four days. To continue to sustain such losses would have crippled the U-boat fleet and all further deployment into the Channel was suspended. Among that huge Armada heading for France on D-Day, were over 100 Air/Sea Rescue launches, who patrolled night and day during June and saved more than 350 lives.

The French Resistance had been alerted a few days beforehand that the invasion was imminent, conveyed by a hidden message when the first line of a poem was broadcast by the BBC on the European network. The second line was the signal for them to carry out extensive disruption on the eve of the landings. The Resistance carried out hundreds of attacks throughout France - railway tracks were blown up, signalmen diverted German troop and supply trains, telephone maintenance workers cut communication lines and sabotaged vital circuits. Denmark too organised a general strike which prevented reinforcements of German troops getting to France. It was part of the pre-invasion plan to put the French railways out of commission for a radius of a hundred miles or so and Allied air attacks had already succeeded in inflicting severe restrictions on the movement of troops and supplies. They were having to make long detours on the remaining serviceable tracks and to avoid detection, were forced to operate mainly at night.

From dawn to dusk on D-Day, fighter squadrons based in southern England patrolled the shipping in the English Channel and provided constant cover over the invasion troops who had established a foothold in Normandy but there was little combat action as the Luftwaffe didn't show. But the flak from German coastal defences was intense and accurate and in the combined air operations, including other inland raids and the diversionary decoy invasion attack in the Calais area, over 100 Allied aircraft were lost during the first day.

There had been reports of German atrocities which many people dismissed as war-time propaganda but we were now getting proof from the parts of France being liberated. A Panzer Division based in southern France were ordered north on 8 June to support the German defenders in Normandy. A convoy of 200 tanks, over 1,000 vehicles and some 15,000 troops set off by road on a journey which should only have taken two days but they had reckoned without the determined efforts of the Resistance to prevent those reinforcements from reaching Normandy. It eventually took over a fortnight to reach their destination but the French paid a high price in human lives for this delay. When the Panzers reached Tulle, they found the French had liberated their own Town during the night of 7/8 June and had killed 139 German soldiers. The S.S. were indignant that they were being delayed to deal with this nuisance but the Panzers re-took the Town and seized over a hundred civilians, 99 of which were hanged from lamp posts and other suitable gallows. Another 21 escaped a similar fate only, it was reported because the Germans had no more rope.

They continued northwards but at Oradour-sur-Glane, a commander of one of their Panzer battalions had been captured by the Resistance and later killed. A widespread interrogation followed and as a reprisal, the male inhabitants of Oradour were rounded up and put into barns, where they were shot. German troops then herded the women and children of the village into the local church. The door was securely locked, the church was doused with petrol and set alight - everyone inside was burned alive. A total of 642 French civilians were brutally murdered on 10 June 1944. The village was never rebuilt but its ruins remain as a reminder of the ruthlessness of Nazi retaliatory methods which typifies the cruellest regime of the 20th Century.

Otto Dickmann, the S.S. Major in control of these atrocities did not live beyond the end of the month - he was killed in Normandy on 30 June. *(After the war, 21 of his troops were charged with war crimes. Some received goal sentences, others were acquitted and two N.C.O's were sentenced to death but later commuted).

Only nine days after the D-Day landings, fighter squadrons were taking up occupation of airstrips in Northern France - this dispensed with the need to return to England several times a day over that dreaded stretch of water which had cost so many pilots' lives. They could now re-fuel, re-arm and have their aircraft serviced in France and soon be airborne again, providing continuous air support where needed. For easy identification, all Allied aircraft had been painted with three white stripes above and below their wings and around the fuselage. This was carried out the night before the invasion.

All the Canadian squadrons of 126 and 127 Wings that we had regularly listened to and taken bearings on at some time or other, were now established on the other side of the Channel and no longer under the control of English based Sector Operations Rooms, As far as my tale goes, I intended leaving the Canadians at this point as our D/F association with them had ended but the following brief excerpts from squadron records, well describes the weather conditions they encountered on arrival in France and their innovative attempts to improve their living accommodation under canvas:-

> *"19/6/44. It rained during the night and most of the day, turning the ground into stodgy mud. The boys spent the day digging 'funk' holes inside their tents to save themselves the trouble of getting up if Jerry decided to pay a nocturnal visit. These trenches also proved a comfortable way of warding off any shrapnel which might dent one's skull. As there was no flying, scrounging parties went out to a wrecked German Radar Station, gathering wood and planks for slit trench building, to improve the protection of their dug-outs. The best find was a German refreshment van which was towed to the airfield and set up as the squadron Orderly Room. A 3-ton truck was acquired to house parachutes. Putting these two vehicles parallel to each other, with a covered archway between, gave us a fairly good but small dispersal.*
> *The Bar and Mess tents were functioning on the 19th and a member of the ground staff had his portable cinema operable in one of the large tents. Weather good in England but lousy in France - the ground*

underfoot is like a quagmire and quite unsuitable for motorised vehicles. The squadron 'found' several German saddles . . . . now to find a horse! (And four days later they did - a horse they called Myrtle was taken in tow by F/Lt. Bob Hayward.)

New potatoes and fresh peas made the tinned meat meals more palatable. Dog biscuits are no substitute for fresh bread, which is sadly missed."

It was also discovered that the converted fighter/bomber aircraft which had a rack slung under each wing to carry a 500lb. bomb could, with a slight modification, also carry a barrel of beer instead, when travelling from England to France!

During those first few days after the invasion, we were told that all five beaches where the landings had taken place had been secured and that the Allies were making steady progress. We were, of course, unaware that the advance had fallen far short of the proposed objectives, and that Caen was expected to be taken during the first few days. In fact the Germans defended it strongly and it took several weeks of heavy bombardment to dislodge them. For the first time in four years, it seemed that the tide was at last turning and we were also looking forward to a quieter period on this side of the Channel, while the Germans were otherwise pre-occupied in repelling the invaders.

Chapter 15

THE V-1 ONSLAUGHT

Our optimism was short-lived and shattered in just 10 days when we realised that Hitler had produced another deadly weapon to send across to terrorise the civilian population. Since the beginning of the war, the bombs dropped on England had gradually got bigger and more fiendish in the destruction they could cause; the blast of high explosive bombs extended far and wide, tossing roofs off houses far from the main crater. The Germans deliberately included many unexploded bombs in their raids and each one that landed in a residential area meant that nearby houses had to be evacuated until the Bomb Disposal Squads could dismantle them and temporary accommodation had to be found for the inhabitants, adding to their stress and increased the growing number of homeless. We were then subjected to incendiary bombs which started massive fires that were difficult to control and then came the land mines, capable of demolishing a whole street of houses with just 1 mine. We were soon to find out what havoc this new threat could cause.

On 16 June, I wrote in my diary - Germany are using pilotless 'planes. Watched a lot come over and one came down. Couldn't get to sleep for ages. They started again in the morning. Biggin was hit last night. We got eight of them down this morning.' During the next two days, there was an American G.I's wedding in the village and Eileen Bond's 21st birthday to write about, so I was short of space to expound on these latest projectiles. But having endured them night and day for several months, I am never likely to forget what they sounded like - their ominous deafening roar can best be described as an enormous vehicle, badly in need of a new exhaust system. It was quite uncanny watching these strange unconventional flying objects pass overhead and even harder at first to comprehend that it had no cockpit and no pilot on board. They were completely alien to anything we had ever seen or heard about before and far more sinister - like something out of science fiction, we thought at the time.

There was practically no warning of when they were about to plunge earthwards in their death dive. The engine would cut out, followed by an eerie silence, except for the whistling noise it made on the descent - a matter of only a few seconds before the blast of a ton of high explosive. On that day, the 16th, London had the longest air-raid warning of the war and for 16 hours Londoners sat in cellars, shelters and tube stations. The following day, I was on night duty at nine and during the night, they were coming over

A Diagram of a V-1 Flying Bomb

The gas emerges in a series of impulses at a frequency of 45 per second giving a forward thrust of about 600 lbs. The engine power is about equivalent to a 600 H.P. ordinary aero engine.

Firey Gas emerged here

Rudder

Rear elevator

Power unit length 11.25 ft thickness of metal about 1/8 in.

Air Intake

Petrol tank 150 gallons (consumption 1 gallon per mile)

Petrol Filter & Lifting Lug

TOTAL WEIGHT FULL AND READY FOR FLIGHT 4800 LB

How length of flight is controlled. The 'Propeller' causes a counter to move back every 30 revolutions. When it reaches zero the flight is terminated

War head containing 1,060 KG of Explosive

Span of planes 17.67 Ft. made of mild steel .034 in in thickness in a steady stream - we just could not resist going outside and watching them, more in fascination and disbelief than anything. Against the night sky, the flame that exuded out the back was like a huge fiery blow torch and could be seen from a long way off. Luckily for us - but not for nearer London - that lot kept on going but the next morning we had out first experience of several 'near misses' when one exploded in mid-air just behind our billet and broke some of its windows. Jill, our landlady's daughter and I went looking for a piece as a souvenir but the explosion was so tremendous, it had all disintegrated and whatever fragments there were, had dispersed over a wide area. When Jill and I returned, Joan Wedgbury was in the garden and called us over - "Come and have a look at this" she said. We found her staring in disbelief at some of her washing that she had only put out about half an hour before. It was literally just hanging there in shreds from the blast of the V-1. Our WAAF issue of service clothing on enlisting consisted of 3 Air Force blue shirts, 6 detachable collars, vests, grey lisle stockings, 2 pairs of striped 'convict' pyjamas and long-legged navy knickers (referred to as 'passion killers'). When any of these items wore out, the drill was to hand them in for new ones on an Exchange Clothing Parade, after an inspection by a WAAF Admin. Officer who would say 'Yea' or 'Nay'. When clothing was getting a bit thin or tatty, we often helped the process along by putting our fingers through the thinnest part, to make sure of getting a replacement. The Queen B . . . 's must have known this was frequently done but I am sure 'A likely story' must have crossed her mind when Joan presented her shredded underwear accompanied by a barely plausible explanation of how they got in that condition!

At first, these missiles were called Pilotless 'Planes (P.P's for short), then Buzz Bombs, Flying Bombs, but trust the Cockneys to come up with 'Farting Furies'. which well described the noise they made at their rear end! Officially they were referred to as V-1 missiles but 'Doodlebug' became the most popular name for them.

On my next duty in the D/F Tower, I heard the blast of a V-1 at the other end of our direct line, when it landed just outside Biggin's Sector Operations Room at 'Towerfield', Keston Park, situated about two miles from the main aerodrome.

During that first week at being on the receiving end of this new menace, there was a casualty in the village. Teddy, one of the Wittersham G.I's was blown off his bike and broke a couple of ribs and then on night duty, I heard the blast of another one landing near the Ops Room. The following day, on my way to the village with Eileen, the engine of one petered out just as it was passing overhead and at that stage, we weren't quite au fait with the drill i.e. fall flat on the ground tout de suite! We just stood mesmerised as it hurtled to the ground in a dive, followed by a massive explosion which vibrated like an earthquake under our feet but luckily, we were just out of range of the debris it threw up, although we were covered with the dust it created. They just seemed to be everywhere.

This was the start of an incessant stream of these dreadful weapons, with little respite from them night or day. On the other side of the Channel, there were over a hundred catapult launching ramps between Calais and the Seine Estuary, spread out like a fan along the French coast and converging closer together as the missiles approached Kent and Sussex, on their way to London. This was dubbed 'Doodlebug Alley' and we were poised at the entrance of this infernal one-way traffic. They flew at an average height of around 2,000ft. and being on elevated ground, to give the maximum range for our receiver aerials, they were exceptionally low as they flew over our D/F Tower. Sometimes, when a salvo was launched at the same time, we could see as many as six or seven abreast, on parallel tracks heading for London and the noise was deafening. Even today, when low flying jets pass overhead, I immediately put my hands over my ears and my instinctive reaction is to want to dive under cover. At times, when on duty, we were very thankful that the leads connected to our headsets were long enough to allow us to make a swoop under the bench. It didn't take us long to realise that our D/F Tower was right under the flight path of a regular V-1 route, which continued in a direct line towards Biggin Ops Room and beyond if it did not cut out before, so when one passed directly overhead, we were able to warn the WAAF in the Ops Room that one was coming their way and sure enough, in less than five minutes or so, she would say they could hear it.

Barrage balloons were gathered from various parts of the country and thousands were erected within a matter of days of the first onslaught, forming a formidable barrier right across the immediate south-eastern approaches to London and formed the last line of defence. It was a masterly achievement with all that the operation entailed and many WAAF's were employed on the sites. Biggin Hill's fighter squadrons had to be dispersed to other airfields because the Bromley/Croydon area was within a Barrage Balloon zone. The person who wrote the following contribution (probably the Station Adjutant) in the Biggin Hill Station Record Log book on the day the aerodrome was covered by an umbrella of Barrage Balloons, obviously found it difficult to come to terms with the realisation that from the height of its fame as the premier Fighter Aerodrome in the Battle of Britain, it had fallen in prestige to the depths of anonymity as a no-account Barrage Balloon Centre! Furthermore, he seems to have been unable to find enough adequate expletives in the English language to express his antipathy at Biggin's humiliation, that he invented some of his own!

23 June 1944   "It may not be out of place to record here that the news that our famous and much advertised neighbour (Kenley?) had been afflicted with a new type of pest known as the Bal-lunatic and that it had fallen from the pinnacle to the low level of a Balloon Centre, was received on this unit with ill-concealed humour. This humour was boojamistic and snarkish in the manner of its disappearance however, for the laconic signal announcing the limits of the balloon barrage was received by this Unit from higher authority. An equally laconic plotting of the co-ordinator on the map by the C.O. served to considerably quicken our interest when it became horribly clear that we were also to be engulfed in the surging tide of 'jelly bags'. At about 18.45 hours on this fateful Saturday, the first of an incredible number of these monstrosities ascended lousily into the sky in a position uncomfortably near the Officers Mess and by the end of Sunday (25th) the ambient air was be-spattered with a bevy of bloated bladders which floated with bovine content and cat-like detachment in the heavens.

27/6/44   As a result of this bladder disease, Station Flight Biggin Hill moved to Redhill and 1004 S.W.H.Q. to Gatwick.

28/6/44   At approx. 09.10 hours a Flying Bomb 'pranged' among requisitioned properties just south of the Camp. doing considerable damage to houses and rendering the Camp Cinema unserviceable. The history of this unit for the remainder of the month, consists of bladders, more bladders and still more bladders. Surely never since that long forgotten dawn which revealed for the first time the existence of the North and South Downs, can so evil a blight have settled over the south-east Counties."

The Sector Operations Room at Biggin Hill, as ever, was to play an important part in the defence campaign. It was the nerve centre and directed the operations of 'Diver' Control - the code name for the battle against the V-1 menace. Six of them had landed within Biggin's boundary - a target the Jerries would have been pleased to know they had hit but those crudely built proto-type missiles were incapable of being set to pin-point a cut-out with that degree of accuracy. Once launched on a straight and level course at varying speeds of between 300/425 mph., they were beyond any further ground control, although a head, tail or cross wind could affect the time it took to reach London - approximately 15/25 minutes, also depending on the variable distances from the French coast launching sites. Before being catapulted into the air, the cut-out mechanism could only be roughly calculated to crash land within the vicinity of a 15 mile radius and it wasn't long before most parts of London had been hit. If the cut-out did not function, it continued until it ran out of fuel and then crashed.

Tempests, Typhoons, Mustangs and the latest type Spitfire aircraft were given the task of tackling the Doodlebugs in the air but the defence strategy for coping with this new threat was a bit of shambles at first along the coast, with the Ack Ack guns firing at the V-1's and the fighters in danger of being fired on when in hot pursuit. There was controversy on both sides - the gunners complained that the fighters should not be flying within range of their guns and the pilots took great exception at being shot at by 'friendly fire' when they were poised for the kill. As you can imagine, the language we heard from the pilots over the intercom then was fiery enough to make our ears singe around the edges! The odds were somewhat improved over combat with conventional enemy aircraft as there was no pilot about to stalk them from behind. When they first started chasing them, I remember a pilot saying over the R/T that it was a change to fire at something in the air that couldn't shoot back. Even though the V-1's flew straight and level and were incapable of taking evasive action, we could see from watching our fighters tackling them that they were still not an easy target to hit, as many pilots found out to their cost. Whatever range they fired at, the main problem was getting out of the way quick enough to avoid being hit by the far flung wreckage caused by a mid-air explosion. It was a comparatively small target, with a wing span of just over 17ft. and a fuselage length of 21.5ft., with the added advantage of speed over the pursuing fighters. Several measures were used to improve the performance of the Spitfire - they were stripped of external paint and the outer surfaces were polished to a gleaming mirror-like finish. This, with all unnecessary fittings removed, gave them an increased speed of several m.p.h.

Two of the worst major disasters occurred during the first week-end the V-1's started coming over. On June 17 one fell on a crowded shopping centre near Clapham Junction and being a busy Saturday afternoon, the street was full of shoppers. 24 people were killed and about as many injured. The following morning, the Guards Chapel at Wellington Barracks, near St. James' Park, received a direct hit while a Sunday morning service was in progress and the death toll was 119 killed outright and 141 injured.

It was obvious we were going to have to come to terms with this new

24-hour threat on our doorstep. Psychologically, it was much worse than a normal air-raid, where the siren warning would sound and the danger would only last for a certain length of time. When the All Clear sounded, it meant that the danger of being bombed had passed, until the next Alert. Not so with the V-1's - they could strike at any time during the day or night, with only the silence of the cut-out as a warning - the threat was constantly there putting people under long-term stress, depriving them of a peaceful night's sleep so they were less able to cope with their day's work. The enemy had increasingly endeavoured to disrupt the bodily life of the country with every means in their power.

Getting adequate sleep was our biggest problem. After a busy 12-hour night duty (and the chase went on through the night as well), it was impossible some mornings to even nod off because of the menacing drone and the vibration of our wooden-built billet, when one passed low overhead. Neither did we feel very safe sleeping upstairs on the first floor. I suppose we gradually got more used to the damn things going over in droves and occasionally landing nearby, eventually resigning ourselves to . . . 'Whatever will be, will be'. It was a pointless exercise listening to everyone that came near, and worrying whether the engine was going to peter out - a recipe for becoming a nervous wreck! Having said that, the volume on wireless sets was kept at just a background level, otherwise that life-saving warning of 5/15 seconds might not be heard.

Taking a bath was a chancey and hurried affair at times - bet your bottom dollar, as soon as you decided to take the plunge, a few would decide to come over and then someone would keep watch outside to give a warning if the engine stopped - those few seconds did at least allow enough time to wrap a towel around and duck under somewhere, away from flying glass - at least you would be half-way decent should a fireman have to rescue you from the rubble. One day when I was keeping cavey for Jill, she had to get out of the bath five times but only two of those Doodlebugs crashed nearby, the others glided on a bit farther before exploding. Thankfully,, the bath at 'The Oast' was on the ground floor - when the house was built it didn't have a bathroom at all and there wasn't room upstairs to put one, so the bath was installed off the kitchen and when not in use was covered with a wooden top.

I think I felt safer on duty than anywhere else at Wittersham. We had a 6ft. high anti-blast brick wall around the Tower and the bench we dived under would hopefully have supported any falling debris from the unsubstantial Tower construction. It was the heavy steel shaft for the aerial which might have been 'the death of you'.

Eventually, the Allied defence strategists sorted out the air space problem and designated zones for each defending force - the fighters to have first crack after the V-1's were launched, with patrols over the Channel trying to down their prey in the sea where it could do no harm. The Ack Ack guns were moved to the coast and placed in position from Dover to Brighton as the second line of defence - and further inland over the Kentish Weald a second fighter patrol would be ready to pounce if any Doodlebugs got through the first two lines of defence. The Barrage Balloons formed the last barrier and looking at an aerial photograph of the massive cover of these 'jelly bags' right across the horizon of south-east London, it is amazing how many still managed to squeeze through - in fact, during the first seven weeks, 2,000 did. We were never told at the time that Biggin airfield was in a Balloon area and that all their fighter squadrons were dispersed elsewhere. The later V-1's were fitted with a knife-edge attachment fixed to the front of the wings, designed to penetrate the balloon defence. Flying at over 350mph, it proved quite effective in slicing the steel cables with its blades and over 600 balloons were let loose from their moorings. A few V-1's landed without exploding, which presented a fresh challenge for the Bomb Disposal Units.

With improved defence tactics, the success rate steadily improved. The Sector Operations Room at Biggin was plotting an average of 100 V-1's per day on its map and the combined defence forces were bringing down a respectable percentage but about 50 were still getting through and hitting the London area every 24 hours. The challenge put an added strain on RAF fighter resources as many squadrons were already established on airstrips in France, giving air support to the advancing Allied troops. By mid-July, a total of 8 single-engined and four twin-engined (Mosquito) night fighter squadrons were required to remain behind in England to deal with Operation 'Diver'. It only took a Doodlebug approximately five minutes to reach our coast and No. 150 Wing, based at Newchurch on Romney Marsh were in the most forward position to be used for Diver confrontation. The three squadrons of the Wing led by W/Cdr. R.P. Beamont, were No. 3, 56 and 486 (RNZAF) and on their first major encounter, No. 3 squadron flying Tempests, knocked down eleven Flying Bombs on 16 June. Different tactics had to be tried and tested to tackle them in the air - the Hawker Tempest had only a slight advantage of speed when flying straight and level and the Spitfire was barely able to catch one. A Spitfire pilot chased a V-1 from Beachy Head to Gatwick before he was able to get within firing range but eventually succeeded in shooting off its wing. As the pilot broke away, he hit a balloon cable which severed the tip of the Spit's wing and the aircraft began to spin. He was able to make an emergency landing at nearby Gatwick. It was frustrating for many a pilot chasing a V-1 only to have to break-off and watch it weave majestically through the forest of balloon cables, unscathed.

Before these pests infested the air space over Kent and affected our daily lives both on and off duty, the intercom we previously heard did not give us much of a clue as to where the fighters were, their destination or what operations they were engaged in. But now the Controllers and pilots were not quite so cautious about the information they imparted and the R/T became much more informative and quite exciting at times because we became more involved with what was happening. Maybe it was a source of conveying to the Germans, through their 'Y' service who monitored our air waves, that many of their missiles were NOT even reaching our coast, when they heard a pilot say he had shot one down in the Channel or mentioned that one had been hit by Ack Ack.

On duty, whether in the Tower or one of the D/F mobile trucks, we would be on the frequency of either the aircraft patrolling the Channel, waiting to pounce when a V-1 was sighted after launching, or taking bearings on the fighter patrols over Kent. It was sometimes a question of luck whether the Channel patrols were in the right place at the right time because one could be launched from any one (or several) of the 100 ramps and if it got too much of a head start, the fighter only had about 5 minutes to get within range before it reached the Ack Ack zone. With the gunners now using the new proximity fuses, it was an area for a fighter to avoid. He would abandon the chase - go back and latch on to those that were following.

This was the start of another very busy period for D/F Stations and on every duty we were kept fully occupied taking bearings. The Controller needed accurate positions of his fighters to intercept launched V-1's from the information provided by radar plots. After the night fighters had landed, the day patrols would take over about 05.30 and the Controller would direct them to patrol between Dover and Hythe, where the V-1's would be crossing at a steady rate. Different code words and abbreviations were used for the 'Diver' operation -

Beachcraft and 'trade' were the code names for the V-1's.
'The edge' was the coast-line where the V-1's crossed into the Ack Ack zone.
Ground control call- signs - Bluefrock for Manston - Kingsley for Biggin -

Birdcage for ? (can't remember!)
Fighter squadron call-signs - Vendor (274) Husky (501) Spider (No.3) Fairway (486) Bombshell (56)
Angels = height in thousand feet.

Vendor Red 1 to Bluefrock Control - "Vendor Red Section now airborne. Where do you want us to patrol?"
B'frock to Red 1 - "Between Dover and Hythe but make for Ashford now - its getting quite busy there. . . . and Red 2 can stay over Dover."
"Roger Bluefrock - Will do"
R1 to Bfk - "I am now over Ashford - Angels 4"
Bfk to R1 - "1 Beachcraft has crossed west of Hythe, travelling towards Ashford. Vector 140° and you should make contact"
Red 1 - "Yes, its just a speck at the moment - ready and waiting"
Bfk to R2 - "There's one crossing in due south of Dover"
Red 2 - "Its just exploded in mid-air. The Ack Ack got it"
Red 1 - "Good timing there - met it bang on and it crashed in a field. Any more?"
Bfk to R1 - "Yes, Beachcraft 5 miles south of Folkestone as yet"
Bfk to R2 - "Return to edge, keep a sharp look-out for B'craft approaching east of Folkestone. If you miss it there, leave it to Red 1 - he might have a better chance"
R2 to Bfk - "The guns got the first one but there was another right behind which I managed to get a squirt at but I didn't see it go down"
Bfk to R1 - "Stay 5 miles n.w. of Hythe - first one crossing in there - second one over Sandgate"
Red 1 - "Have you course on the second one?" Bfk. "Yes. 300°"
Red 1 - "Red 2 is nearer first one - I'll latch on to the one behind"
Red 1 - "No joy that time I'm afraid"
Bfk to Red - "Not much doing now - you can throttle back. Trade is slackening off. Maybe one or two odd ones around"

The most interesting patrol for us was the one from Dymchurch, Dungeness and Rye, which covered our area and quite often the action was taking place over 'our patch'. Sometimes the fighters would be flying over the top of our D/F Tower and we would hear the engine of the pilot we were listening to and the drone of the Doodlebug he was chasing. This gave us a certain personal involvement and we often egged the pilot on to get 'it' before 'it' landed on our doorstep.

When Spider Blue Section were airborne, they would ask for instructions. Birdcage Control would tell them to patrol 6 miles inland between New Romney and Rye.

Birdcage to B1 - "Keep to the south of your patrol - there's some trade coming your way"
Birdcage to B1 "B'craft now about 15 miles south of Dymchurch on 300°. Should cross edge at Dungey Point"
B1 to B'cage - "Roger - will keep a sharp look-out"
B'c to B1   - "Can U C it now"
B1 "Not yet - the sky is a big place up here!"
B'c to B1 "Sorry, false alarm - it disappeared but there's another one behind on same course - good hunting"
B1 "Yes, can C it coming - will wait over the marshes - a good place to knock it down there"
B1 "Got in a good burst at that one - large lumps flew off and it nose-dived into the ground. Got in too close though and think I've got a few holes in my kite. Will return to base and inspect the damage"

Birdcage Control would also be having similar intercom with Blue 2.

Approaching a V-1 from the rear diminished the size of the target in the view of the pursuing pilot as the wings were only 8 inches thick and the width across the fuselage, around 3ft. Concentrating gunfire at such a small target squandered ammunition and the patrols could not remain airborne for long, if they ran out of ammo: When this happened to one determined pilot, he discovered another tactic for disposing of them. He flew alongside the Doodlebug and manoeuvred his wing under the wing of the V-1 and it tipped over - this upset the gyro mechanism and it would twist into a spiral dive and hurtle to the ground. This technique was often adopted thereafter but it was a highly dangerous exercise and many a pilot returned with bent wings, the fabric burned off the tail rudder or minus a wing tip because the V-1's wings were covered in sheet steel and theirs only had a skin of light alloy.

We sometimes watched this operation, in fear and trepidation for the pilot's safety, if he misjudged it and got too close. I remember on one occasion a fighter and a Doodlebug were approaching from the west, which was strange as they usually appeared from due south. It looked as though their wings were locked together but as they got nearer, we could see that the fighter had already turned it 90° . . . . then a bit more, and eventually it did a complete 'about turn', heading back in the direction from whence it came! The pilot broke away, doing a Victory roll and we all cheered like mad. Too much to hope that it might have gone 'home' to explode and given the Krauts a taste of their own medicine. Wouldn't they have been surprised to see one back again!

Sometimes on duty we would be listening to some interesting intercom and then they would switch to another channel, so we missed the ending. One day, when we relieved 'A' crew, Polly was deep in thought as she handed over the headphones - "Ah well" she sighed "I'll never know what happened now" and went on to explain "I've been taking bearings on a fighter who attacked a Doodlebug and as it was diving towards the ground, he realised it was going to land on the railway line north of Canterbury, in the path of an oncoming train. The Controller asked how far away was the train and would it be able to stop and where did the V-1 land? The last Polly heard was the pilot saying it had crashed but did he mean the train or the Doodlebug? The Controller then told the pilot to switch to Channel D-Dog to give them a fix for an immediate landing and he was told to ring Kingsley (Biggin Ops) and tell them what had happened. The Ops Room were not very communicative when it came to imparting information, so there was no way of finding out.

I have since discovered that there was a serious crash in August 1944, involving a train from Victoria to Ramsgate (which passes through Canterbury). An eye-witness saw a fighter tipping over a V-1 with his wing-tip and it exploded on a railway bridge in the path of an oncoming train from Victoria. The driver was unable to pull up in time and the engine fell through the gap and overturned. The coaches immediately behind the engine were poised in the gap, pointing upwards in the shape of a 'V'. Eight people were killed and about 16 seriously injured but in view of the seriousness of the crash, casualties might have been a lot worse. I don't suppose many Doodlebugs landed on railway lines in Kent but without being able to match up the time and dates when Polly was on duty, a probable coincidence and the mention of Canterbury, is the only link that they might have been the same incident.

It is very true that 'what cannot be cured must be endured' and we went about our daily tasks, trying not to let the Doodlebugs disrupt our lives any more than could be helped. Wherever we went on our day off, to places like Hastings, Tenterden, Ashford etc. or the occasional trip home, we couldn't escape the blighters so we carried on as normal . . . but Friday, the 30th June was not the best day for Donnie and I to have chosen to head for London. We had just come off night duty, having previously decided to go to our respective homes - regardless of how much sleep we had managed to get (practically nil). Donnie lived in Finchley. We hitched a lift with the postman to Tenterden and we were lucky enough to get a lift all the way to the West End with an American Red Cross girl. We arrived at the Regent Street entrance to Piccadilly Underground around mid-day and at the top of the steps we were having a discussion whether it was worth paying the tube fare to go one station or walk the short distance to Leicester Square. A crucial decision when it was a question of how best to eke out our meagre pay! We hadn't had time for much breakfast after night duty, and hunger was the deciding factor in choosing the Tube as the quickest way to satisfy the pangs. Voting for the Underground was a providential decision as we had barely got to the Booking Office when there was a huge explosion above - debris and dust began falling from cracks in the ceiling and the blast rushed through from the Regent Street side like a tornado and out again at the Haymarket end exits. We didn't wait for tickets but made a dash down the escalator as fast as we could to the safety of the tunnels below. After our meal at the Athens Restaurant, we walked back to Piccadilly to see where the Doodlebug had landed. By this time the area had been cordoned off to allow access for rescue teams to operate - we could see that it was in the vicinity of the Regent Palace but it wasn't until later we learned that it had actually landed on the annexe of the Regent Palace Hotel, destroying the top three storeys. Miraculously, all the residents were out of the hotel and the only fatal casualty was a chambermaid but outside in the street, 168 people had been injured and we realised we'd had a very, very lucky escape. It was the ferocity of the blast which swirled any flying debris into lethal weapons that caused so much injury to passers-by. At such speed, even a slither of glass was like a dagger, flying through the air, inflicting dreadful wounds. Had we known at the time that as many as <u>37</u> other Doodlebugs had hit Greater London that very morning, we wouldn't have hung around in Town but made tracks for home. As it was, we went to an afternoon dance at Covent Garden, also unaware that only streets away a V-1 had crashed in Aldwych at 2 o'clock, landing in the vicinity of Bush House, Australia House and the Air Ministry. The photographs taken (though not published at the time) show a scene of appalling carnage - 198 people were killed and hundreds more seriously injured.

 Donnie and I went our separate ways and I reached home about 7.30 - I began to feel tired through lack of sleep after night duty, so I went to bed comparatively early but Doodlebug activity woke us early and once disturbed, I thought I might as well get up, although it was only 06.30. I

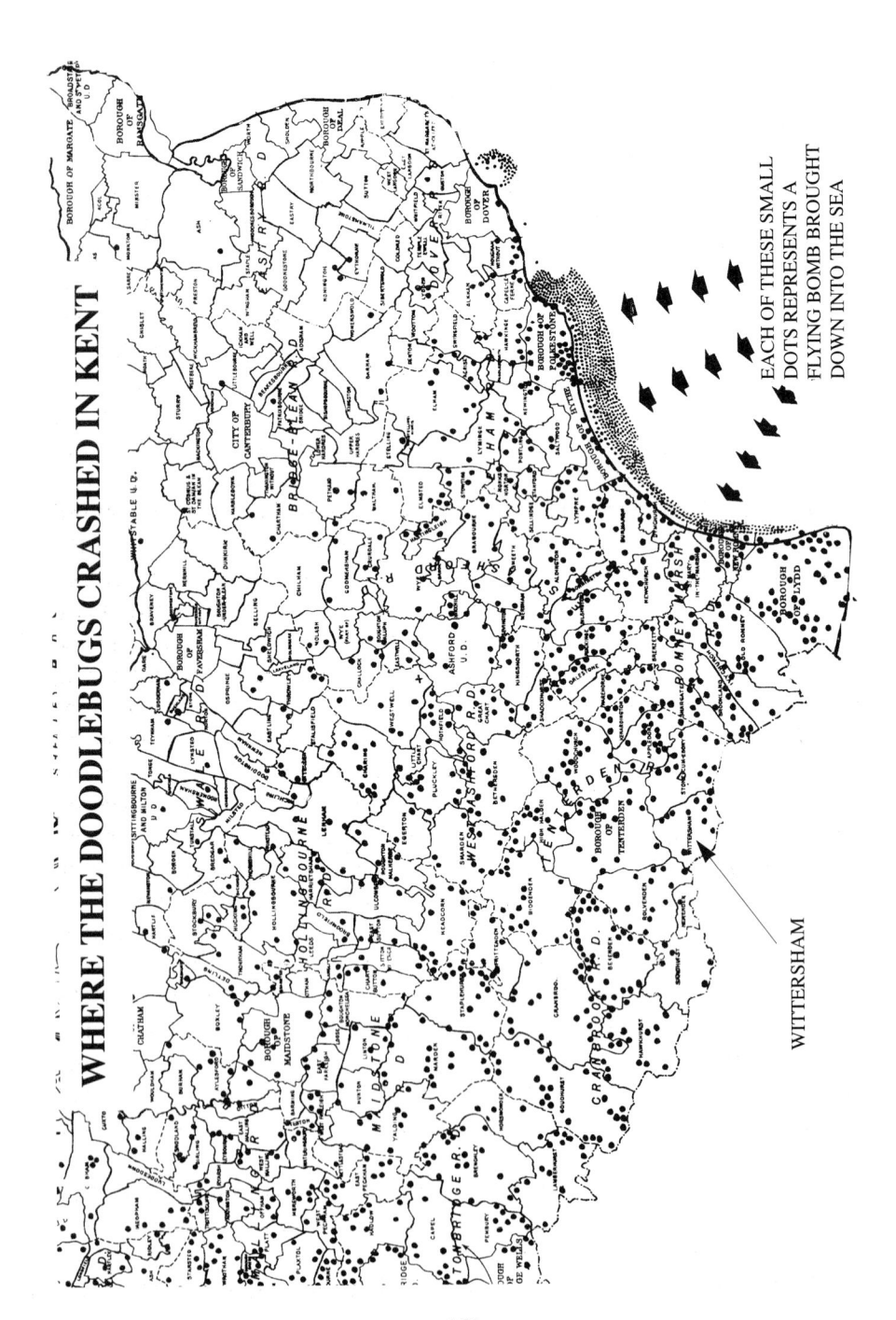

WHERE THE DOODLEBUGS CRASHED IN KENT

EACH OF THESE SMALL DOTS REPRESENTS A FLYING BOMB BROUGHT DOWN INTO THE SEA

WITTERSHAM

was surprised that V-1's overshot London to reach the northern suburbs but altogether 14 crashed in Wembley during the main onslaught and even landed as far out as Bushey, Elstree and Chesham.

Donnie and I had to get back for afternoon duty at 1.30 and we had arranged to meet at Charing Cross but she was half an hour late and we missed the 9.15 train. Plan 'B' was a dash to London Bridge, a train as far as Lee and hitch from there. Our first lift was a rather windswept ride in the dicky seat of private car. (Several makes of small pre-war cars had extra seats outside the car, which opened like a boot . . but from the top and had no protection from the elements.). Then an American jeep stopped for us - he was only going as far as Headcorn but took us right to Wittersham. We got plenty of fresh air that morning but hitchers couldn't be choosers and we always appreciated any lifts we got, especially when people were kind enough to go out of their way to get us back on duty in time.

For the first few weeks, Government restrictions had prevented newspapers from reporting the full horror of casualties and the extent of the damage these Flying Objects were causing. The veil of secrecy was finally lifted by Winston Churchill, who gave a few facts and figures in the House of Commons on 6 July. Up to 6 a.m. that morning - 2,754 V-1's had been launched, inflicting 2,752 fatal casualties and a further 8,000 injured people had been detained in hospital. These figures were alarming - in only <u>three</u> weeks? It was no consolation to the British public either when he added that had it not been for concentrated attacks by Allied aircraft on the launching sites, the bombardment might well have started at least six months earlier. They were thinking of the coming months and making composite calculations of likely casualty figures yet to be endured - the prospect was gloomy. Hitler's ambition and that of Field Marshal Erhard Milch was to launch up to 500 of their Vergeltungswaffe (revenge) Weapons every day. The people of London will never endure it, they thought.

The battle against the 'V' weapons had begun in the summer of 1943 when it was discovered that research and secret trials were being carried out at Peenemunde, on the remote Baltic island of Usedom. The whole area was attacked and devastated - which resulted in a set-back for the programme by several months. Thereafter, any information from the slave labour used in factories, underground plants, from the Resistance or from aerial reconnaissance photographs as to any further development was acted upon and had it not been for the Allies relentlessly attacking any 'V' related activity, the onslaught would have begun a lot earlier, as Mr. Churchill said.

The launching sites erected along the French coast were only small units consisting of a ski-type catapult and a few huts, often hidden in a small wood and well camouflaged, they were not easily detectable from the air. When located, they were sought out and destroyed but they were quickly repaired and were not out of action for long. The hammering of road and rail links in Northern France in readiness for the invasion, also prevented the Germans from maintaining a non-stop round the clock V-1 onslaught and there were periodic lulls in launching, when supplies could not get through. Bad weather and poor visibility could ground RAF aircraft but V-1's could be dispatched in any adverse weather conditions. During the whole offensive, 26 August was the only day when none were launched at all.

One thing that puzzled us during the Doodlebug era was the strange searchlights we could see at night in the direction of the coast, east of Rye - in pairs of two, spaced apart, they remained absolutely stationary, two shining vertically up to the sky, parallel to each other and the other two at an angle pointing out to sea. They were poised like that at night on many occasions and they were a topic of some speculation roundabout, as no-one could understand what purpose they were serving. A German pilot was not likely to obligingly fly into the path of a static searchlight and the V-1's could be seen easily enough. Fifty years on, a Tempest pilot of No. 3 Sqdn. based on Romney Marsh has provided the answer. "Control had a system of searchlights on the coast between Hastings and Dungeness and this was the point around which the Tempests were stacked, flying figures of eight, waiting for the V-1's to come over. When the bottom aircraft left the stack, the others would move down. The searchlights helped you know where you were but it was an unpopular operation, as it was necessary to fly with navigation lights on to avoid mid-air collisions. The Germans often tried to infiltrate their own aircraft into the pattern and then Control would tell us over the R/T to 'Close your windows' - the code informing pilots there was an intruder in the area and a signal to switch off navigation lights."

It was a 24-hour defence battle on this side of the Channel and although they were easy to see in the dark, the night fighter squadrons had a problem at first in gauging the exact range at which to fire, until a British 'boffin' devised an optical gun sight which reflected two images of the V-1's exhaust and when they came together, was the right time to fire. Mosquito aircraft joined in the nightly vigil and they destroyed a total of 428 V-1's.

The Doodlebug attacks lasted for two and half months until it eased off in September for Kent, Sussex and Surrey because the advancing Allied troops were over-running the French coastal launching sites. In September

1944, the Kent Messenger weekly newspaper, published a map of Kent showing where all of the 2,400 Doodlebugs had crashed. Later statistics put the figure somewhat lower but there is no disputing that more V-1's littered the countryside of Kent than any of the neighbouring counties and our area around Tenterden topped the list for the greatest number landing within its rural boundary - 238. We used to cycle into Tenterden at least a couple of times a week, as it had our nearest cinema and we enjoyed a drink in the Cellars. My diary remarks were quite matter of fact, such as:-
'Had a couple of close calls in Tenterden'
'They were shooting D.B's down like flies today'
'While in Tenterden, a D.B landed near the cinema and broke some windows'
'With Johnny Garrett in Tenterden when a D.B. fell close by in an orchard'. .
It was no big deal experiencing 'near misses' 'cos everyone was having them!

There were other disruptive elements besides the high casualties and massive destruction of property. Factories in and around London, engaged in the manufacture of essential items for the war effort, lost production because of direct hits or damaged premises. Businesses, shops, hotels, restaurants. theatres and cinemas, all lost trade as people were not staying in London, unless absolutely necessary. Over a million residents chose to leave the capital. Although they could not be aimed to strike a specific target, some of these projectiles caused a lot of chaos. One struck the narrow Hungerford Footbridge and railway line which spans the Thames and brought Charing Cross Station to a standstill, as it was the only access for trains in and out of that station.

The crudely built V-1's were cheap and easy to manufacture and for all the devastation they caused, they cost no more than £150 each to produce. The defence campaign cost the British exchequer in the region of £62 million, including the cost of rebuilding 23,000 destroyed houses and repairing the damage to a million more.

Approximately 10,000 were launched but more than a third failed to reach our coast.
No. Destroyed
By fighter a/c 1,847   By Ack Ack 1,866   By Barrage Balloons 231
Casualties
No. of Civilians killed - 6,184   Seriously injured - nearly 18,000

Amongst my war-time memorabilia, I found this poem

ODE TO THE DOODLEBUG by R.H. Sauter (Abridged)

Stands Wittersham still, looking over to France,
Beneath the Flying Bomb on the nape of the hill
Stands Wittersham - where this morning she stood
When I rose and set out and departed from there

For the hunt was up at the break of day
Over Sussex and Kent towards London way
Where the evil black fox goes streaking away
To the sound of the siren's warning.

For I've seen the whole pack of them hunting at noon
Spitfire - Mosquito - Mustang - Typhoon
Tempest and Thunderbolt - hot to the tune
And the baying of guns in the morning.

For today I have known the snarl and the bite
The sudden quiet and the twisting flight
And the glare and the bang and the sight and the kill
Of the plume of smoke on that Kentish hill.

For the chase will be on with the full of the night
When the Doodlebug flickers its sinister light
In the horns of the searchlights and tracer is bright
From the view to the blast and the burning.

Over Sussex and Kent, the Wittershams stand
Though many's the home lies blasted and bent
Though many a site on Down and on Weald
From Town to the sea will be rubble this night.

If you ken the grim Fox with his coat so black
And his fiery red brush - cocked over his back
You will ken the heartbeat with the run of that pack
And the lift of the heart at returning.

Chapter 16

NO ODDS TOO GREAT FOR THE POLES

We frequently listened to the intercom of and took bearings on a number of Polish squadrons and in the air, they were relentless Hun killers - anything with a Swastika on it was attacked with ruthless ferocity. Before escaping from their Homeland, Polish men had been outraged at the indiscriminate destruction of their defenceless cities, purposely calculated to kill thousand of helpless civilians. Harbouring undying loathing towards the Germans who had ravaged and overrun their beloved country, they left their families, knowing there would be no communication allowed for the duration of the war, however long that might be and they would have to live with the constant anxiety of not knowing how their families were faring under that brutal regime. By various means, many Poles managed to reach England, determined to fight with the Allied forces who were united and resolute in ultimately defeating Hitler. The Polish Air Force were eventually able to form 15 squadrons of fighters and bombers during the course of the war and their aircrew and ground staff rose to 10,000 strong.

Two of the Polish fighter squadrons, 306 and 315 flew sorties along the French coast, demolishing railway stations, marshalling yards, trains and rolling stock and if the Luftwaffe put in appearance, they would pursue them to the death, with little regard for their own safety. They hated the Germans vehemently and Fritz got no mercy at the hands of the Poles.

This encounter on 23 June 1944 illustrates the overwhelming odds they were prepared to face in combat. 306 Squadron had successfully bombed buildings and track on the railway station at Verneuil when they met 30 bandits at 14,000ft. and F/Lt. Potocki, leading four aircraft of Blue Section, flew into the fury of the fight, undismayed by the odds, and attacked them from the rear. He scored hits all over the cockpit of one ME109 and it went down trailing smoke and flames. He then found five more fighters on his tail, took evasive action and managed to out-turn one and get on his tail, in a position to fire. It rolled over and dived down out of control, exploding on the ground in a sheet of flame. But the fourth ME109 hit F/Lt. Potocki's aircraft and he had to make an emergency landing at B4 (Beny-sur-Mer) one of the newly acquired airstrips occupied by the three Canadian squadrons of No. 126 Wing. He left his damaged Mustang and returned to Holmsley South in a light aircraft. In the same encounter F/Sgt. Czezowski saw four German aircraft a mile away and undeterred that the odds were four to one, he engaged them all until he ran out of ammunition.

He ducked down to zero feet and skimmed across the Channel to base. That day the squadron claimed 5 ME109's and 5 ME190's destroyed and two FW190's damaged but their success was marred by the loss of their C.O. and two Flight Commanders.

There are countless stories of the audacity and fearless daring of Polish bravery in combat. During the week following the invasion, when No. 315 squadron were attacking tanks south of Cherbourg, W/O Tamowiez was seen to crash-land on the marshes by his C.O. Sq/Ldr. Horbaczewski, who immediately landed on a half-constructed airstrip nearby, 'borrowed' a Jeep, drove to the crash site, and waded out on the marshes to extricate the injured W/O from his Mustang. He managed to get him into the Jeep and back at the airstrip, both pilots squeezed into the cockpit of the Mustang, which Horbaczewski flew back to England, where astonished ground crew watched as two pilots emerged from the cockpit, which was hardly big enough for one!

Two months later, 315 Sqd. lost their courageous leader. From Brenzett A.L.G. on Romney Marsh, No. 133 Wing put up 36 Mustangs for a Rodeo on 18 August 1944 and pilots of 315 Sqd. sighted an estimated 60 FW190's taking off from airfields around Beauvais. They swept into the attack and in a running dogfight, claimed 16 for the loss of only 1 Mustang - that of their C.O. Sq/Ldr. E. Horbaczewski, D.S.O., one of Poland's most brilliant war-time pilots. He was posthumously awarded the Virtuti Military Class 1V, their country's highest combat decoration.

Courageous though they were, the reason I remember the Polish pilots so well was because to us they were always 'those naughty boys' who were the bane of our lives on D/F Stations. When it came to R/T procedure in the excitement of a dog-fight or chasing a Doodlebug, they forgot every rule in the book. They frequently omitted to switch off their intercom after transmitting and then we would hear this boisterous gabble, all talking at once and yelling encouragement to each other in their own language and it was virtually impossible to tell one from t'other. So, after taking a bearing, our dilemma then was - "Which aircraft was it?" because they also regularly forgot another golden rule - always give an identification when transmitting. Besides the squadron call-sign, pilots were either 1, 2, 3, or 4 in Red, Yellow, Blue or White Section and they jolly well ought to say so! Otherwise, we didn't know who they were. Sitting all alone in our little round Tower with no-one to talk to, I often used to put a 'spoke' in when listening to this one-sided conversation but it was just as well they couldn't hear what I said! Amongst other things I would shout back "Say who you are, you silly . . . . " It was a useless exercise taking bearings on unidentifiable pilots because there could be no cross-link with bearings from other D/F Stations. The Controller sometimes 'lost control' and tried in vain to get them to go in a certain direction or to return to base - if they were in combat or hoping to bag 'just one more Doodlebug', they would make out they either hadn't heard or didn't understand his instruction! They often left themselves dangerously low on fuel as they coasted back to base on a near empty tank. We were secretly amused at their antics but occasionally, we had to ask the Controller to remind them of proper R/T procedure, because it would be to their disadvantage should they need to bale out, as their position could only be established by two or more D/F Stations taking bearings on the same aircraft.

For several years now I have been attending the Aircrew Association's annual Memorial Service at St. Clement Danes in the Strand and at one of the receptions in the Royal Courts of Justice afterwards, I met an ex-Polish fighter pilot who married an English girl and remained here after the war. I was relating our intercom experience and in the telling, it suddenly triggered off the call-sign of one of the Polish squadrons - BAWBEE - which I hadn't thought about in over 45 years and wasn't consciously aware that it was even stored in my memory box! That call-sign jogged his memory too and he was able to tell me that Bawbee was the call-sign of 306 squadron, which I never knew until then either. That was before I had even thought about putting it all down on paper. I have been trying to regurgitate more memory revelations like that by disturbing the cobwebs of my mind but no further joy! The rest I have found out the hard way - by researching. After D-Day, the call-sign for No. 133 Wing was CAMPUS but we probably heard the call-signs for the individual squadrons more often. Besides BAWBEE for 306, CENTRAL was the call-sign for 315 (Polish) and TURNIP for 129 Sqdn.

The Wing operated from Brenzett (9 miles east of Wittersham) from July to October 1944 and performed many 'anti-Diver' patrols in those hectic Doodlebug months. Ground crews worked long hours keeping the Mustangs in air-worthy condition and the pilots also slept in tents, not far from their aircraft, with little time for anything else but Doodlebugs and the best way of knocking them out of the sky. A pilot from 306 squadron was on leave at his home in Heston, Middlesex when a V-1 crashed on his house, killing his wife and child and injuring himself. Tragedy again struck at the end of July when another of 306's pilots was hit by our own anti-aircraft guns and he was killed when his Mustang crashed into the sea, a few miles off shore, south of Hastings. Mustangs were also capable of long-range escort duties and during that time they accompanied Beaufighters of Coastal Command on a shipping strike off the Norwegian coast, when they destroyed eight intercepting fighters for no loss to themselves.

Boleslaw Drobinski was a commissioned Polish Air Force fighter pilot when he escaped to Romania, took a train journey to Paris and got a passage from Cherbourg to Southampton, arriving in England just after war broke out. He joined No. 65 Spitfire Squadron during the Battle of Britain and later, flew numerous low level sweeps with No. 303, a Polish Squadron, eventually becoming its Commanding Officer in 1944, with the call-sign GLENCOE. He shot down seven ME109's and scored many hits on enemy shipping. He was awarded the DFC in 1941 and received five Polish decorations. After the war, when he attempted to register as a British subject he was told he would have to wait five years because he had arrived in Britain without permission. The fact that he had been fighting for Britain since 1940 and had married an English girl in 1943 was of no avail, so he left in frustration and went to the United States. He later returned and was granted British citizenship.

316 (Polish) Mustang squadron operating from Friston, west of Eastbourne also took part in the V-1 battle. They were in Tangmere Sector, under the control of Tangmere Ops Room and during the campaign they destroyed 74 Doodlebugs. No. 133 Wing at Brenzett accounted for 179.

Collectively, Polish squadrons destroyed more than 500 enemy aircraft and 190 V-1's . A total of 1,660 Polish aircrew were killed, missing or taken prisoner.

Chapter 17

GOOD-BYE WITTERSHAM

During 1943/44 there had been quite a few changes in WAAF personnel at Wittersham for various reasons and anyone leaving, a promotion, an engagement or a birthday was always a good excuse for a party. Most of us 'old hands' had done a year and a bit at Witt and I had been under threat of being posted to Tolleshunt D'Arcy a month or so earlier but I was reprieved at the eleventh hour because another WAAF didn't want to be parted from her best friend and volunteered to go in my place. I was pleased to be staying on - better the devil you know - and I would have been quite happy to spend the rest of the war there, but it was not to be.

Stew and I were not dating as often as we used to and seemed to be drifting apart. We'd had a tiff about something or other and I confided to my diary "Saw Stew 3 times today but he wouldn't speak to me - he can lump it!" I had been meeting a Yankee pilot in Hastings on my days off and maybe it got back to him. Anyway, it didn't upset me too much and the carefree life I was leading suited me just fine!

Among the American D/F operators at Wittersham belonging to the 57th Fighter Control Squadron was a handsome Tech/Sgt. called Norman Hoglund - he was the best looking guy out of all three units - over 6ft. tall and for a G.I., rather reserved and shy. Every new WAAF who came to Witt thought he was 'dishy' and cast their eye his way but we told them they were wasting their time hoping for a date, because he hadn't been out with a girl locally in the ten months he'd been in the village. We knew he wasn't married but guessed he probably had a steady girl friend back home, to whom he was being faithful. Within a couple of days of Stew and I finally splitting up, Norman asked me to go out with him, which I did. We were on different shifts and as he was working on my next day off, I decided to hitch-hike to Wembley. I had only just arrived home when I received a telegram from our Cpl. i/c Bart, saying I was posted - but he didn't say where - just that I was to return immediately. So after only three hours at home, I had to hitch all the way back to Witt. I called in at the Tower and found that my destination was Tolleshunt D'Arcy. How many times have WAAF's asked "Where the hell is Tolleshunt D'Arcy?". It sounded more like somewhere in France than a small village in Essex. Joycie was far from pleased at this news which meant my new romance was being nipped in the bud! Curly and Jay were on duty in the Tower and I asked them not to let on that I had returned because if I could keep out of the way of Bart and

Vic, I might be able to delay my departure and keep my second date with Norman the next evening. It was getting dark as I walked down our lane and I dived in the ditch at one point because I thought it was Bart or Vic cycling away from our billet to find out if I was back, but panic over - it wasn't either of them. The next morning, I got a message from Vic telling me I was to be packed and ready to catch the 2.30 bus. Defiantly, I wrote "He's had that". I turned up at the Tower at 1.30p.m. for my normal afternoon duty and got through to Sgt. Farrow at Biggin, and whatever reason I gave, there was no objection to my leaving tomorrow. Vic was rather annoyed that I blatantly defied his instructions and had managed to undermine what authority he thought he had at Witt. My memory of Vic is a bit hazey but I believe he was a diminutive civilian squirt, who because of his more mature years, thought he could boss us around. By hook or by crook, I had manoeuvred a last evening with Norman and a Farewell Party at the Swan. After 'chucking out time', we loaded up with a crate of beer and a crowd of us adjourned to the haysticks outside our billet to round the evening off. The G.I's sometimes gave their graduation ring to girl-friends when they were 'going steady' but of course the girl's finger is smaller and the ring in danger of slipping off. Peggy Clinker suddenly realised that Gep's ring was missing, so we all started to search for it. Looking for a ring in a haystack is just as impossible as looking for a needle and all the disturbance we were making looking for it, probably made it sink further into the depths and we never did find it that night. I was reluctant for the party to end - neither did I want to leave Wittersham and all the good friends I'd made during my 14 months service there and as for Norman, we had hardly had time to get to know each other. A favourite expression of the G.I's (putting on an exaggerated English accent) 'It's tough don't you know - in the E.T.O' (European Theatre of Operations). It had been a pleasant warm August evening but gradually as the night wore on, we found we were being engulfed in one of those chilly summer ground mists which covers everything in dew and suddenly we felt cold and damp. So at 3.30, we had run out of booze and the party ended.

A few hours sleep is better than none at all and I had to be up bright and early to finish packing and catch my train. Had I received some advance warning of the impending posting, I could have taken and left some of my belongings at home the day before but at short notice, I still had all my kit with me at Wittersham, which I had to transport up to Biggin first and then on to Tolleshunt D'Arcy.

It was the first time I had set foot on this most famous of Fighter

Stations because when Kenley closed down last March, we were automatically transferred to Biggin Hill Sector. The aerodrome had suffered 25 air attacks between August 1940 (the Battle of Britain period) and April 1941. The Operations Room had received a direct hit and an emergency Ops Room was set up in Biggin village (it was back to blackboard and chalk) until a permanent new one was established at Towerfield, Keston Park, 2 miles from the airfield. Biggin Sector comprised Hawkinge, West Malling, Gravesend, Lympne and Biggin Hill airfields.

When I got there I duly reported to Sgt. Farrow (whether male or female I remember not) who told me that I and other WAAF's from various places, were to make our own way and report to Tolleshunt D'Arcy the next morning, so I had the rest of the day 'to play'. I found two old chums on duty - Lilian Thornton and Chris and we caught up on all the gossip. I was able to dump my loaded kitbag in Lilian's billet and as she had no plans for the evening, we decided to go up to London for my 'last fling' before I was banished to Biggin's most northerly and remote outpost in the wilds of Essex. We went first to the Nuffield Centre and when we left there, I don't think we realised that we had forgotten to put our WAAF hats back on. Not a very bright thing to do in the centre of London where there were Military Police of all three Services wandering around, any one of which could apprehend you for being improperly dressed. It was Lilian who first heard the commotion behind us and summed up the situation at once - "Scramble" she said "Bogeys on our tail". I took a brief look round and saw two WAAF Officers frantically waving for us to stop and gaining on us at 180°! Not Pygmalion likely. Other than getting put on a charge, there was only one alternative - make a run for it, so we took off like bats out of hell. They took up the chase but we had a slight head start and the advantage of youth on our side! We scooted down a couple of side streets, dodged round a few corners and eventually realised that they had given up. We didn't want to hang around there in case we bumped into them again and as we were scurrying down the Haymarket, we were confronted by two Yankee Officers, who dodged sideways in front of us, so that we couldn't pass. "What's the hurry girls?" they enquired, and as we kept looking behind us, they thought we were running away from a couple of guys. They were quite amused when we told them of our chase and escape and never slow to take advantage of the main chance, one of them said "We"ll walk a ways with you and if those two old dragons show up again, we'll say you've been with us all afternoon and they must have mistaken you for two other gals". We quite liked the idea too - brave knights saving damsels in distress and we needn't worry if the Queen B. . . s recognised us again. They seemed like a couple of nice guys, so why not? We took a stroll in Green Park and then they asked us to spend the evening with them. We went first to the Orchard Club and then to a place called the Miami Club, recommended by the taxi driver (who probably got commission for sending clients) but it turned out to be a bit of a dive. £2.10 shillings to get in and £5.10.0d. for a bottle of whiskey, which even in those days was 'way over the top'. After a while, we noticed that couples round about kept disappearing for much longer periods than it took to go to the loo!. It began to dawn on us that the Club provided additional facilities, other than drinking and dancing!! It wasn't until Lilian and I were in the Ladies that we had a chance to talk things over but we definitely decided this was no place for us and agreed on a plan. I went back to the table and said that Lilian had gone outside for some fresh air as she was not feeling well and I was going to take her home, so we made a hasty exit. To be fair, I am sure the Yankee pilots only took us there because of the taxi driver's recommendation and that they had no ulterior motive but they might have been ready to take advantage of the extra perks on offer, had we also been willing!

It was gone 3.30 a.m. when we got away from there and the trains to Bromley didn't start until 06.15, so we went in Lyons Corner House in the Strand and drank coffee for an hour or so, which helped to keep us awake. Missing a night's sleep and only a brief couple of hours the night before hadn't yet hit me - I was still on my feet! It was a bind to have to go back to Biggin just to get my kitbag, when I could have parked it at a Left Luggage office in Town but I had intended to stay in Lilian's billet and had not expected to stay out all night! Lilian had to go straight on duty after a quick change in her billet and a snatched breakfast. I collected my belongings and made my way back to Town again, heading for Liverpool Street this time, to catch a train to Maldon, via Chelmsford - a journey I was to make many times.

Chapter 18

WELL - HELLO TOLLY!

The newly arrived WAAF's assembled at Maldon Station and we were taken in an RAF truck to Tolleshunt D'Arcy to be allocated billets in private houses. We had not been selected for individual places on the housing list so I thought I would position myself at the back of the truck, ready to jump out at a likely looking 'home from home', as far as could be judged from the outside. We stopped first at a few cottages and semi's in and around the village, where some of the girls got off. Then we left the village, turned into a country lane and half-way up was a large isolated farmhouse with a tall weeping ash in the centre of the front lawn. "Only one WAAF here" said the Billeting Officer, so I jumped out and staked a claim. At Wittersham I had shared a small room with Joan and Eileen for over a year, with our beds lined up against one wall (like the three bears!) and the chance of having one all to myself this time, seemed like a good move. Besides, I did not know any of the other girls and its

Brook House Farm, Tolleshunt D'Arcy. My Billet

always a gamble whether you will get on with whoever you might get shacked up with. The farmer and his wife, David and Lorna Golding were a young couple, only married three years and as yet no children. I was shown my room which had a comfortable divan, a wardrobe, ample drawer space and carpet on the floor. As I looked out of the window at the rural scene across the farm, there was barely another roof-top in sight. My first impression was that I couldn't have made a better choice and I knew I would be very comfortable and happy here. But would Mr. & Mrs. G. feel the same about me?

Lack of sleep after my Farewell Party at Wittersham and my night on the tiles in London had begun to catch up with me and I was dead beat.

After unpacking, I went to bed early in the evening and crashed out for a solid <u>14 hours</u> I fear this did not create a very good first impression.

It was just as well I was totally refreshed because straight away I was put on duty that same afternoon and I needed to be 'on the ball' because it was quite hectic - as for expecting life would be more leisurely away from the south coast - no chance! On my first night duty the following evening, I sat at the wheel for nine hours on the trot without a break. At Tolly, we started at 6.30 p.m. instead of 9 - a long 14 hour shift. I had Ellen on duty with me but she was still under training and not yet allowed to take control on her own. At 3.30 a.m. I had to ask her to go and wake Edna, as I was finding it hard to remain alert and when Edna relieved me, I trundled over to one of the Mobile trucks for a nap. I had obviously been involved in a busy night of operations but at the time I wouldn't have been told which fighter or intruder squadrons were prowling the skies during the night of 16/17 August 1944. During my recent research, I found nothing of any significance relating to that night and then I wondered whether an aviation buff I know, might be able to provide a starting point. He is compiling a list of all RAF crashes and any that were 'Missing' on that night, might give a clue as to which squadrons were airborne. I was certainly not prepared for a list pages long, covering 90 crashes world-wide during those two days and my main reason for mentioning this at all, is to emphasise the heavy toll of aircrew and 'planes lost in such a short period during those years of intense air activity.

Off duty, I soon settled down to a much quieter existence, as the pace of life was very different from Wittersham and the Doodlebug menace. David and Lorna treated me as one of the family and involved me in visits to their relatives who lived in all the surrounding farms. They were not short of anything much in the way of food because they could always exchange eggs and farm produce for whatever they needed, such as tea, sugar and flour etc. I revelled in the luxury of being able to have an egg for breakfast whenever I liked - hitherto, I used to record such an event in my diary, as it was a red letter day.

During August, the outdoor tomatoes were ready for harvesting and I often lent a hand. It was a good crop that year with a yield of between 2,000/2,500lbs. per day. I also used to feed the chickens occasionally and help look for the eggs - they were all free range in those and what a difference in the flavour - there is no comparison. Getting the turkeys penned in for the night was enough to try anyone's patience - they are even more stupid than sheep.

The Goldings had a friendly black and white mongrel called Chum, who looked as though he had some Collie in his mixed pedigree although not very noticeable when he was rounding animals up. Amid a certain fiendish delight, David did find he was very useful in getting me up in the mornings, when I had to be on duty by 8.30 a.m. One of my great failings, then AND now, has been an inability and distaste for wanting to see the light of day. When a knock on the door and a shout from Lorna 'Time to get up' failed to get any response, David would then call Chum, who would take a giant leap on my bed, landing on all fours and proceeded to lick me all round my face. He was a great pal and I was very fond of that dog - although I didn't appreciate his caresses at that time of the morning. David was a bit of a practical joker too and I was invariably the one at the receiving end - coke in my Wellies, a blank cartridge filled with water, placed precariously over the door ready to fall on me as I walked in. I always had to be on the alert.

The lane leading to Brook House Farm continued on as far as the River Blackwater and at high tide it was ideal for swimming, otherwise it was too muddy. The son of a friend of Lorna's, came to stay to help with the harvest during his school summer holidays. He was a young lad of 16 called Michael and down by the river, he liked nothing better than to indulge in mud-slinging and I was often a stationary target, unable to get out of range. Standing in one position for a few minutes, your feet gradually sank further down in the mud and when I tried to move, I invariably fell flat on my face because the other foot was up to its ankles in stodge and I couldn't budge. As I gradually prized my foot free it made a revolting squelching noise. Not exactly my idea of good clean fun but mud does have therapeutic qualities, I understand. Its good for the complexion as it detoxifies, strengthens and tightens the skin . . . but without a good hose down, I always experienced difficulty in removing it from all my nooks and crannies! (There is now an annual Maldon Mud Race across the 200 yards estuary of the River Blackwater to raise money for charity. Hundreds struggle against the mud's pulling power, sinking thigh-deep in the stuff).

Life on the farm was very pleasant and I knew I was very fortunate in having a first-rate billet but I soon began to wonder what I was going to do for amusement during my off duty hours in this quiet backwater, where you would not have known there was a war going on. Some days I could hardly find enough worthy of mention to fill the lines in my diary - not even the sight or roar of a Doodlebug to deafen the sound of the birds - no disturbed nights and assured of a morning's peaceful sleep after night duty - all that to me was bliss. The locals had never experienced the terror of a V-1 and I began to think I never would again either, but that hope was short-lived.

The Allies had been steadily advancing through France and eventually over-ran all the V-1 launching sites as far as the Pas de Calais but the retreating Germans managed to take with them many of the mobile V-1 firing catapults, which they were soon able to re-establish at sites in Holland. To reach London from there, the V-1's were coming over the North Sea, across the coast of Essex and during the next few months, an appreciable number were still getting through to London, but about 412 came down in Essex, although there were nowhere near as many, or as frequent as I had experienced in Kent. I can't recall as much air activity overhead trying to shoot them down either but probably the patrols were operating out at sea and trying to catch them before they reached the east coast. Radar would have been able to provide better early warning over the North Sea than the short expanse of the English Channel. Even so, having thought I had managed to escape them for good, it was a bit shattering to encounter them a second time - just my luck!

I did not discover until after the war (because we were never told) that the Germans had found another way of launching their Doodlebugs - in the air from Heinkel III bombers. The Heinkel's took off from airfields in north-west Germany with the V-1 fixed by a bracket under the wing and to avoid detection by British radar, they flew only a few hundred feet above the North Sea. When about 40 miles off our coast, they needed to climb to over 1,000ft. to be high enough to launch the missile. From take-off to release, it was a very dangerous flight for the Heinkel crews. They had to get airborne with a ton of high explosive and extra fuel on board, fly low over the sea, mostly at night, then the hazardous operation of starting the V-1 engine, and unless released promptly, the restricted exuberance of the motor could result in both machines plunging into the sea. Just over 400 Flying Bombs were launched by this method and together with those dispatched from ramps in Europe, there were still a fair number being sent across. Places farther up the east coast were having their first experience at the receiving end of these vile weapons of war. Suffolk had 93, Norfolk 13 and Yorkshire 7.

Compared to my social life at Wittersham, I began to wonder what I was going to do with myself every third day. I felt a bit intrusive hanging about the farm all day and probably getting in the way. So at first I used to either go home to Wembley or visit an aunt and uncle (my father's brother) in Chelmsford. Their only child John, had been killed in the Army in the early part of the war and after such a tragic loss, they felt their lives were meaningless and empty. They were always pleased to see me and I hope my visits helped to temporarily divert their melancholy. The wireless was the main source of entertainment indoors and they were quite keen on a game of cards. Sometimes, they suggested I go out and enjoy myself at one of the local dance halls in Chelmsford and there I met a Yankee Havoc pilot called Bob Wallace who was stationed at Gosfield. He walked back with me to my uncle's house and asked for my address and telephone number but a week or so passed and no word from him. Not to worry - plenty more fish in the sea I often told myself but they were harder to find in Essex than they were in Kent!

Lt. Bob Wallace - USAAF

The following week, after a trip home, I was on the train back to Tolly sitting at one of those long carriages with tables for four, when two G.I's came and sat opposite - inevitably chatting me up. They were quite amusing and helped to pass the time on a boring train journey. Paul went to get some refreshments and when he was out of earshot, Tommy Sugg asked me to meet him in Colchester and to bring along a friend for Paul. Then when Tommy went to the loo, I had an identical conversation with Paul, who asked me to bring along a friend for Tommy. I had letters from them both, still in competition and I arranged to meet them in Colchester, taking along a WAAF friend. Later on, I often wondered whether this was a little betting game they played together, testing their male charms, as to who would succeed in dating the girl. Tommy Sugg came from Louisiana and had a fascinating southern accent and right from the start, I decided he was my first choice. It all worked out

M/Sgt. Tommy Sugg - USAAF

alright because my friend and Paul liked each other too.

Then Bob, the Havoc pilot telephoned the farm a couple of times when I was out and eventually reached me the third time he rang and would I meet him in London? So bemoaning the fact there was no-one to go out with in this neck of the woods, I now had a choice. Tommy thought he would be going back to the States in a month or so and Bob was expecting to move to an airfield on the Continent, so neither might be around for long. With a bit of luck, they were far enough afield for me to see both and I could leave it to the USAAF 'powers that be' to make the decision which one left me first, because I'd be sure to make the wrong choice! I used to meet Tommy either in Colchester or Ipswich - I believe his 861st Bomb Sqdn. was based somewhere near both and I also met Bob quite frequently too. I probably told each I could only see them once a week, not letting on that I had every third day off.

Around that time, I went back to Wittersham for a few days to see the old crowd. Not that you were ever welcomed with open arms - you were far more likely to be greeted with "I thought we'd seen the last of you" or "You must be a glutton for punishment wanting to come back to this hole". Quite a lot of the old gang were still about - Eileen Bond, Donnie Mayhew, Peggy Clinker, Curly Dunsmuir etc. and Lilian came over from Fairlight when she heard I was back. We had a raucous get together in the Swan, joined by Stew and some of the other G.I.'s. I think Norman must have left because he wasn't around. Eileen Bond was made Corporal soon after and was posted to Noak Hill in charge, and several of the long-serving Wittites went to other Biggin D/F Stations. Joan Wedgbury had been Mrs. Hall for over a year and was out of the WAAF's, pending the arrival of her baby but still living at Wittersham.

****

Before actually embarking on writing my war-time story, the deciding factor was whether I would be able to uncover sufficient information about the Mayday incidents with which I had been associated, after an interval of nearly fifty years. I systematically went through my diaries and made a list of those I had mentioned but I left out a few because they were so vague, I did not think there would be the remotest chance that I would ever discover any relevant information or find out who the pilot might have been. My first course of action was to write a letter to the Aircrew Magazine which was published in the Summer Edition of their quarterly magazine 'Intercom'

- the gist of which was to enquire whether the aircrew who baled out over the Channel/North Sea during WWII, ever reflected afterwards on the organisation that located them and led to their recovery. I was hoping to get some belated appreciation of the efforts of the Air/Sea Rescue Service but the response on the whole was rather apathetic, except for one letter from Hugh Ross, an ex-Tempest pilot who said that as one who needed to call Mayday, he had read my letter with interest, adding "We were all grateful to those who helped get us back but there was no way of passing on our thanks at the time and I for one would like to read an account of the work performed by D/F Stations". He only briefly mentioned his own 'splashdown' so when I acknowledged his letter, I asked for more details and this was his reply -

"I was stationed at Manston (Kent) flying a Tempest with No. 80 Squadron and on 14 September 1944, I baled out a mile or two off the Dutch coast. I was picked up by a Walrus and taken to Martlesham Heath . . . . now then Joyce, could I have been one of yours?". Thinking it very unlikely, I nevertheless consulted my diary and lo and behold, one of the vague clues I had not thought worth including in my Mayday list turned out to be:-

'14 Sept.1944. On duty at 2 p.m. Worked for a spell - a/c in trouble. One baled out but he got back O.K.'.

Our D/F Tower at Tolleshunt D'Arcy was one of the nearest to the Dutch coast and Martlesham Heath aerodrome was just over the Essex/Suffolk border. Hugh Ross did not mention the time of day he baled out, but on checking No. 80 squadron records, it revealed on that day . . . .

'Recalled from 12.50 Recce at 13.00 hours because of targets being bombed by the 'heavies'.

15.35 Big Ben armed Recce in the Hague area. Strikes observed on 3 large barges and on sailing vessels on Grover Canal; also on various M.T. and gun emplacements. R & R (road and rail) attacked and left burning at D750901 (map reference). Light flak from wood at D714975 and intense at D684943. On the return trip an a/c piloted by W/O Jock Ross developed mechanical trouble and the engine cut. W/O Ross baled out successfully and within a very short time was picked up by A/S/R/ Service.'

The same incident in No. 278 Squadron (Martlesham) records stated - 'Search 17.20 - 18.50. Two Spitfire aircraft piloted by F/Lt. S.T. Thompson and P/O A.A. Hyde were ordered to search for a pilot who had baled out in position N8030. Vectored to position by Ops and found the pilot in a dinghy being orbited by a Tempest. Dropped a smoke float and circled until

SEPTEMBER 14

Thurs 1944 Got up & caught the 10 o'clock train back. Nearly missed it again! Took bus to Maldon. Got back just after one. On at 2·0 in the Tower. Worked for a spell - a/c in trouble. One baled out but he got back OK. Pressed my battledress, tunic & the rest of my things. Bed 11 o'clock.

Diary entry 14th September 1944

Hugh Ross

the survivor was picked up by a Walrus, piloted by P/O J.E. Meeklah and Sous Lt. J. Felice, Free French. No cloud. Visibility 5 miles. Sea static.' (This was the only afternoon rescue on the 14th)

In my brief correspondence with Hugh Ross, he has admitted that he is a reluctant letter-writer, so I was very fortunate to have received the following detailed account of his personal experience in 1944:-

"On that morning, September 14th, I was told I would be flying No. 2 to Sq/Ldr. Bob Spurdle, the C.O. of No. 80 Sqdn. and that there would be just the two of us on the op. Time dragged on and then I was informed the op was off and then it was on, but instead of the C.O. it would be F/Lt. Johnny Heap and myself. For some reason I couldn't take my own aircraft and was given the Tempest of the 'A' Flight Commander, Tony Seager. His two ground staff had just spent hours polishing every square inch of the aircraft and a Tempest is surprisingly, a very big aeroplane. They were not too happy that someone from another section was going to take up their Flight Commander's aircraft, as the two flights each looked after their own aircraft, with due pride and personal care. Polishing a Tempest with bees wax was really hard work but it looked superb, gleaming from end to end. One of the ground crew joked - "If you scratch it, don't bother bringing it back!"

A quick briefing and Johnny and I were airborne and on our way to the Hague. We were to look for and note any enemy movement inland of the Hague and then finish off with the odd attack, to make it look like an ordinary op. Of course, Arnhem wasn't mentioned but that was obviously the reason for the op. We crossed over the Dutch coast and flying at between 2-4,000ft. we searched for any out-of-the-ordinary enemy activity but found nothing unusual. As our sweep was coming to an end, we looked for the odd target and found a big white boat or barge which we attacked with our four 20 mm Hispano cannon. Shortly after pulling away, my oil pressure started to drop and I realised I would not be able to make any more attacks. I called up Johnny, who said "Set course for home and I will cover you".

It was obvious I was not going to make it back to England in that Tempest, which left me with the choice - either bale out now while over land and point aircraft westwards to ditch in North Sea or make a forced landing in Holland - both options resulting in becoming a P.o.W. Or getting as far out to sea as possible - bale out and hope parachute and dinghy worked alright and that Air/Sea Rescue would pick me up. It was a lovely day, no cloud, visibility over land was good but there was a fine low mist over the sea which restricted visibility and could possibly worsen. I decided to take my chance in the North Sea. I had been rescued from the sea once before in the middle of the Atlantic when the troopship 'Anselm' was torpedoed and sank with the loss of 300 lives but miraculously about 700 of us were picked up. I reckoned there would be a good chance of me being picked up off the Dutch coast, hopefully by our own A/S/R.

We flew on towards the coast, gradually gaining height as I nursed the engine along, with Johnny flying above and behind me. We kept R/T silence as we did not want to draw attention to our plight any sooner than need be. The oil pressure was dropping off rapidly and it seemed I would never reach the coastline but I was very relieved when it passed under my tail unit. The oil pressure was now practically zero. My thoughts were fully occupied with how I was going to bale out as abandoning an aircraft is the tricky part. I decided I would trim the aircraft to fly hands off and simply dive over the side. There was a grinding jolt and the propeller stopped dead. I called Johnny telling him I was going to bale out and left him to give the Mayday call. I jettisoned the canopy and the side panel and carefully trimmed the aircraft to glide gently down. Then I unplugged the R/T, undid my safety harness and scrambled into a crouched position, with my feet on the edge where the side panel had been. I tried to dive outwards but was brought up with a jolt as my R/T cable had caught on something. I tore my helmet off and this time succeeded in baling out, pulling my rip-cord after a few seconds. My parachute opened and in mid-air, I watched Tony Seager's immaculately polished aircraft gliding towards the sea. Slowly its nose came up and after a gentle semi-stall turn, it dived vertically into the sea. I splashed down soon after and in no time, I was sitting in my inflated dinghy. Johnny Heap circled overhead until two Spitfires arrived and relieved him.

Eventually, I saw a Walrus approaching at about 50ft. above the sea. As it came near it dropped a smoke cannister and landed into wind. It taxied alongside and I half-climbed and was half-dragged through the side hatch. As soon as I was aboard, the Walrus took off in the direction of Martlesham Heath (an aerodrome between Ipswich and Woodbridge in Suffolk). Arriving there, I was taken straight to the Station hospital where two American doctors stuck discs all over me and spent ages trying to get their little black box to give some readings. I'm still not sure whether they were more concerned about their little black bos or me! They kept me in hospital until the 16th September, much to my disgust, when an Oxford arrived to take me back to my squadron at Manston. I did not even get a chance to thank the Walrus crew.

Shortly after my return, a young L.A.C. came up to me practically in tears. It was the young chap who had said "If you scratch it . . . . ". He felt his remark had brought me bad luck and had been blaming himself ever since. I assured him I bore him no hard feelings nor considered he was in any way responsible for what happened and I eventually managed to console him.

No. 80 Squadron had rather a disastrous time between the 14th/25th September when we lost six experienced pilots, including my best friend, Pete Godfrey. Within a day or two, I resumed flying and on the 29th September the squadron moved over to the Continent.

And finally Joyce, a belated but none the less sincere thank you for your efforts on my behalf on 14th September 1944."

As for my small contribution in the team effort of helping to get Hugh Ross back safely, I would have been sitting in my D/F Tower, not yet realising there was a ditching about to take place because they were maintaining R/T silence for a while. The first intimation I would have had was when Ross told F/Lt. Heap he was baling out. Then his Flight Commander would have transmitted - "MAYDAY, MAYDAY this is Railroad Blue 1, calling MAYDAY. Blue 2 has abandoned his aircraft and baled out. He has landed in the sea and about to climb into his dinghy". The Controller would acknowledge and probably ask him to continue transmitting at intervals, so that the D/F Stations within range would get a good bearing. Having an a/c circling over an airman in the sea up-dates any drifting of the dinghy position and helps the Spitfire spotter a/c to locate him more speedily. I was probably the closest D/F unit, as The Hague was almost due east of Tolleshunt D'Arcy and I would have passed a bearing in the region of 080°. When Ross's position was 'fixed', No. 278 Squadron at Martlesham would 'scramble' two Spitfires and a Walrus, as the nearest available rescue facility.

Three days later, operation 'Market Garden' - the airborne landings at Arnhem began and the end of the month summary of No. 80 squadron records stated:-

<u>18 September 1944</u> - The invasion continued and we were again detailed to attack flak positions around Flushing. Airborne troops were being led in over us. Concentration of light flak. Attacked - several guns silenced and the place generally strafed. F/O P.S. 'Lofty' Haw was hit by flak. He attempted to ditch but eventually baled out at 1,260ft. and is 'Missing Believed Killed'. F/o Haw and Tempest were seen to crash into sea 20 miles west of Hook, his parachute being only half opened. F/O R.H. 'Bob' Hanney mysteriously disappeared and no facts are available about him. As reported, it was a day of suicide flying. W/O Hugh Ross re-commenced flying duties on 19 September.

It was such a extraordinary coincidence and a sheer stroke of luck that Hugh Ross replied to my Aircrew Association letter and all these years later, most gratifying to discover a pilot still alive that I had lent a hand (or more modestly . . . . a finger) in helping to save. This early success in solving such an obscure diary clue gave me great encouragement to tackle others.

Chapter 19

BATTLING AGAINST ALL THE ODDS

The last half of 1944, from June onwards, was I believe the most frustrating period of the whole war. Until then there had been little cause for optimism - it had just been a plain struggle for survival to prevent this beleaguered island fortress from being invaded and ravaged as had happened throughout Europe, whose people had been deprived of freedom and treated like slaves of their so-called German masters. When the Allies were militarily strong enough to reverse the defensive position into an invasion attack, not only had the Bosche's aggression been halted, but we were now set fair to liberate those countries that Hitler's troops had terrorised and pillaged since 1939/40. People's hopes began to rise but that glimmer of light at the end of the tunnel, dimmed again with every set-back that followed and there were many disappointments during those six months.

The invasion on 6th June 1944 had started well and a good foothold had been established. The British people were understandably expecting a break from air bombardment, thinking that the Germans would be utilising most of their military power to repel the invaders. There was barely an interval of ten days before the V-1 Flying Bomb attacks brought even worse death and destruction to London and the south-east corner of our shores, which continued day and night for several months. Then the invasion thrust in Normandy towards the east had ground to a halt because the French town of Caen was still in German hands and being strongly defended because it was the most important road junction in the area. Only seven miles inland from Sword Beach, where some of the invasion troops had landed, Caen was expected to have been in Allied hands during the first few days but the Germans held out there for over a month, with practically no support from their Luftwaffe until it was eventually annihilated by an endless stream of hundreds of Lancasters and Halifaxes who unleashed their bombs on the Town.

For what should have been the blooming month of June, the weather was atrocious and the worst storm for half a century blew up on 19 June and raged for three nights and days. Many of the Allied off-shore vessels sank at sea and hundreds more sought any kind of shelter to ride out the storm. Catastrophic damage was inflicted on the artificial 'Mulberry' harbours which had been erected to get supplies ashore. The invasion troops already established on French soil were awaiting reinforcements but three British divisions were unable to land and the Americans had to postpone their proposed break-out because supplies could not be brought ashore. It seemed that even the elements were against us.

Field Marshal Erwin Rommel was in Germany celebrating his wife's birthday when the invasion began but he was immediately recalled and a conference was quickly arranged with two Commanders of his Panzer troops, Generals Bittrich and Dietrich. When he was returning to Army Group Headquarters in his staff Mercedes, his driver diverted along side roads to avoid the many smouldering and burned out vehicles littering the main roads - targets of marauding RAF fighters who were able to fly the Normandy skies practically unhindered. When the Mercedes emerged once more on to the main highway, Typhoons were circling overhead and two of them dived down, roaring along the road after the car. attacking it with cannon and machine gun fire. The Mercedes went out of control and overturned, killing the driver instantly. Rommel and the other three occupants were all wounded and taken to the nearest hospital. Rommel recovered from his injuries but he took no further active command in the defence of France, in fact his military career was almost at an end.

But by far the most lamentable news was the failure of the German Generals in the plot to kill Hitler on 20 July 1944, which would undoubtedly have helped to shorten the war by many months. Two previous attempts had been made the year before but the participants were unable to 'pull it off' and fortunately for them, the attempts were undetected.

Even before the Allied invasion, there were within the realms of the Third Reich, dissatisfaction among the military hierarchy at Hitler's strategy and his reluctance to heed their expert advice. By July, the Nazi Generals realised they were going to lose the war and suggested to Hitler that they negotiate peace to prevent the fight finally ending on German soil and all the destruction it would create in their Fatherland. Hitler would not listen to them and a plot was hatched to assassinate him and set up a government who could negotiate peace terms with the Western Allies. Count Claus Schenk von Stauffenberg, aged 37 was in personal contact with Hitler. He had been seriously wounded in Tunisia and had lost his right arm, right eye and two fingers of his left hand while serving with the Afrika Corps. No longer able to participate in active service, Hitler promoted him to full Colonel and he was given the post of Chief of Staff to General Friedrich Fromm, the Commander of the Reserve Army. An opportunity to assassinate Hitler presented itself on 20 July when Count von Stauffenberg was due to attend a Conference at the Fuhrer's military Headquarters in East

Prussia. He arrived by air at Rastenburg with his brief case, which contained two bombs and he intended to set the time fuses just prior to the Conference. The operation was bedevilled by several unforeseen circumstances - in the process of timing the fuses in the toilet, he was disturbed and only had time to prime one, which he hoped would be adequate. The Conference was going to be held earlier than first planned because Mussolini was visiting Rastenburg that afternoon and one further disappointment - the underground bunker where the Conference should have been held, was being re-inforced and the alternative location chosen was a wooden hut. The blast of an explosion in the confined space of a solid concrete bunker, would have been far more destructive than in a construction made of wood, where the blast could escape through open windows and reduce the impact on the intended target.

Inside the hut was a large table covered with maps which Hitler, Field Marshal Keitel and other military chiefs were studying. Von Stauffenberg placed the lethal brief case on the floor, leaning it against the table support, about six feet away from where the Fuhrer was standing. Without arousing suspicion, he made a plausible excuse to leave. After he left, Colonel Brandt who had been standing behind him, moved forward and in so doing, kicked against the brief case, which he picked up and moved away from the table, and shielded Hitler from the worst of the blast. As Stauffenberg reached his waiting staff car, although out of sight of the hut, there was a loud explosion and smoke and flames rose from that direction and he assumed that his mission had been successful. He made his way to the airfield and flew to Berlin to join the other plotters in the revolt but many conspirators had been reluctant to act and hard line Nazi chiefs and S.S. Leaders had not been arrested, even before it was known that the attempt had failed.

Within the Fuhrer's conclave, it was first thought that the Russians were behind the assassination attempt but it soon became evident that it was an internal coup when details of Von Stauffenberg's hasty departure to Berlin were linked. Three of Hitler's military commanders were killed but the Fuhrer, supported by Kietel, emerged from the scene cut and bruised, with his uniform ripped but the only long-term effect was permanent loss of his sense of balance and deafness in one ear. Having miraculously survived the explosion, he now believed he was immortal but he was also deeply shocked at the disloyalty of those who had betrayed him. He was ready for ruthless revenge on anyone connected with the conspiracy. Count von Stauffenberg and those found with him were arrested, court-martialled and shot almost immediately. Several others wisely committed suicide, as the rest suffered a far worse fate at the hands of the Gestapo. On direct orders from Hitler, they were strung up and suspended by wire nooses on meat hooks, like animals in an abattoir and as they were slowly being strangled, Goebbels made a film of their agonising deaths for Hitler's special enjoyment. The Gestapo purges into the plot went on relentlessly and thoroughly and altogether about 5,000 people were executed, including innocent relatives and children of suspected conspirators. Field Marshal Erwin Rommel had known of the plot, although he had not participated but he was given the choice of taking poison by his own hand or being court-martialled as a traitor and condemned to death. He chose the former. Nine months later, in the ultimate stages of final defeat, executions of people thought to have been connected with the attempted assassination were still being carried out.

Countless wars throughout history have been waged in the earnest belief that 'God was on their side' and World War II was justifiably being fought for the highest of principles to rid the world of the most evil aggressor who, for his own megalomaniac vision of a Third Reich that would last a thousand years, had subjected most of Europe to the cruellest chapter in the history of the 20th century. Yet the tiniest bit of Divine intervention at that point would have spared thousands upon thousands more lives, by ending the war many months sooner but Hitler survived and three non-intended victims perished.

By the time the Allies had liberated France and entered the Low Countries, hopes were running high that the war was almost won. After all that Britons had suffered, it did not seem possible that there could be any further horror they would have to endure, but the ultimate weapon was yet to come. The first barrage of V-2 rockets landed in England on September 8 and continued for six months. I didn't mention in my diary when the V-2 rockets commenced because there was no official announcement for some time and people could only speculate on the cause of these mysterious explosions. Unlike the Doodlebugs, nothing was seen or heard before impact - no air-raid warning could be given - just an unexplained blast out of the blue - how did it arrive and where did it come from, people were eager to know? Only those at the receiving end rightly suspected it was another deadly weapon, indiscriminately aimed at defenceless civilians - and only the experts who examined fragments from the craters knew the whole truth, but were not permitted to disclose their findings. Once again, the press and radio were under strict censorship and the British public were kept guessing for a month. German Radio first broadcast that V-2 long range rockets were being launched against England and on November 10, Winston Churchill made an announcement in the House of Commons.

As with the V-1's, the general public could not comprehend at that time how a 46ft. long rocket, weighing 12½ tons, including a 1 ton warhead, could be thrust into the stratosphere and in a matter of seconds, have travelled just over five miles at a staggering speed of 3,600mph ultimately reaching 55/60 miles above the earth and within five minutes of being launched in Holland, would make its deadly nose-dive over some part of Greater London. In 1944 such advanced technology was beyond most people's grasp.

Directly on orders from Hitler, the V-2 long range rocket programme was intensified and priority was given to its production, supply and transportation to the launching sites. Hitler had become obsessed with the notion that another blitz on London with his V-2 weapons would bring him the victory that had eluded him in 1940 and he also wanted to avenge the destruction of Germany's main cities by Allied raids, ignoring the plain truth that Germany had begun the indiscriminate bombing of London, Coventry, Southampton, Exeter, Plymouth etc. in the first place. The first V-2 to descend on England fell in the west London suburb of Chiswick on September 8, killing three people and badly injuring another ten. An underground assembly plant in east Germany had the capacity of turning out 900 V-2's a month but the Fuhrer was unable to sustain a steady barrage of his rockets because the Allies were constantly seeking out and bombing the launching sites, as well as road and rail routes to prevent supplies reaching their destination. During the six months of the onslaught, 1,115 V-2's dropped on English soil and over 500 reached the London area. In addition to the V-1 casualty figures, the V-2's accounted for a further 2,754 deaths and about 6,500 people were seriously injured.

September held yet another disappointment for war-weary Britons - on the 17th the Allies launched the largest airborne force ever attempted - thousands of 'planes, gliders and paratroops descended within a 50 mile radius of Arnhem but they were unable to hold their position due to strong German opposition and after nine days of bitter fighting they were forced to withdraw. Out of the original 10,000 troops, only just over 2,150 made it to safety, with 1,200 dead and some six and a half thousand captured, wounded or missing.

Encouraged by the press, it was widely rumoured that the war would be over by the end of 1944 and the British people readily wanted to believe it. It did seem within the realms of possibility with the rapid advance across Europe and for this reason, Londoners and those at the receiving end of the V-2 rockets were less tolerant at having to suffer further hardship and mounting casualties. After five years, how much more could London be expected to take? They had had enough of living like rabbits, scurrying down their underground warrens whenever the air-raid siren sounded but with this latest terror, there was not even that safety warning. Once launched nothing could stop a V-2 on its course of deadly destruction. The Allies were boasting continued air supremacy over Europe as the Luftwaffe seldom took to the skies, so it was understandable that Britons were impatient that the V-2 launching sites were not being found and obliterated, which was the only defence against them. After the retreat at Arnhem and the realisation that the war was not in its closing stages, morale was at its lowest ebb with the same old diet of hope followed by despondency and the Bull-dog spirit was flagging. On 9 November, Antwerp was liberated and the German crews who had been launching V-2 rockets from an off-shore island surrendered but it had little effect on the number of V-2's launched during that month. 82 were dispatched from trailer platforms in and around the Hague and under their camouflage netting, they were almost undetectable from the air. Several of the factories supplying the liquid oxygen rocket fuel were deliberately built in densely populated residential areas in Holland, knowing full well that the Allies would not bomb them and risk killing Dutch civilians.

    The final bad news in 1944 was that the Wermacht and Panzer divisions were able to mount a counter-attack on December 16 and managed to break through the American lines along a 50 mile front and 1,000 tanks and 250,000 German troops poured back into Belgium, with the intention of recapturing Antwerp, which had barely enjoyed a month of freedom from Nazi occupation. The RAF and American Air Forces were once again grounded by fog and foul weather and were unable to assist in halting the German advance. The rockets and Flying Bombs were now being aimed at the Belgian port and the combined offensive of both weapons destroyed a good part of the city. Londoners were having a lull of barely one rocket a day but over the Christmas period, 52 V-2's hit Antwerp and one of the worst incidents was a direct hit on a cinema, killing some 270 people. Allied servicemen comprised the major part of the audience.

****

Meanwhile back at the farm . . . . a WAAF called June Harmer was posted to Tolleshunt D'Arcy and became part of my crew. Up until that time I had not made a particularly close friend amongst the girls but June and I hit it off at once and became firm friends, on and off duty, as I had with Donnie at Wittersham. There was one snag though - June was billeted with Lorna Golding's mother and father at a farm on the border of Tolly and Goldhanger. As previously mentioned, there were relatives in nearly every farm around and I had already experienced how quickly any gossip spread through the family grapevine. David and Lorna were teetotal and pubs were not the sort of places they would approve of young unattached females frequenting, so I kept quiet that I had seen the inside of quite a few! One evening I was having a drink with a couple of WAAF's in The Lion when in walked Molly Golding, David's sister, selling flags and there was I caught with a half pint of beer in my hand . . . . and what is more, by the time I came down to breakfast the next morning, David already knew! Not that it was really any of their concern what we did away from the billet but they had welcomed us into their houses and to make for a peaceful 'home' life, a little subterfuge was sometimes the best policy. So when June and I had been on a jaunt to Colchester or Ipswich, whoever we might be meeting, it made life less complicated by saying that we had been to the cinema rather than be asked questions about various boyfriends and what we had been up to. But we had to make sure we picked the same film, in case notes were compared between mother and daughter!

David used to call me a 'bad-do-er' because I had a good healthy appetite and never put on any weight. It was an East Anglian expression used about cattle they wanted to fatten up for market but never got fat. In spite of all I ate, I managed to remain slim which was no doubt due to all the exercise I had dashing, here, there and everywhere and the amount of cycling involved to get to the nearest railway station.

Tommy Sugg returned to the States in November and we corresponded for about six months. His letters were always quite affectionate and he said he would come back for me when the war was over but he was inclined to be flippant about most things and I didn't really take him seriously until he asked for my ring size. Bob Wallace, the Havoc pilot had moved to France but just before Christmas I had a surprise 'phone call to say that he was back in England on a short trip but had to return the next day. It was nice to have a chat, even though no chance of meeting. Then he telephoned to say that they were unable to fly back because of fog - the same foul weather as on the Continent which grounded RAF and USAAF aircraft and prevented them from attacking the German infiltration back into parts of Belgium. The turkeys were being killed at the farm and I had already planned to take one home to Wembley on my day off, so I was able to see Bob after all. I met him in Town for the evening and we went to Del Monico's and L'Auberge de France for dinner. I noted in my diary that I had a most scrumptious ice-cream - my first one for years. Turkeys were in short supply at Christmas 1944 and had I not lived on a farm, I doubt if my family would have had one, so they were particularly pleased to receive my Christmas surprise and a whole <u>dozen</u> eggs which Lorna had given me.

I 'chickened out' (?) of having anything to do with the slaughter of the turkeys but I did help with the plucking - it was an itchy job as most of them had lice, who were anxious to quickly find another live host! Farmer David and his brother Geoff came back with two cut up pig carcasses which had to be hung, as none of the farms had refrigerators - not many people did pre-war and freezers were still very much a thing of the future. Sides of bacon were usually hung from the ceiling of farm kitchens in those days which would probably be frowned on now as being unhygienic but the bacon certainly had more flavour than it does today, when pigs were bred in a more natural way.

The fog persisted and I was able to meet Bob again in London on my next day off. I had travelled by train with my precious turkey cargo but I couldn't afford two train fares in one week on WAAF pay, so hitching it had to be. On the main London road from Chelmsford, I met up with a couple of G.I's who were also hitching to Town but they weren't having much success in getting lifts. It turned out to be the most hilarious and longest hitch-hiking escapade I ever made with two of the craziest G.I's I ever met,

3 small prints of Joyce and 2 G.I's - Hitch-hiking

bearing in mind that it was the day before Christmas Eve and there was a lot of goodwill about! They would leave me on the pavement by myself to thumb a lift while they kept out of sight or hid behind a hedge until the vehicle stopped and with not so much as a 'by your leave' to the driver, they would pile in after me and the astonished driver wasn't sure whether they were with me or not and sometimes I pretended I had no idea where they had appeared from. Some of the lifts we got would have sped us on our way to London but the sight of a pub open during the lunch hour and they'd 'want out', so instead of making progress, we kept stopping at numerous pubs on the way, getting tanked up with Xmas spirit. If there wasn't enough room in a vehicle for us all, they wouldn't let me go on by myself, pleading that they would never get to London if I wasn't there to get them rides. I was virtually a hi-jacked hitch-hiker although not too unwillingly, I have to confess. One of them was married and the other one had a camera - I was holding a bunch of flowers for my mother and married Yank was carrying a week-end bag - there wasn't room on the path to walk three abreast so when tail-end Charlie called out, we both turned round and as we did so, he took our photograph. Now he was chuckling to himself that he could make some mischief with married Yank's wife - that he'd snapped him going off to London with his English girlfriend and what was it worth? That started a bit of horse-play between the two of them - every now and again married G.I would try and get hold of the camera to expose the film so that it could not be developed and his friend would pretend to be off-guard but remained very sharp and managed to thwart each attempt. We must have eventually reached London and parted company - I can't even remember their names, but married G.I. obviously did not manage to sabotage the film as one of them must have sent me the three photographs, which I still have. I never saw them again but I do recall they were two of the most amusing jokers I had the good fortune to meet and they made that hitch-hike such a lot of fun. I got home to Wembley mid-afternoon still clutching my bunch of chrysanthemums for Mother which surprisingly I hadn't left in a car or a pub. (Diary comment 'really felt happy' which I think was a bit of an understatement after the numerous gin and tonics I'd knocked back).

    Bob 'phoned soon after and we arranged to meet at 7 p.m. at Piccadilly and we went to a Dinner Dance at the Lansdowne Restaurant. I deposited my WAAF greatcoat in the Ladies Cloakroom and it looked rather conspicuous amongst the fur coats of the majority of females who were in evening dress. Their escorts, at least those in the Services, were all high ranking officers - the RAF Officers were Group Captains or above - there were no Army Officers below the rank of Major and being unfamiliar with Naval Ranks, I can only say they had an abundance of rings and gold braid. While we were dancing, I could see over Bob's shoulders that some of the couples sitting at tables around the edge of the small dance floor, seemed to be looking me up and down and passing some remark or other. Americans didn't really understand the class snobbery that existed in England and that it was 'infra dig' for high ranking officers to consort socially with the lower rank and file. Bob only laughed when I tried to explain that I was being given the cold shoulder because I was a lowly LACW amongst all the brass. English fellas seem to be slightly embarrassed to remark on a girl friend's appearance and as a rule were not over-generous with compliments but the Yanks knew how to make a girl feel 'special'. Bob took hold of my hand and whispered "Well, if you think you are being noticed its because you are the loveliest girl in the place and I bet the women are envying you your slim figure, English rose complexion, beautiful hair and innocent bright eyes". After dinner and a few more drinks, we spent a lovely romantic evening dancing cheek to cheek and soon forgot there was anyone else in the place. Bob came as far as Baker Street and I caught the last train home. I got talking to a couple of Sgt. Pilots in my carriage who had just returned from training in South Africa and I remember thinking that with a bit of luck they might be spared becoming involved in aerial combat, as the war was not likely to last much longer. I hope that Bob Wallace survived the war too - he flew Havocs with the 647th Bomb Sqd. in 410th Bomb Group and lived in Orchid Lane, New Hyde Park, New York.

    Christmas week 1944 was proving to be 'All go'. I returned to Tolly the next morning in time for afternoon duty at 1.30p.m. - this was Xmas Eve - and a Section Officer and a Flight Sgt. came out from Bradwell Bay aerodrome with our Christmas Hamper and we were invited to go back with them for a Xmas Eve 'Do' at the Sergeants Mess. Now, its a wonder I agreed to go because a month before several of the Tolly WAAF's went to a dance at the Sgts. Mess there and we weren't a bit impressed. Of that visit I had written "We were all put in different huts - everywhere is filthy and the food isn't fit for the pigs. And the dance band didn't turn up until 10 p.m. either. I didn't think breakfast would be worth leaving my bed for, so I didn't bother. There was no transport laid on to get us back to Tolly and we had to hang around the NAAFI all morning - it eventually came for us at 2 p.m.". My comments about the Sergeants were not very complimentary either! So I must have been a glutton for punishment to risk another possible dismal 'Do' but it WAS Christmas and probably the only invitation we got! On this occasion my diary records . . . ."We are all in the same hut this time. Went to the pub first and then to the Sgts. Mess. We were snowed under with mistletoe when we arrived. Bags of spirits and the beer is on the house. Newman was behind the bar (someone I must have known then). Met an Aussie Warrant Officer but Deadly* kept trying to get him away from me. Don't think there was a sober person there. When the ceiling started moving, I quit. The others saw it through. Got in just after 1." (* I remember we used to call one of our WAAF's 'Deadly' - as in 'Deadly Nightshade' but the tie-up escapes me!)

Christmas Day- 'Froze all night. Didn't hear the rest of the gang come in. Got up at 7. Per usual there was no transport organised for us. The M/T (Motor Transport) Officer poked his head round the hut door and requested 'One hot WAAF to defrost my windscreen'! Cheeky sod!

In the end Len, our civilian maintenance operator came and fetched us and June and I must have gone straight on duty when we got back. Poor June was suffering from that 'morning after' feeling and crashed out on the mattress for an hour or so. She felt better by the time we went off duty and I told her the freezing temperature outside would soon sober her up! We were back again for night duty at 6.30 with no likelihood of anything to monitor up there in the 'wild blue yonder' so we hit the sack early and we felt less like Zombies after a sound undisturbed night's sleep. Remembering the 1943 Christmas I spent in Hastings Hospital, this wasn't exactly the Xmas I had in mind to compensate but never mind - spare a thought for all those troops on the Continent, sleeping rough in all this freezing weather.

On our day off, June and I had intended going home for Boxing Day but felt too tired. I would probably have made the effort if Bob had still been in London but as he hadn't 'phoned, it was likely the weather had improved sufficiently for them to be able to take off for France on Xmas Eve. Instead I spent it at Tolleshunt's Farm, where the Golding's parents had a family gathering on Boxing Day with 18 people to supper and as much Xmas fare as you could eat.

V2 rockets were still coming across although not quite so many during December - out of the 88 that landed, only 33 hit London, averaging about one a day but in the final days of 1944, Islington suffered two serious incidents. The publican of the Prince of Wales pub in Islington had converted the cellar into a bar, where customers might feel safer from V-1 and V-2 attacks. On Boxing Day evening it was crowded with revellers, when a rocket crashed in the street outside, demolishing nearby shops and houses and the pub building collapsed on top of the cellar, trapping the occupants underneath. Rescue workers were unable to reach them and to add to the chaos, fire broke out and nearly all the people in the cellar bar were either killed or seriously injured. The crater in the road burst the gas and water mains, which caused flooding and rescue vehicles were further hampered by a dense pea-soup fog. The final death toll was 68 dead and nearly a hundred badly injured. A few day's later, just before midnight on New Year's Eve 1944, Islington was again the indiscriminate target of a V-2 which crashed in the region of Crouch Hill, killing 15 people and 34 seriously injured. During the four months from 8 September to 31 December 1944, 382 rockets landed in the south-east corner of England. So what would the New Year bring . . . .

****

War-wise and weather-wise, the outlook for the start of the New Year brought very little in the way of good cheer. For more than a dozen Allied airfields on the Continent, including our ex-Kenley/Biggin Canadian Wings at Heech and Evére, New Year's Day was heralded by an early morning attack by a formidable striking force of over 900 Luftwaffe aircraft. They approached at low level to avoid radar detection and made simultaneous attacks on various airfields in southern Holland and Belgium. At one airfield, Allied aircraft were lined up in rows, wing to wing, like cars in a car park, providing such an easy target. Had it not been for the icy conditions on the improvised runways, more Allied aircraft would have been airborne but despite the freezing conditions, many fighters took off immediately and inflicted severe losses on the Luftwaffe. Reichsmarschall Hermann Göring had planned this New Year surprise believing that it would be less costly for the Luftwaffe to destroy Allied planes on the ground than in the air but the Germans paid a heavy price for that attack. It was the greatest loss in one day of Luftwaffe pilots during the entire war - over 250 aircrew were killed, many through lack of combat experience and 270 Luftwaffe aircraft were destroyed and 40 damaged. It crippled what was left of Hitler's Air Force and in spite of destroying many Allied aircraft on the ground, they were still out in force on the afternoon of New Year's Day, when the weather improved, managing to fly about a thousand sorties.

New Year's Day fell on a Monday and on the following Friday, the 5th, June and I had our closest frightening encounter with a V-2 rocket. We were on afternoon duty and I was carrying a kettle in my hand as we walked over to our D/F Tower, when a rocket landed in the next field. To be caught unawares by an earth shattering explosion loud enough to blast your eardrums without any warning, is a tremendous shock but we instinctively threw ourselves on the ground which was trembling beneath us. It was the first and only time in my life that I ever saw stars and thank goodness the kettle only contained cold and not boiling water. That incident made me realise how trivially we had treated the perils of living in that dangerous south-east corner during the past couple of years, when that rocket could just as easily have come down in the field we were walking across. If anything, I should have felt less threatened in rural Essex than I did in Kent. When I returned to the farm, David was in the process of covering up the windows which had been blasted out, and my bedroom was one of them. At the time, January 1945 was said to be the coldest month in living memory and with sub-zero temperatures, the boarding cover over the windows was far from weather-proof and let in too many draughts. The farmhouse kitchen had an Aga type cooking range which threw out a good heat and there was a cheerful log fire in the Living Room but the rest of the house was only a degree or two warmer than the temperature outside during that bitter January. We existed without the creature comforts we now believe we cannot live without - no central heating or electric blankets.

June and I had spent our last two days off 'farm-bound' with very little to do, so on our next free day we decided we would relieve the monotony and make for Ipswich, staying overnight at the YWCA which provided a cheap night's kip for Service gals. Without any qualms about the stupidity of venturing out on those treacherous roads hoping to get lifts, we obviously had given little thought that not many cars would risk the icy conditions unless their journey was absolutely necessary. We could so easily have got stranded way out in the sticks along those 10 miles of country roads to Colchester but from there to Ipswich, the next 18 miles were on the main highway. Anyway, we got a lift most of the way to Ipswich in a lorry, but when we got there we realised that 'only mad WAAF's and Yankee guys go out in the freezing snow!'. The place was deserted except for a couple of Yanks who pelted us with snowballs. They were doing their best to dodge the U.S. Military Police as Ipswich was 'off limits' to American Forces for 24 hours as a routine check for deserters. They decided the safest place was in the cinema and asked if we would join them. There didn't seem much else for us to do either, so why not? It gets dark quite early in January and when we came out of the cinema after seeing "Goldwyn Follies', we thought it was a bit of a giggle helping them to evade their Military Police, who were still out in force. We took devious routes round the back streets and before turning a corner, June and I would venture out first and signal if the way was clear (just like they do on the movies!). We got them safely to the 'Mulberry', where we had a few drinks and then they saw us back to the YWCA in the same evasive manner. We had to be in by 11p.m. otherwise we'd be locked out. I expect those two G.I's convinced us they were just a couple of rebels who didn't want to spend their day off confined to Base but re-reading and remembering the episode again, we might well have been aiding and abetting a couple of American deserters! June and I were on afternoon duty, so we returned by train rather than risk hitching and maybe not getting back on time. It was still freezing and the roads were like glass.

Chapter 20

THE END IN SIGHT

Two more days of duties and then I was homeward bound on ten days leave with nothing in particular planned now that Tommy and Bob had left. Keeping up a steady correspondence with other fellas I had met previously, often worked out rather well because eventually, they would get a 48 hour pass or a leave and head for London. My social life was seldom in the doldrums for long and when I arrived home, I was very chuffed to find a telegram from Derek Hamilton, asking me to ring him in London. He was a Fleet Air Arm pilot from Christchurch, New Zealand, based somewhere in Scotland and I hadn't seen him for a while, as visits down south were not very frequent. I had first met him last October on my 20th birthday at a dance at the New Zealand Club which was a central meeting place for all Kiwis in London. Being a small country, they invariably met someone they knew or hadn't seen for a long time and on our first visit on this leave, two of his school-friends turned up unexpectedly and what a party we had that night! Peter was a F/Lt. in the RNZAF and Rob, who was a marvellous pianist, had joined the Navy. Everyone took notice when he played boogie-woogie - all the rage then - he could play almost any tune people requested and I was one of his biggest fans.

The New Zealanders were an incorrigible bunch with a strong tendency towards being 'anti-establishment' - they indulged in a lot of friendly rivalry between the different Armed Forces they served in and Derek seemed to like having a few of his friends in tow, which I didn't mind either! One evening, two more friends, Bull Henderson and a guy called Clive turned up at the Fernleaf Club with six Kiwi Pilot Officers and we all went to the Hammersmith Palais. They were quite happy propping up the bar but I did manage to entice some of them on to the dance floor.

Derek Hamilton - Fleet Air Arm

It was a hilarious evening and thankfully, only Derek came to Baker Street because Father was on the platform waiting for the Wembley train. He had been fire-watching at Finchley. What would he have said had he seen his daughter earlier, strolling along Hammersmith Broadway arm in arm with 9 New Zealanders from various

189

branches of the Armed Services!

The Uxbridge and Watford trains stopped running both ways about midnight so Derek only came as far as Baker Street with me, as he wouldn't have got back. The carriages on both lines were non-corridor and as a sensible precaution when on my own, I would always make a point of getting in a compartment with several occupants. There were 10 stations to Preston Road so there was no guarantee you would not be left in a carriage with an 'undesirable' when other people got out at stations along the way. The only risk really was being alone with someone who had had too much to drink and thankfully that never happened to me. Occasionally though it turned out to be quite advantageous! Later in the week, I was alone in a carriage sitting opposite a handsome RAF Fl/Lt. pilot with DFC and we got chatting. By coincidence, he too got out at Preston Road because he also lived there - he saw me to my door and asked to see me again. His name was Dick Clarkson. I had only planned to see Derek the following day and again at the week-end, so a few days later, Dick called for me at home and we went up to Town, saw a movie and then went to a Dinner Dance at Oddenino's. By an even stranger coincidence, when I told him I was an RT/DF operator listening to intercom and Maydays etc., it transpired that he was Lounger 'J' for Johnny, one of the call-signs of the squadrons on our frequency, so I would have heard his voice over the intercom. He did tell me that he had finished two tours of Ops but I cannot recall that he said anything about his exploits, how he got his DFC or the number of his squadron. We caught the last train from Baker Street and it was a nice change to have someone to see me to my door. But as invariably happened, however quietly I crept indoors father would still be awake waiting for me and create a helluva fuss about coming home at 1 o'clock in the morning, with some justification. I was often admonished by stern parent for frequent similar offences, without realising that they were unable to relax until their wayward daughter was safely indoors.

I saw Derek on the last day of his leave and after a cinema show, we took the Underground to the Regent Palace for a Dinner Dance and blow me - who should get in our carriage at Leicester Square but Dick Clarkson on his own. He sat opposite us with his penetrating gaze firmly focused on me and if looks could kill . . . . I was so taken aback, I didn't know whether to speak or not but in the end I didn't, because he didn't say anything either. I was thankful that Derek and I were getting out at the next Station as it was an embarrassing situation but I couldn't help thinking that of _all_ the people milling around London and of _all_ the hundreds of carriages on the

Underground - it was rotten bad luck that Dick happened to board the one I was in! It didn't concern me unduly whether or not any of the fellas I corresponded with and met occasionally had other girl-friends at home or where they were stationed - in war-time I preferred to remain foot-loose and fancy free.

Not surprisingly, that was the last I saw or heard of Dick Clarkson as although we both lived in the same area of Wembley, our paths did not cross again after the war. Until I re-read my diaries, I had long since forgotten that rather trivial encounter on the Underground but I have recently discovered that LOUNGER was the call-sign of No. 692 Mosquito Squadron, based at Graveley, south of Huntingdon. My informant, an ex-Navigator also added that as the squadron operated on six nights of the week, with individual crews flying on Ops two nights out of every three, they thought someone had a warped sense of humour allocating No. 692 the call-sign LOUNGER.

Before I established the connection between the Lounger call-sign and 692 squadron, Graveley was one of the bases I thought that the Coulsdon crash Mosquito might have been heading for and was one of the squadron records I checked through at Kew. When I dealt with Wagtail One-Niner's Mayday on night duty 12/13 May 1944, Dick Clarkson was also airborne at the same time, from 02.45 until 05.45. "692 on operation to mine Kiel Canal in a 3½ miles stretch. To aim mines accurately it was essential to fly in at low level (300ft.) Route was marked by green Verey lights dropped by 139 squadron. First six a/c arrived at target at 03.36 identified with the help of the moon and light of dawn just breaking. Second wave of 7 a/c due on target at 03.52. Length of Canal where mines were laid was practically undefended - 1 or 2 light guns. One Mosquito did not return and crew reported Missing. 692 was the first Mosquito squadron to carry 4,000lb. bombs."

A few months later F/Lt. R.H.W. Clarkson DFC completed his second tour of Ops (which on Mosquitos meant 80 (50 + 30) raids over enemy territory.)

****

When I returned from leave, snow inches deep covered the ground everywhere and the bitterly cold weather persisted beyond January. On night duty we were frequently closed down for good around midnight as there was practically no night flying. My feelings on those occasions were expressed in my diary with remarks such as YIPPEE - HIP-HIP - OH JOY or WHIZZO and once I had begun to write HALLELUJAH but obviously couldn't spell it! To fully enjoy this welcome bonus, we would bed ourselves down early to keep warm and listen to the radio. At any time during the night Biggin Ops Room might ring through to give us a time check but we suspected it could also be to make sure we were still there! I hadn't made a note of any Maydays during that bitterly cold weather but the poor devils who might have baled out would have stood little chance of surviving for long in choppy seas and icy temperatures. The fact that we were kept in ignorance about rescue failures may also have been 'by design' to keep us detached and remote from personal involvement and on reflection, I'm rather thankful that we did not know exactly who they were, otherwise we might have dwelt on the loss of yet another young life with a momentary lapse in concentration from the job in hand. After being involved in a Mayday call, we optimistically hoped that it resulted in a successful outcome and we were often told when it did. We were kept from knowing details of those who didn't make it and in many instances, we probably heard the last words spoken by those brave young pilots as they plunged to their deaths. There were frequent abrupt breaks in the intercom rapport when a pilot failed to respond to repeated calls from the Controller to answer . . . "Come in, Monarch Blue 2 - I am not receiving you - over". We often feared the worst but we rarely had our suspicions confirmed. After looking through squadron records, I now know the reason for many of those unexplained silences and I could not help becoming misty-eyed and choked with emotion, as I read brief accounts of such narrow margins between life and death, when with just a little more time they might have survived. To quote a few examples :-

F/O . . . . was either hit by flak or an FW190. He baled out over the Channel. Two pilots of his squadron circled and watched him go into the Drink. He was not seen to climb into his dinghy and as yet no word has been heard of him.

Beachy Head patrol - two dinghies seen floating in the water. One inflated but empty and the other one not opened.

Flying Control requested a Walrus to search Channel as customer reported to be in sea 22 miles out from Deal. Area searched but found only an oil patch and a small amount of wreckage.

Sq/Ldr. . . . hit by flak over target. His a/c was carrying a bomb which exploded and disintegrated in mid-air. Pilot killed instantly.

F/Sgt. . . . had engine failure after changing from his auxiliary tank to main tank. He was escorted back by Blue 4 when half-way across the Channel, Blue 2's a/c was seen to roll over on its side and drop into the sea from 2,000ft. Blue 4 watched the a/c plunge into the Channel. He orbited for 15 minutes but Blue 2 sank in his a/c and nothing surfaced.

Pilot killed after being hit by his own drop tank off the coast of Holland.

A Spitfire pilot flew into a German road convoy while shooting it up. He tried to bale out but his parachute got entangled with his 'plane.

A Walrus orbited an airman being dragged through the water by his open parachute. On investigation saw the pilot was still attached to it but no longer alive. Continued patrol for a further 7 miles and investigated another pilot being dragged by the wind, also with open parachute - he was also dead.

****

I have often thought what a junk-yard the sea-bed of the English Channel must have been after the end of the war littered with wrecks of Naval and Merchant shipping - sunken submarines - crashed aircraft - hundreds of Doodlebugs - discarded auxiliary fuel tanks - bombs that were jettisoned on the return flight for a safer landing - and a watery grave for so many who drowned in those vessels.

When relating or reading about the war-time exploits of these courageous young fighter pilots, who regularly faced the perils of flak, encounters with the Luftwaffe or engine problems, we are apt to lose sight of just how young most of them were. Many joined the Air Force straight from school and after flying training, found themselves posted to a squadron and at the age of 19 or 20, plunged into a world of 'kill or be killed'. Survival depended on quickly learning the skills of combat and to gain enough experience to help him stay alive a bit longer. They were often given the junior role of acting as Number Two to a Flight Commander, Squadron or Wing Leader. 'Sir' was able to concentrate on increasing his score of the number of Huns he knocked out of the sky, knowing that he had a faithful and dogged No. 2 who would stick with him and protect his 'derriere' but there was no-one behind the 'Minder' to watch over him and that was how some of the younger less experienced pilots 'bought it'.

****

Because of the precarious situation of the war during the last half of

1944, I suppose we were inclined to be over-cautious about sighting victory too soon, in case Hitler had anything else to knock us out with - like the dreaded 'V' weapons but it seemed at the time those were his last trump cards. We were spared the knowledge of the V-3 bunker at Mimoyecques, near Calais with its complex of tunnels dug by slave labour, capable of receiving railway trains, and in which were concealed five shafts, containing five guns, each 420ft. long with a muzzle velocity of 5,000ft. per second. Additional charges were to be fired every 12ft. along the shaft to accelerate the missile. Half of the deep underground complex at Mimoyecques was destroyed by the RAF early in 1945, using huge Tallboy bombs and the site was eventually overrun during the Allied advance before it was completed, when the lower levels were sealed off by Canadian and British engineers. Who knows what might have been in store for us, had the V-3 become operational?

By early March, the Allies had reached the Rhine, despite a late German counter-offensive and they were now ready for the final thrust into Germany - the Russians were also closing in from the East. But there was no let-up in the V-2 rocket attacks coming this way. During March, 166 were launched and one of the most serious incidents was the mid-morning disaster which befell Smithfield Market in Central London, killing 110 people, when the streets and market stalls were crowded with shoppers. The very last V-2 fell on March 30 at Orpington, Kent. During the six months duration of the onslaught, 2,754 people had been killed and 6,523 seriously injured.

American President Roosevelt did not live long enough to see the end of the war. On 12 April 1945 he died peacefully at his country home in Warm Springs, Virginia, after an attack of cerebral haemorrhage brought on, it was reported, by the strain of heavy duties. At the age of 63, Franklin D. Roosevelt had achieved the unprecedented record of being elected to four consecutive terms of office as President of the United States. The following day, the Russians captured Vienna.

At the end of April, 'Il Duce' Benito Mussolini and his mistress, Clara Petacci, were captured by a group of partisans in a village beside Lake Como in Northern Italy, while trying to escape to neutral Switzerland. Only a few hours after his arrest, the former arrogant Italian Dictator and the 12 Fascist followers with him, were shot by their captors. The bodies of Mussolini and his mistress were taken to Milan for public display in the same square, where 15 patriots had been executed by the Fascists. They were strung up by their feet and angry Italians unleashed their pent-up anger by spitting and hurling abuse at the already disfigured corpses. One irate mother fired five bullets into the already bullet-riddled body of Mussolini, crying "Five shots for my five assassinated sons".

Lord Haw-Haw, still regularly broadcasting his "Jairmany calling - Jairmany calling" was now becoming a bit of a joke. Within a fortnight of the end of the war he broadcast a last appeal to Britain to join Germany in saving Europe from the 'Red Menace'. He declared that Hitler had thrown in all his strength to fight the Russians. "We have given Britain an opportunity to save Europe" he said. "If reason does not prevail, the British people will have to pay a terrible price". During his final broadcasts, he spoke with a hoarse and often slurred voice, obviously drunk, at times nearly crying but vainly attempting to keep up the facade. He fled from Hamburg when the British arrived and occupied the broadcasting station but he was discovered gathering firewood near the Danish border because of his distinctive voice. He was arrested and tried for treason at the Old Bailey later in 1945 and hanged.

It was about this time that June told me the shattering news that she was pregnant. She had known Bill, an American G.I. for over a year, long before she came to Tolly. He was stationed at Cambridge and June often went over there and I had met him when he got transport and came over to see her. He was her first real serious romance and her first affair - he eventually persuaded her to spend her leave with him in London. We had longer periods of inactivity on duty, now that control of air operations was mostly beyond these shores and to pass the time, we discussed and aired our views on nearly every topic imaginable. She was well aware of my thoughts on getting pregnant and probably ruining the rest of your life for a brief moment of uncontrollable passion! I also had a stern and not very understanding father who would have chucked me out on my ear if I ever 'got into trouble'. From the cloistered upbringing of a girls' boarding school and at the tender age of 18, I was rather shocked and secretly amused, at some of the 'goings on' in the Forces but how they behaved was no business of mine! We had both known of some pitiful cases of the down to earth consequences - left in the lurch and penniless by fathers who either wouldn't own up to their share of responsibility or disappeared from the scene tout de suite. Women are very gullible when it comes to flattery and utterances of undying love, because its something they want to believe! Some had been seduced by vague promises of marriage, and this proved a convenient let-out for many a married man, who could eventually confess he already had a wife and the pregnant girl-friend had no comeback. There are always lessons to be learned from other people's misfortunes and I took heed - look after No. 1 and don't let your heart rule your head - advice which stood me in good stead but in all honesty, I could see no point in complicating the wonderful carefree life I was leading. Knowing my views on that subject, it had taken June a couple of months to pluck up enough courage to tell me. The important thing now was the best way to deal with her predicament. She was the only child of elderly parents and she was sure they would not be sympathetic if she told them the truth or come to terms with the shame she'd bring on them. As she had no brothers or sisters or any other close relative to confide in, I felt she ought to give her parents a chance and if they really cared for their only daughter, they would surely put her welfare first, before worrying about what friends and neighbours might say. But June was adamant that she wasn't going to tell them and I knew her well enough to know that once she had made up her mind, she wouldn't budge. She figured the best plan was to get compassionate leave, have the baby, get it adopted and hopefully return to the WAAF's, without her parents ever finding out. She wouldn't entertain an abortion and by the time she told me, it was too late for that anyway. She reminded me of the time I had met her in Chelmsford (after a doctor confirmed her pregnancy) and I had written in my diary "Met June off the London train - she looked like a ghost. She just managed to make it to Maldon. I took her into a chemist who gave her some medicine which helped. I was on duty at 2 p.m. and had to get a taxi because we'd missed the bus." The thought that she might have been pregnant never occurred to me but now she needed a friend and I would do all I could to help. She wanted to keep it a secret at Tolly for as long as possible and even though she sometimes looked ghastly after sleepless nights worrying about the future and retching her heart out from morning sickness, no-one else suspected. Watching Jean suffering the early stages of pregnancy, strengthened my resolve to avoid such temptation but I suppose at that time I had not been put to the ultimate test! Besides, I naively thought it was accepted that men could 'sow their wild oats' but they did not <u>wed</u> the girls they 'slept around' with, preferring a wife who was 'virginibus puerisque' when they decided to marry!

Bill and June still met frequently either in Cambridge or Tolleshunt D'Arcy and I am a bit vague why marriage wasn't an option, but Bill was being very supportive towards her and I had no reason to doubt after the baby was born that he would give financial support as well.

At the end of April/early May, rumours were rife that the war was in its final stages but could it really be true? As anyone who has served in the

Armed Forces knows, there is no better breeding ground for the inventing, distorting, expanding and spreading of rumours, so that eventually it bore no resemblance to the original concept. How some rumours ever got bandied about has baffled us all but the source of some of the most outrageous was the biggest mystery of all. Rumours were an integral part of service life and we thrived on them . . . . but we also became the most disbelieving lot of so and so's imaginable!

So it was the week preceding VE-Day (Victory in Europe) - 8 May 1945. We felt a bit out of touch in our rural outpost and we were continually asking the Ops Room girls at Biggin for some 'pukka gen'. At the end of April, Himmler was supposed to have offered unconditional surrender but only to the British and Americans (not to the Russians) and the offer was refused. On 1 May, we were told that Hitler had committed suicide and that the Russians were occupying Berlin the following day, but meeting with stubborn last stand resistance. My diary entry on the 5th said "The Germans have surrendered in Denmark, Holland and north of Berlin - they can't hold out much longer." The reality that the war was finally coming to an end began to sink in and people were beginning to have mini-celebrations before the official announcement .

<u>VE-DAY (minus 1)</u> - June and I cycled into Maldon for the express purpose of buying a couple of hand-waving Union Jacks to take to London and we decided to visit the cinema. As the Allied Forces were penetrating further into Germany, the full horrors of the Concentration Camps were being revealed and June and I were absolutely horrified at the first pictures of the inmates of Belsen, shown on the Newsreel. We watched in disbelief at the camp littered with corpses, and those hollow-eyed creatures, more bone than flesh, clad in striped prison clothing, with barely enough strength to move about. Their dead-pan faces seemed unable to express any human emotion. Now that we have become more or less de-sensitised at viewing such atrocities, it is difficult to try and explain in those pre-television days, how appalled we were when exposed for the very <u>first</u> time, to scenes of such brutal treatment of fellow human beings. We had hitherto considered Europe to be the most civilised Continent in the world and yet it was the German race who had committed these barbaric acts. Nor could we comprehend how the German staff who worked in the camps and herded thousands upon thousands of Jews and dissidents, day after day into the gas chambers, could have been a party to such atrocities or tolerate the human suffering stretched beyond the limit of endurance, the dying screams and

stench of bodies, without showing a modicum of compassion. It seems hardly credible that so many Germans were willing to renounce a decent moral code of behaviour to incorporate the Nazi dogma of brutality and genocide.

The British public were unaware and unprepared for the stark reality of the Concentration Camps, as more and more were liberated and the pits full of emaciated bodies were exposed. We had heard rumours of such atrocities but they were dismissed as war-time propaganda. The films on those newsreels are a permanent record of the Nazi's indelible shame. Hitler was the archetypal monster of this century, the prime cause of the death of millions and for the mindless destruction of beautiful cities throughout Europe. Stalin's cruelty was not fully exposed until after his death but in 1945 we were shocked and frightened at violence of this dimension.

June and I were very subdued when we left the cinema after witnessing such appalling scenes and we were thankful to divert our thoughts to the buzz of excitement in the streets outside. People were spreading the news that tomorrow was the official Public Holiday to celebrate Victory in Europe. We headed for the Swan where a bunch of pilots were already getting tanked-up for a night of unparalleled jubilation and everyone soon caught the party mood and joined in the communal rejoicing. I don't know if all the aircrew came from the same 'drome but above the din of that joyful crowd, one of the pilots called Johnny gave me an invite to their Victory Dance at Rivenahll, near Witham. I gave him my telephone number at the farm and he would let me know the exact date. It was a sobering thought that we would have to cycle the 6 miles back to Tolleshunt D'Arcy but June and I were in buoyant mood and nothing seemed to matter except that the war in Europe was finally over and the best news of all - ADOLPH HITLER had been driven to commit suicide and was really and truly D E A D. We shouted and cheered all the way back, proudly waving our newly acquired Union Jacks. The farms and cottages along the road all had their lights blazing to celebrate the ultimate ending of the black-out.

Chapter 21

THE BEST MAY-DAY OF ALL

TUESDAY, 8TH MAY 1945 - At last, the long awaited day had arrived - a wonderful, glorious, absolutely stupendous day when we could all indulge in the most patriotic demonstration of national celebration in our history, to mark the ending of WWII in Europe. It had lasted nigh on six wearisome years, several times on the brink of defeat but our survival depended on ultimate victory over the Nazi strangle-hold on the Continent and in the end we had triumphed.

The official announcement of the date of VE-Day was only given the night before and we had received no instructions from Biggin so we turned up at the D/F Tower for our normal morning duty, quite expecting to be given permission to 'shut up shop' - go and have fun. Instead, we were dumbfounded to be told that we had to stay on duty as the Ops Room at Biggin was still being manned. God dammit, the war was over - this was a momentous day - history-in-the making - Mr. Churchill had declared a Public Holiday - and I had set my heart on being in London, the focal point of the biggest gathering of celebrators and I wanted to be there and join in the fun. I asked to speak to someone in higher authority to plead our case but they wouldn't put me through. Who was likely to be roaming the Wild Blue Yonder on this day of all days? Maybe a flypast or an exuberant pilot taking to the skies to do a victory roll but in either case, couldn't they jolly well find their own way home for once? Hadn't they often, in good visibility found their way back to Biggin by following that reliable landmark - the railway track from Folkestone to Redhill, which ran straight as a ruler from Ashford, turn right at the house with the green roof at Marlpit Hill to Westerham and you can't miss it! I wasn't convinced that our presence on duty was of vital importance and I was in the right frame of mind to be rebellious, 'jump ship' and hang the consequences. As I pointed out to June and Betty - "What can they do to us if we go?". In civilian billets it wasn't practicable to 'confine us to camp' or dish out 'jankers' as there was no-one in authority to supervise the punishment. At worst, we might be dishonourably discharged for disobeying orders and deserting our post but that didn't seem such a bad deal either because if we were chucked out, we would jump to the head of the queue in the rush to get back to civvie street, instead of a long wait for our turn. Any future employer would hardly expect to get an adequate reference from a member of the Forces and would they be any the wiser if we said we didn't get one? Weighing up the pro's and con's. it didn't seem that we had much to lose. June was willing to join in my scheme but Betty was a little in awe of officialdom and would never to do anything 'naughty', so she said she would stay behind and hold the fort, but full of foreboding, she warned us we were embarking on a disastrous course.

We listened to Mr. Churchill's Victory Speech on the radio before cycling to Witham to catch the London train. There were masses of people piling in every Underground station, being drawn like a magnet towards the West End and all inward buses were full to capacity. You could sense the atmosphere immediately - it was magic. We found Piccadilly packed with a steady flow of revellers, releasing their pent-up spirits in mad abandon and exploding with joviality - the like of which I had never experienced before, or since. On VE-Day in Trafalgar Square assembled the largest crowd ever seen there. It seemed as though the entire population had blown a safety valve and was letting off steam after years of keeping a stiff upper lip, suppressing feelings of fear through the many dangers we endured with stoicism. Everyone in the Services got a handshake, embrace or a pat on the back and we girls in uniform were greeted with hugs and kisses. Processions formed out of nowhere, people waving flags and whirling football rattles - anything that made a noise - all marching in step with linked arms, 'Doing the Lambeth Walk' or 'Knees up Mother Brown'. Fathers carried children on their shoulders for a better view, which was the safest place for them in that good humoured throng.

Buckingham Palace was a popular destination, where enthusiast crowds filled every surrounding street and from the forecourt of the Palace, the mass of people extended as far as the eye could see. Periodically, we would chant "We want the King" and in response, the Royal Family would come out on that famous balcony and loud cheers would echo all the way up the Mall to Admiralty Arch. Traffic could no longer get through and the only break in the vast crowd was the fountain moat around the Queen Victoria Memorial. Anyone nimble enough would scale the lamp standards or traffic lights to survey the scene from the best vantage point. The King and Queen had chosen to stay in London during the war - they had shared with the people the horrors of the nightly bombing during the Blitz and the terror of the V-weapons. They made frequent tours of desecrated areas, speaking and comforting many people who had lost loved ones, homes and everything they possessed. Buckingham Palace suffered bomb damage too and so many of London's beautiful historic buildings and churches were just a heap of rubble, as a result of wholesale wanton destruction by the Germans all over Europe.

Winston Churchill, the prime architect of the triumph we were celebrating figured prominently in the day's rejoicing and he appeared on the balcony of the Ministry of Health in Whitehall and spoke to the vast crowds - "This is your Victory" he said and the crowds roared back "No, it is yours" - he then continued "In all our long history, we have never seen a greater day than this . . . We were the first in this ancient island to draw the sword against tyranny . . . There we stood all alone for a whole year . . . I say that in the years to come, not only will the people of this island but of the world, wherever the bird of freedom chirps in human hearts., look back to what we've done and they will say 'Do not despair - do not yield to violence and tyranny - march straight forward and die if need be - unconquered'."

As we had come to expect, our guiding star, who had steered us through so many crises, boosted our morale and inspired us to even greater effort with his oratory, had once again produced exactly the rights words for the appropriate occasion and the crowds wanted to express their appreciation and gratitude for his superb leadership. Winston Churchill later joined the Royal Family on the balcony of Buckingham Palace and when he appeared with them, the spontaneous roar of welcome rose to a crescendo of patriotic fervour and lasted for more than five minutes. It was so exhilarating to be part of such communal rejoicing on that unforgettable day. In memory it surpasses all other occasions and I wouldn't have missed it for anything.

June and I found ourselves in one long wall of people struggling to make headway - we held hands tightly all the time because if we had been parted, there was no way we could have battled against the masses and we had not made any contingency plans for meeting up again, should it happen. Anyway, there was no real choice of movement - you just had to go in the same direction as the crowd. I haven't a clue which street we were in but one half of the crowd were singing at the top of their voices going in one direction and the other half were moving past going the other way, singing a different song. Momentarily, both sides stopped, facing each other and tried to out-sing the opposition - the contest ending in cheers all round. It was then that I saw 'HIM' - a tall dark handsome American pilot - our eyes met in a long lingering look over the heads of the yards of people between us but sadly, we were going in opposite directions. June and I battled on as both sides began to move again - she was slightly in front and I was holding her hand with my left and I hadn't looked behind me for a while to see who was holding my other hand but now it was being gently squeezed and when I turned round, lo and behold . . . it was 'HIM'. How he managed to change course and battle his way through that throng, I'll never know but I was so glad he had and the pleased expression on my face, must have conveyed as much. It was impossible to talk over the din of the singing and shouting, so we decided to 'Stop the World, we want to get off' and the three of us slowly edged our way over to a side street. 'HIM' turned out to be Lt. George L. Duffy, a pilot from 597th Bomb Squadron, based on the Continent. He was over here on leave - his first time in London and May 8th was also his 21st birthday. A double cause for celebration but by this time the crowds had all but drunk London dry and after a few unsuccessful attempts at getting a bottle of anything to celebrate with, we eventually ended up drinking neat rum in an American Bar (foul tasting stuff, I confided to my diary and it did in fact put me off Rum for life!). When it began to get dark, bonfires were lit on the numerous bomb sites, stoked by the vast amount of wooden debris from demolished buildings and the crowds, still intent on making whoopee, kept the festive momentum going, by dancing around the firelight glow.

June and I were on duty the next morning and we reckoned that the milk train to Witham at 03.20 would just about get us there in time. We were sitting on a seat in St. James' Park talking to George until 2 a.m. with ne'er a thought as to how we were going to get to Liverpool Street to catch it. The Underground trains and buses had closed down and cars had been kept out of Central London, while 'people power' took over the streets. During my hitch-hiking expeditions in the WAAF's, I had always managed to get from 'A' to 'B' so far, without getting stranded in some God forsaken place and mostly on time but I was beginning to wonder if I would come unstuck this night. The only vehicle in sight was a Metropolitan Police Black Maria - I don't suppose on any other night I would have had the gaul to even ask for a

Lt. George Duffy and Joyce

lift in a Police vehicle . . . and I'm quite sure that on any other night, they would not have given me one!! The Police Sgt. driver was going to London Bridge and the three of us got in the back door and sat on one side, facing the few offenders they had rounded up. I can boast that it was my first and only ride in a Black Maria. George stayed with us at Liverpool Street until the milk train left at 03.20 and we arranged to meet on my next day off, which in actual fact was then tomorrow. The train was absolutely jammed packed with revellers returning to Chelmsford and stations beyond and I don't think June and I would have survived the crush, had we not managed to get standing room by a window in the corridor. It was still dark when we got to Witham so we laid ourselves down on two hard old benches out in the open - just like a couple of vagrants! Before I dozed off, I thought about the events of the day - made all the more rewarding for me because I had defied authority to be there - the marvellous convivial atmosphere that engulfed everyone, the camaraderie, the satisfaction of knowing that all the European people who had suffered such brutal repression during years of cowed submission, were now free once more but at a terrible cost in human lives. All those brave young men who could not be with us today to celebrate an enemy beaten into total surrender. We must never overlook the ideals for which they fought and died. And of course, the climax of meeting a super guy like George, to whom I was instantly attracted - was he at long last the big romance I was beginning to think would never happen to me. I had a gut feeling he might well be or was he just part of the ecstatic mood I was in? Time would tell.

When it got light, June and I started on our eight mile journey back to Tolleshunt D'Arcy, longing to crash out on our 'biscuits' on the floor as soon as we got on duty. When we arrived at the Tower, we were horrified at the 'Marie Celeste' scene as we opened the door - the place was deserted and where in the devil were the night duty crew who had taken over from Betty and should have stayed until we relieved them? Even though we were a bit on the drag, it was an unwritten law to hang on until the next shift came but they had just upped and left. We could hardly believe our eyes - the Tower was in an uproar, empty bottles strewn everywhere - half the ceiling was down and the place reeked of stale beer. It must have been one helluva party with many more than one over the (VE night plus) eight! Throughout the war, our D/F Towers had been manned 24 hours a day and we wondered how long it had been left empty. Perish the thought if Biggin Ops had rung through and got no answer - there would be hell to pay. Had we not been dog-tired, we might have seen the funny side of the chaos we were facing but having to clear up their debris before we could lay ourselves down, left us quite humourless. In the end, we did manage a couple of hours kip but the stench of stale beer permeated our small Tower for several days because there was no through draught to get rid of it.

We had a few hours off in the afternoon and back on duty again at 6.30pm - straight to bed and luckily an undisturbed night's sleep because there was no night-flying and all was quiet on our normal frequencies. The next morning, with batteries re-charged and quite refreshed, I was ready for another jaunt to London. I cycled to Maldon, got a lift into Chelmsford with Miss Page (whoever she was) and I was in London by 11am with time for a coffee and a tidy up before meeting George at Piccadilly. One minute past the appointed time and all sorts of thoughts raced through my head . . . he wasn't coming! It was his first visit to London and Piccadilly was a big place - had I explained the meeting place clearly? He had been on his own all day yesterday and could easily have flashed that charming Irish smile at someone else. Thank goodness, he was only two minutes late, otherwise I might have worked myself up into quite a state. I was so relieved to see him and that first welcoming kiss dispelled all my fears and from that magic moment, I knew he felt the same way too. We had lunch before going to the cinema and in the evening we went to a Dinner Dance at Oddenino's - a most romantic evening which would have ended far too soon, had I caught the last train from Baker Street at midnight, so I went home to Wembley by taxi and got in at a quarter to three. For once, I must have sneaked in without waking father or else he was away. On several previous occasions, I had been met at the front door by an irate father in his pyjamas who, ignoring black-out regulations, let the hall light stream down the garden path like a searchlight as he directed me indoors. He was rather anti-Americans and usually tore them off a strip for keeping his daughter out so late - not that they were entirely to blame, poor chaps! I think he frightened off a few budding boyfriends because I didn't hear from some of them again and others were too scared to see me right to my door - at least George was spared the performance that night!

Next morning I left in good time to be on duty at Tolly by 2pm. We had 'bods' to spare on crews now because there was much less flying and I asked Carrie, our Corporal in charge for a 48 hour pass. After Pay Parade, I changed into civvies, cycled into Maldon and was back with George by 7 o'clock . . . whew!

Reflecting on those war-time exploits of mine, dashing here, there and everywhere, I must have had boundless energy and I don't know how I managed to keep up the pace. It exhausts me now just reading about all I did! Once or twice I did mention in my diary "Don't know what's the matter with me lately, I feel permanently tired".

At the end of his leave, George had to return to Germany and he came to Liverpool Street to see me off first. We dreaded having to say 'Goodbye' because life was so uncertain in the Services and we did not know how or when we might manage to meet again. Now that the war in Europe was over, he could easily be sent back to the States from Germany at short notice and then on to the Pacific to finish off the Japs. This time I had stayed in Town so as not to waste any of the precious hours we had left together but I told Mother I was going back to Wittersham for a few days. Be sure your sins will find you out - and when I returned to Tolly, I found they had. Officially, I'd only had a 48-hour pass, plus legitimate days off and had I told June where I was, they would probably have covered for me but my absence put Carrie in a bit of a spot. June had 'phoned my home and of course I wasn't there - she spoke to one of my WAAF sisters who, thinking I was at Wittersham, sent a telegram to my old billet but I wasn't there either, so the police were notified and put on my trail. Had I come to grief somewhere, Carrie would have got into trouble herself for not reporting me missing, so she had no choice but to tell Biggin I was A.W.O.L. Unaware of the concern for my safety my prolonged absence was causing, it required quite a lot of explaining all round but apart from a verbal reprimand (and a few raised eyebrows) I was extremely fortunate to have got off so lightly over that little escapade.

I kept a low profile for the rest of May and avoided any further trouble! On my off duty hours, I helped out on the farm and became an expert radish puller, earning 8/3d. for eleven dozen. I was feeling a bit lonely and down in the dumps and it helped to pass the time . . . but boring. My first two letters from George arrived quite quickly and they cheered me up no end as I was finding it difficult to adjust from a busy life to that of recluse. The work on duty wasn't very stimulating now either.

I had completely forgotten about the Rivenhall Victory Dance that pilot Johnny had invited me to when we met in Maldon during VE-Eve celebrations and it was a welcome diversion from my hum-drum existence when he rang to say when it was. Transport was being laid on to and from Chelmsford so I could stay the night with my aunt and uncle. I presumed it was a dance for the whole camp but it turned out to be an Officers Mess Party. I went in civvies so it didn't really matter - if anything it added to the spice of life of an erk-ess entering 'forbidden territory', as I was likely to rub shoulders with the WAAF Officers who came out to Tolly with our pay and to service our needs. The opinion I first formed at Cranwell and later encounters with WAAF Admin. Officers, had not altered or improved and at the dance at Rivenhall, I got quite a kick out of the WAAF Officers sitting around like wallflowers. I went on to add in my diary 'Lined up for chow at 11 pm - what a spread - haven't seen anything like it for years. Chicken and all the trimmings and REAL peaches and ICE CREAM'. There wasn't much room on my limited line quota to elaborate on my encounter with one of the 'wallflowers' but I remember it with a degree of smug satisfaction. When we were helping ourselves to the marvellous buffet spread, she was next in line and said to me "I feel I know you from somewhere?". I recognised her immediately as one of the Queen B. . . 's who brought out our pay and rations but I wasn't going to let on, hoping that in my pretty civvie dress disguise, and flowing shoulder length hair, I looked very different from a female in a shapeless uniform, and hair scraped together in a roll that would tuck under a WAAF hat. "I think not" I replied, not wishing to pursue the matter further because a lowly LACW 'living it up' in the Officers Mess was tempting Providence to its limits, if caught!! But she was not prepared to leave it there. Some time later, I think she purposely followed me into the Ladies and while I was combing my hair, still with a puzzled look on her face, she said "You know, I'm sure I've met you before" and then started on a whole diatribe of possibilities and places and then the obvious one - "You are not in the Forces by any chance?" I did not answer immediately as I was thinking what a pest this woman was becoming and how to get her 'off my back'. Then inspiration dawned - "Well, I have three sisters in the WAAF's and we are very alike - you may have mistaken me for one of them but the war was nearly over before I was old enough to enlist". Typically, she was more interested in pursuing her suspicions, than enjoying herself and having a night off from the job. The dance continued until gone 3am and after the transport dropped me in Chelmsford, I crept into Uncle Wilf's house at 04.15. They let me sleep until noon and then Johnny 'phoned to say he had got the evening off, so he came into Chelmsford and we went to the pictures. He'd told me at the Dance that he had been posted to Calcutta . . . and so ended another brief acquaintance. As for Section Officer, whatever her name was, the next time we had a visit from Rivenhall, I was on leave and the following one, I was going to borrow a pair of spectacles and try and change my appearance but it wasn't necessary as a different Queen B . . . turned up.

  When I got back to Tolly after the Dance, there were two more letters from George and after that they started arriving fairly regularly and he should be getting mine too.

On a couple of consecutive night duties, there must have been some night flying because I worked until 2am one night and 3am on the other, confiding to my diary 'pretty poor show in peace time!'. To pass the time on night duty when we were 'Stood down' we took to washing and setting each other's hair and now the evenings were lighter, for supper we dug a few small new potatoes from the next field, went through the hedge and picked some peas in another field which we shelled and cooked on our small stove and ate with hard boiled eggs and cheese. The tomatoes in the field opposite were not yet ripe enough to add to the supper menu.

I got a week's leave in June and No. 3 WAAF sister was home on embarkation leave. She was a Sgt. now and had volunteered for the Middle East, with a posting to Algiers. Later on, in one of her letters from there she mentioned that several WAAF's were being sent back to U.K. for demob because they were pregnant. "Can't understand it" wrote Molly - "Out here its too blessed hot to even hold hands!".

For the last few days of my leave, I hitched down to Portsmouth and over to the Isle of Wight to see father . . . . so that was where he'd got to. It must have been a spur of the moment decision and I couldn't have let him know in advance because he was very surprised to see me. Mother was born on the Isle of Wight and had lived there until she got married. I often used to spend my long summer school holidays with Granny, who lived in East Cowes and the long boat ride by paddle steamer, was a great treat for me in those pre-war days. Father had his car over there and we did a tour of most places around the Island. Shanklin had been subjected to some heavy bombing during the war and the sea front was badly cratered. The Isle of Wight is somewhere I never tire of visiting and it was so peaceful walking along the cliffs at Alum Bay towards the Needles, where we stopped at a cafe for a delicious fresh lobster tea. Because they were so plentiful then, they weren't considered expensive either. Their scarcity has made lobster prices soar. My few days passed all too quickly and on the ferry back from Cowes, we passed alongside an American troopship pulling out of Southampton, packed with G.I's on every deck, taking a last look at England and no doubt relieved to have survived the war and lucky to be among the fortunate ones returning home. We were so close as they passed that we were near enough to call out to each other. I was about the only person on the deck of the ferry and I got some whistles and cat-calls as I began to wave. One of them shouted across "Where were you hiding all the time I was in U.K.?" and from another deck, someone else called out "Come on jump, honey - there's room in my kit-bag for you!". Before they passed out of earshot I called back "So long Yanks and thanks for everything - we couldn't have done it without you". More cheers and whistles as we went in opposite directions. Quite a moving little scene and it made me realise that it wouldn't be long before George would be on his way home to Oregon.

When I got to Wembley there were five letters from George waiting for me, all of them hinting that he was trying to get over to England and the last one said that he wasn't likely to get here until the week-end - another week on tenterhooks, ending in disappointment. Then he said he had got as far as Paris . . . . then he was stuck in Paris for four days . . . Huh, a likely story, I thought! While in London, we had our photographs taken together in Selfridges and the proofs were now ready. I remember when we were walking down Oxford Street, on our way there, he was forever returning the salute of G.I's who saluted him and in a mischievous mood, I wouldn't let go of his hand so he was unable to raise it to salute - I nearly got a tanning for that! The proofs were excellent and I would soon have a photograph of him I could drool over.

On duty, it was becoming a bit of a farce for a full crew to be there to man three units, as since the end of hostilities, there was far less flying and we were rarely operational on more than one channel at a time. On the last day of June 1945, the axe was wielded. Five WAAF's - Joan Cheney, Ann, Doris, Kath and Joan Bellinger were posted back to Biggin and the two mobile units closed down as from midnight, just leaving the permanent Tower. I was pleased that June and I would be staying on, although now that she was five months pregnant, it might have been a convenient time to make an exit from Tolly but on the other hand, she wanted to stay near to Bill at Cambridge, so that they could see each other as often as possible. Marie, joined our crew and we were quick to realise that we could probably wangle more time off between the three of us, whenever we wanted it. For a start, there was only room on the floor of the Tower for two to sleep on night duty and there was barely enough work to keep two occupied in the daytime, let alone three. In the past, going on duty was never a chore or a bore - I would say we were a dedicated lot (known as 'keen types') but instead of the exciting intercom we used to take bearings on, the flying activity was now mostly routine. Accurate 'fixing' was still important work for us but the duty hours dragged when there wasn't sufficient work to keep us fully occupied. We had time to knit, play cards, write letters and read.

June took off for Cambridge to be with Bill for Independence Day celebrations on July 4. I was quite amazed the way she was still managing to hide her widening girth so that no-one among the WAAF's or the locals had the least suspicion. Now that it was getting warmer, she took to wearing her shirt loosely on the outside of her skirt or trousers. I think I was more concerned than she was at the scandal that would erupt in that small village, if the truth became known. We would all be branded as a promiscuous lot, for sure. June hadn't returned for morning duty but luckily she was back in time for the night shift, because I wanted to take off. I had been sent a message from the farm that George had 'phoned and would meet me at Piccadilly Underground at 1 o'clock the next day. It was our official day off anyway and with Jean returned, there was no need for me to rush back. Our photographs from Selfridges arrived by post just before I left, so I was able to take them with me and we met up again as arranged. He brought over several bottles of Champagne - we drank the first one between us on an empty stomach and suffered the consequences. He also gave me some French perfume, a watch and real nail varnish. During the next few days we wined and dined at the Trocadero, Jules Club, L'Apertiff Grill and the Potomac - it was a bit of a cheek taking along our own champagne and asking them to put it on ice for us, but they didn't mind. I took George home to Wembley to meet what members of the family were around at the time and on our last morning, he came to Liverpool Street to see me off, before going to Euston to catch his own train to Blackpool. Another of those painful 'Goodbye's' I had come to dread, with time running out on how much longer he would be able to stay here before returning to the States. To have met at all in that vast VE crowd was providential but to be parted again so soon before we really had time to get to know each other was tough and I just sat in the corner of the train compartment, alone with my thoughts and feeling very sorry for myself. I bumped into Carrie and Betty in Maldon quite by accident - they were both going on leave and Carrie said she had left instructions at Tolly that I was being left in charge - what a hoot I thought, but this time she did know I had returned!

I was on night duty that same evening and Lorna Golding came up to the Tower with the message that George had 'phoned, saying that when he got to Blackpool, he learned that he would be leaving for the States tomorrow - the news I had been dreading. He said he would ring again within the hour, so I went back to the farm for a quick visit. By the time he 'phoned, the reality that 'this was it' was beginning to sink in and I could hardly speak for the trembling in my voice and trying hard to hold back the tears. There was so much I wanted to say but I was too choked to speak coherently. After I replaced the receiver, I flopped down in a chair in a daze feeling utterly wretched, hardly able to believe that it was ending so abruptly, after such a brief time together. When I returned to Marie for the rest of our night duty, she listened sympathetically to my tale of woe. I stayed around the farm on my day off but there was no further news - he must have gone. Then the following morning, I had to rush all the way back from the tomato field because he was 'phoning from Blackpool. Out of breath, I listened intently as he told me he might be staying a few more days. He was obviously in a Stop/Go situation up there and even though the war was over, the 'powers that be' were still being tight-lipped about revealing personnel movements - either no-one knew or they were reticent to tell and he could only relay what little information he had been given. I might have dashed up to Blackpool only to find when I got there, that he had already taken off. All he could say was that he'd ring again. Its a wonder I wasn't a nervous wreck by the end of that week, the number of times my hopes had been raised and dashed again and now I was on tenterhooks every time the 'phone rang. June finally turned up on night duty that evening, so Marie went back to her billet to sleep. I was getting a bit concerned about June's absence. "Naughty girl", I wrote - "Now that I'm the boss, think I'll have to put her on a charge!". It was just as well Carrie was on leave and didn't know how long she had been away.

    Then I got a 'phone call from George at mid-day - "Come to Blackpool" - he was fairly certain he was going to stay for a few more days. How marvellous - a reprieve. I threw a few things into a bag and I was off like a shot. When I got to London I was most disappointed to find that there wasn't another train to Blackpool until 11pm but I could get as far as Preston on the 7.30, which arrived there at 1am. At least I'd be almost there and I might find some other means of transport for the last 17 miles. It was quite surprising how often on my travels, I bumped into someone I knew because I was seldom on a large Camp long enough to make the acquaintance of hordes of people and D/F Stations were such small units. On the train to Preston, I met Phil Humphreys, who used to be at Wittersham and it passed the time to have someone to chat with as far as Nuneaton, where he got off. When I arrived at Preston, I tried to 'phone Blackpool Central Station but it had closed down for the night. Nothing much else I could do then but to wait until the 04.30 train to Blackpool so I had a few hours to kill. The Station was practically deserted but I wandered around and on an unlit platform, I found a stationary train which didn't look as though it was going anywhere for a while, so I got in one of the empty dark carriages and had a couple of hours comfortable sleep, stretched out on the seat. (I really shudder now, when I think of the risks I ran on my many travels - if someone had been lurking in the shadows on Preston Station and followed me into that isolated carriage . . . .?? But in those days it was really quite safe for a female to roam at will and I don't suppose it ever occurred to me that I might be harmed. Thankfully, men of that generation behaved in a civilised manner towards women and I never had any cause to feel afraid of them, or the dark. I have often wondered during the last five decades why the male of the species has gradually become such a sadistic lecherous beast, that women of all ages can no longer roam freely without fear of being mugged, raped or murdered even in broad daylight).

Luckily I didn't oversleep and woke in time to catch the 04.30 train but when I got to Blackpool Central Station at 6am, I wasn't really surprised that George wasn't there. Goodness knows how we managed to meet up again with no way of contacting each other - I guess I just waited there until he turned up. (There are a few blank pages in my diary which I never got around to writing up when I got back.) We had a reprieve of three more snatched days together and then he came early one morning with the news that they were leaving in half an hour. I went down to the field with him and thankfully that final 'Goodbye' came rather swiftly because a long drawn-out farewell would have been too painful. I put on a brave face because he was with pilots from his squadron and I managed to control the tears until he was out of sight. George hadn't been in Europe long enough to be involved in much combat before the war ended and there was every likelihood that he could be posted to the Pacific to help defeat the Japs. I can remember very little about the train journey back to London but I decided to spend a night at home and return to Tolly in the morning. A few days later, I received seven letters from George, which had been written while at Blackpool but for some reason had been held back until he had actually left. Now that the war in Europe was over, it did seem rather unnecessary for the movement of returning US. personnel still to be kept secret but I suppose old habits die hard and once again - ours not to reason why.

Chapter 22

IN LIMBO

I settled back into the old routine, after coming down to earth once more. When not busy on night duty, we always listened to the A.E.F. programme for American troops in England, which kept us up-to-date with all the famous singers, Big Bands and hit records in the USA, so the news that the Station was closing down in July 1945, was heralded with much lamentation. 'Spare us from the dreary BBC' was my comment at the time but all was not lost - by scanning the air waves, we found we could get excellent reception on the American Forces Network on the Continent and we became regular listeners to 'Midnight in Munich' on night duty.

Prisoners-of-war had been put to work on some of the farms roundabout Tolleshunt D'Arcy and Goldhanger but to me, they were still 'the enemy' and I ignored them completely, unwilling even to muster a smile - but on the morning I received three more letters from George, I felt on top of the world and completely out of character, I even said "Good morning - wonderful day" to a group of Italian prisoners.

On August 9, I got a cable from George that he had arrived back in the States and the news from the Far East was that the Japanese were on the point of surrendering after the American Air Force had dropped the first atomic bombs on Hiroshima and Nagasaki, razing both cities to the ground with the citizens suffering the most appalling injuries and burns from the radiation. I happened to be home on VJ Day and joined in the celebrations in London on August 15 but it lacked the exhilaration of VE-Day and in comparison, was a bit of a let-down for me personally.

When I rolled up at the Tower the next day, I found the girls on night duty had done a fair bit of celebrating. Not quite as chaotic as the VE-Day aftermath but I was told that Ellen and Rene had to be carried off duty. Cpl. Carrington was in buoyant mood too and reckoned she'd be out of the WAAF's at the beginning of December. We were asked to attend a Church Parade at Goldhanger for a National Day of Prayer on 19 August. I duly cleaned my buttons, pressed my uniform and dusted off my WAAF 'titfer', smart and ready for the big event. The WAAF's were out in force - all five of us - and we marched behind the British Legion, some of whom were so frail, I doubted whether they'd make it as far as the Church.

June was now in her sixth month of pregnancy and it must have taken great courage to hide her condition for so long but still no-one had suspected, although I knew she wouldn't be able to conceal the fact for much longer. Then, providentially at the end of August, a Records posting to Winchester came through for her. Unbelievably, she left Tolly without anyone else knowing besides me and I got 48 hours leave so that I could help her back to Biggin Hill with all her kit - she had accumulated quite a lot. Lorna Golding's sister gave us a lift to Maldon, which saved a bus journey but we still had to lug it across London on the Underground from Liverpool Street to Victoria, where we caught a train to Bromley - stopped there for lunch and then took a bus out to Biggin. This was only my second brief visit to Main Camp, the first being when I was posted from Wittersham to Tolleshunt D'Arcy. WAAF's were housed in the Rookery which overlooked the airfield and this time, even though the rain was bucketing down and lashing against the windows, as I looked across that most famous airfield, it wasn't hard to conjure up the scene of activity during those crucial months in 1940, when the 'So Few' courageous fighter pilots took to the autumn skies so often and deprived the Luftwaffe of the air supremacy they so desperately sought, without which Hitler knew that an invasion attempt would not succeed. I regret that I did not pay a visit to the Memorial Chapel when I was there, as it was burned down the following year. During the war-time period 1939/45, 453 aircrew from 52 squadrons lost their lives while operating within Biggin Hill Sector. Their names are inscribed on the reredos, either side of the altar of the St. George's Chapel of Remembrance, which was eventually built in 1951 to replace the original chapel. A Spitfire and a Hurricane are positioned in the foreground of the entrance approach.

It was a dreary, miserable wet day for August when June and I ventured across to the Mess and I commented at the time 'We lined up for chow and then it wasn't eatable. Dirty Mess and food dished up by greasy erks - uggh! I'd hate to be back here for good.' How fortunate we were to be living on 'the fat of the land' in our farm billets and to have escaped for so long from the poor standards of communal Messing.

June made an appointment to see a WAAF Admin. Officer to ask for compassionate leave to have the baby and then to hopefully return to the WAAF's afterwards. The reply she received was blunt and to the point . . "What do you think we are running here? This is not a convenient welfare service for WAAf's who get themselves into trouble. You will be given a dishonourable discharge and dismissed from the service forthwith etc." An absolute bitch is the only way to describe the attitude of that Queen B. . . . She was unwilling to muster an ounce of compassion and when she had finished her tirade, she had reduced June to uncontrollable sobbing. I was angered and disgusted that she could be so heartless. In my experience, the Admin. types who were selected as 'Hoffisar material' only needed two main qualifications - mature years and a bossy nature. Tact and the ability to handle the welfare of a group of women was apparently not an essential requirement.

Bill must have still been in the picture at that time because June 'phoned him that evening to relate what had happened. I had intended to spend the night at home before returning to Tolly but I felt I couldn't leave her all alone in such a depressed state, where she did not know anyone, although I couldn't extend my stay any longer as with June gone, we had no spare crew members to double up and I was due on duty in the afternoon. I wasn't sorry to leave Biggin - the dreadful weather and the reason I was there, had a depressing effect on me. I hoped that the next time I set foot there, it would be for my own release at the end of my WAAF service.

I can't remember how June and I managed to communicate during the next couple of months - by some devious means I suppose, because I wouldn't have risked writing anything in my diary. I managed to knit some baby clothes without arousing any particular interest, as one of my non-WAAF older sisters was married and already had one child. June gave birth to her baby in late Autumn and I got leave and went down to see her at Torquay, where she was living in a home for unmarried mothers, called 'Hazelwood'. June was in rather rough company there - some of the mothers did not even know who the fathers were, although it was obvious from the dusky skins of some of the babies that black American service men played a part! There were many unhappy tales of regret and "What a fool I was to trust him" and June herself was faced with the ultimate heart-break over Bill. Suddenly there was no word from him, although up until that time he had accepted his responsibility. She eventually 'phoned the Base at Cambridge and was absolutely shattered when she was told that he had been shipped back to the States - not so much as a hint did he give, although he would have had some prior notification. The final devastating news was to learn that he already had a wife in Nebraska. The American authorities were very adept at shielding their service men from their responsibilities when they got into any sort of trouble. If they ran up debts they couldn't pay, contemplating an unsuitable marriage, or a married man with a pregnant girl-friend - the solution - whisk them off to another theatre of war, beyond the reach of the jurisdiction of their last base. The majority of war-time unmarried mothers were left 'holding the baby' and had to bear the burden of bringing them up alone, without official financial support from

American fathers and fifty years on, the U.S. authorities are most uncooperative towards war-time illegitimate children who are trying to find out who their fathers really were, as TV programmes and newspapers have illustrated.

So all the time that sod Bill was married and had strung her along. Poor June, I felt so sorry for her but all I could really do was to give her as much sympathy and support as I could muster and not just because I was really the only friend she had in the world now. She still would not tell her parents. It is easy to talk glibly of adoption before a baby is born, when it all seems rather impersonal but it is a very different matter when mothers hold that little bundle in their arms and their natural, maternal and protective instinct comes to the fore. Many then realise that they would have a guilt feeling for the rest of their lives if they allowed he/she to be adopted, never knowing if the child was happy or being well looked after. The curfew at 'Hazelwood' for the unmarried mothers was 8.30p.m. and after having this discussion with June, I made my way back to the Y.W.C.A. where I was staying but it was too early for me to turn in and I thought a little light relief from June's problems might temporarily help to stop me churning it all over in my mind. The music from a local Dance Hall as I passed, tempted me and I went inside. I happened upon another of those chance meetings in Torquay of all places, when I was least expecting to bump into someone I knew. A Canadian airgunner called Pete recognised me from three years ago. In the summer of 1942, before I joined the WAAF's, I had spent a holiday in Bournemouth with two girl friends, Nona and Lenore, where many Canadians from a nearby O.T.U used to spend their evenings. Apparently at the time, I had been going out with his friend Vince, another Canadian airgunner but even when Pete showed me his photograph, I still couldn't remember him clearly but a reminder of what we did (and something I later acknowledged as THE dumbest thing I have ever done in my life) I remembered only too well! The six of us were walking along the sea front at Bournemouth and Vince and I crawled through the barbed wire fortifications, which were mounted all along the south coast to deter any invasion attempt and to keep people out because the beaches were mined. We gingerly walked down to the water in single file, had a paddle in the sea and then returned up the beach, walking in the same footprints we had made in the sand on the way down. We called to the other four to follow us - that we had made a safe path for them but they had more sense and thought we were quite reckless and stupid - how right they were! Pete then told me that Vince had since been killed in action.

When I went to 'Hazelwood' the next morning June told me of her plans - she had decided to bring the baby up herself, although she knew it was going to be a struggle to make ends meet. She was a very caring person and I wasn't really surprised when she found she couldn't part with it.

I returned to Tolly and June stayed at Torquay until the baby was a few weeks older and then I received a heart-rending letter from her. She had managed to find a job with accommodation where she could keep the baby with her but no more information than that. She felt she had caused me a lot of worry, as I had been so closely involved in all that had befallen her and she thought it best if she faded out of my life and then I needn't be concerned about her any more. She was grateful for my staunch support and for standing by her when she most needed a friend - she would always remember me with affection but she had made up her mind and I must not try and find her. At first I was very upset that she felt it necessary to end our friendship in this fashion and so abruptly but she had this stubborn, independent chip on her shoulder that she did not want to be beholden to anyone or feel she was a burden but we all need the help of a good friend when problems arise and I was also somewhat resentful that she was spurning the last one she had. I had no idea where she had gone and it was more than likely she had changed her name to Mrs. something or other to make tracing her more difficult so I soon accepted the fact there was little I could do. I thought about her a lot in the following months and wondered how she was making out. I wrote periodic short notes to her parents' address, in the hope that she might eventually contact them . . . . just saying that I had lost touch and would they let me know where she was. Apparently, she did contact them briefly, telling them she was alright but had decided to live her own life and she would rather that they did not try to find her. To get a message like that from your only child, not knowing the real reason, must have been a shattering blow to her elderly parents. They asked the Salvation Army to try and trace her whereabouts and they did eventually find her. She went home to live and I resumed spasmodic contact with her and although I asked, she never told me what had happened in the intervening period. A year or so later, she got married and our correspondence then was little more than a short note with a Christmas card each year and a postcard from holiday destination with an occasional photograph, which included two later children.

Some 18 years later, I wrote saying that I would be visiting her immediate area and she invited me to stay the night with her. She lived in one of those depressing Northern Towns of street upon street of drab terraced houses with no front gardens, although the inside was cheerful and comfortable. Her husband was on night shift and the children were also out, so we were able to have a few hours to ourselves in which to talk. Years ago, her parents had persuaded her to come home and live with them and to keep up appearances, neighbours and friends were led to believe that she was a war widow. Things didn't work out and I got the impression that as an escape from an unhappy situation, she virtually married the first chap who asked her. He had treated her well enough and adopted Bill's child as his own and at that time, they had not told any of the children the truth. I suppose she was reasonably content and didn't grumble about her lot - nor would she, as she always accepted full responsibility for her actions and never blamed anyone but herself for the mess she had made of her life. She had been an attractive girl and in different circumstances, things could have turned out much better for her but that brief affair with Bill, and having an illegitimate child, virtually ruined her future prospects. Some 18 years later she admitted that she didn't know what she saw in him and could hardly remember what he looked like.

That meeting was a sad ending to my relationship with June. She wrote soon after, saying that she had thought things over and even though she regarded me as the sister she never had, nothing would alter the fact that she would always associate me with that unhappy period in her life she had desperately tried to put behind her and seeing me again had been a painful reminder of that time. She wanted to terminate our association altogether, which was something I fully understood and could appreciate from her point of view but I felt so sorry that there seemed to be no other solution, after all we had shared together.

Chapter 23

I WANT OUT

To return to 1945 . . . . with George and June's departure, I was left feeling depressed and thoroughly miserable, my days were long drawn-out and empty. I helped on the farm to give me something to do on my days off but I was becoming 'cheesed-off' with Service life - there wasn't the interest or the job satisfaction now that the war was over. I was just longing to get demobbed and head for America. George and I wrote to each other every few days - I was down in the dumps when there was no mail and on cloud nine when there was. The post was rather erratic - sometimes I would get several letters at once and then there would be a gap depending on what ship, States side his letters managed to catch. He sent me an engagement ring soon after he got home and welcome parcels of items he knew we were still unable to get. Our correspondence was full of future plans. He lived in Oregon, way over on the west coast of America and he said he would come to New York by car and meet me off the boat - commercial flying had hardly got off the ground (!?!) then. He would show me America as we drove from coast to coast and then we would get married at his home. So many G.I. brides had been strung along with a grossly exaggerated picture of American life, and led to believe that they were going to live in luxury in a movie-type home but the reality was very different and many had a disillusioned awakening when they reached their destination and then without financial means, there was no way back. So what we planned seemed like a good idea, as still with that level head on my shoulders, I wanted to have a 'look see first' at where I might be spending the rest of my life. He lived in timber country and looking on the gloomy side, it might be a 'liddle old log cabin in Beaver Creek'. Love does not always conquer everything and it seemed sensible to err on the cautious side because I'd be a long way from family and without any friends I could turn to if (heaven forbid) things didn't work out.

In November, Bradwell Bay aerodrome closed down. It was just across the River Blackwater from Tolleshunt D'Arcy and alternating with Rivenhall, we received regular visits to service our equipment and for supplies etc. It was a black day when on their final visit, they made us relinquish our constant companion and life-line with the outside world - the rotten so and so's had come to take away our most prized possession - our/their RADIO! How would we ever survive without it? Sitting all alone for hours on end in the middle of a field, with damn all to do now, it was the only thing that prevented us from 'going round the bend'. Besides which, we were plagued with mice in the Tower - 'over-run with them' I wrote, which no doubt was a slight exaggeration. I was often on night duty for 14 hours on my own and I'd be able to hear them trying to gain access without a radio to drown their scratchings. I took to sleeping on the table - 'that'll fool 'em' I added, but knowing how I loathed the little perishers, that was sheer bravado. They were probably field mice looking for warmer winter quarters.

Just before Christmas 1945, I again took a turkey home for my folks but I lacked any enthusiasm for entering into the festive spirit and I magnanimously offered to do two x 24 hours shifts of duty in the Tower on my own, so that a couple of the girls could have a longer Christmas break at their home. They had done duties for me before George left. It meant taking enough food to keep me nourished for a night and a day but how was I going to keep it safe overnight and prevent my four-legged friends from nibbling at it while I slept? I put my under-taxed brain to work to try and outsmart the intruders. What cupboards we had were made of wood and that wouldn't be much of a challenge for them. We had no tin or metal boxes to hide it in and my eventual brainwave was to somehow hang it from the roof. I can recall with some amusement, standing on the table with hammer, string and tacks and wrapping my meals in several packages which I dangled from the ceiling. The thinking behind the multiple parcels was that if I had kept it in just one and they had managed to have a nibble, I wouldn't have fancied eating the rest that they might have crawled all over! I felt well pleased that my efforts had out-witted the little pests because my grub hadn't been touched.

My second 24 hour stint of duty was from mid-day Christmas Eve until 1.45 on Christmas Day, when Marie would relieve me but WHO in the RAF in peacetime for heaven's sake, needed to be 'Up-Up-and-Away' on Christmas Day in 1945, so that we couldn't be stood down for 24 hours? With no radio and no other distractions, it would have been a golden opportunity for me to have begun writing about our exciting war-years and interesting work, as with the end of hostilities, the restriction on secrecy would no longer be important. Why didn't I think about doing it when still comparatively fresh in my memory?

My good deeds accomplished and out of 'solitary', I was due for a few days leave. I went home first and then on to Noak Hill D/F Station, near Romford, to spend New Year's Eve with Donnie. I decided that a hermit's life was not for me - for one thing it was self-defeating because the time dragged even more and I was too young to shut myself away from all the fun. I had begun going out with the girls, sometimes to dances and wearing my engagement ring, led to meeting a few kindred spirits who were parted from their loved ones and just wanted a partner to dance with or a bit of companionship. But I was 'always true to George in my fashion' and in the comparison, no-one else came close.

Monday, New Year's Eve 1945 was one of the coldest days that winter and London was engulfed in a filthy fog. I was going to hitch to Noak Hill but went by train instead. I met Donnie and the rest of the D/F operators, including Eileen Miller from our Wittersham days. We were all on our way to Hornchurch aerodrome for a New Year's Eve Party when the transport broke down, but with uncanny navigating by the driver on this particular night, where did he come to an abrupt halt? Just outside 'The Plough' pub so we had a nice comfortable place to shelter on this freezing night and a head start getting the New Year spirit under way. My diary records . . "When we got to Hornchurch, found the beer was 'on the house'. Kept bumping into RAF types with bottles of whisky - they were very popular till the bottles were empty. Then we left them flat and found someone else with another bottle. Was still pretty sober tho' I had certainly put away a few drams. Beryl had really 'had it' - she was snogging with some Canuck every chance she got. I had a white party hat and I put "Oregon Kid" in large letters on it. Thought of George at midnight when we were singing "Auld Lang Syne" but I'll be with him this time next year tho'. Piled into the transport and sang all the way back. Will be surprised if I've got any voice left when I awake. Ours was the second stop. Donnie, Eileen and I piled out of the truck. Couldn't find the darned house (Donnie's billet) at first and then the key wouldn't fit in the lock - only because it was so dark and not because we were too boozey to see the keyhole! Got in at 2.15." It had been a good party and on the way back, the transport driver was asked to 'stop for a leak'. The RAF lads went to the front and the WAAF's found a grass verge at the rear. As each one of us de-flagged our 'passion killers' and squatted . . . . there echoed through the silent night a series of loud 'Ouches' and other painful squeals as our bare bottoms touched what we thought were blades of grass but in the dark, we had settled on a bed of stinging nettles. Those who were not fully committed, were able to move to another place but the rest had to go on suffering. The men were wondering what all the commotion was about and thought it a huge joke when we explained.

I had so much to look forward to in 1946 but the more optimistic I was about getting demobbed in the near future, the more despondent I became when it didn't happen. The war in Europe had been over seven months - sisters and friends were getting back into civvy street in a steady stream but for those like me who had not joined up until late 1942, we just had to wait our turn. It was only fair of course that first in, should be first out and there was no short cut or extenuating circumstances, apart from having a baby I guess. I had been to the American Embassy and filled in forms etc. and a Shipping Line thought I would be able to get a passage in June but I would first need WAAF discharge papers to get emigration clearance. Obviously the reason for the slow demobilisation was to prevent the job market being flooded with too many people at once seeking employment but for those of us left in the Forces, it seemed such a waste of time, with not enough work to keep us occupied. I gave up my daily diary scribble because there was very little of interest to write about - life was tedious and the months dragged on and on. George's letters kept my spirits up but we had been apart from more than a year and it was becoming increasingly difficult to know what to write about. We both lacked the background knowledge of each other's environment - I didn't know much about his family. although his mother and sister had written to me and George wouldn't have been particularly interested in hearing about the people with whom I worked. It was that ill-timed posting of mine to Honiton Clyst in Devon in the summer of 1946 that led to a serious misunderstanding.

There I was poised and ready for my discharge from the WAAF's and when it came they wouldn't see the back of my heels for dust. But instead, this bolt from the blue and "Why" I thought "am I being sent all the way down to Exeter, when so near to getting demobbed?" It gradually penetrated my thick skull that it had only been wishful thinking on my part that I was near to getting free - the Air Force had other ideas. When the realisation eventually sunk in, my hopes were dashed for the umpteenth time and what could I say to George? I don't know how many times I had written that we would have to be patient a little longer. The situation was very different on the other side of the Atlantic - U.S. Forces were soon back as civilians. Unemployment figures spread over such a large country would barely be noticeable and hardly a reason for keeping them in uniform any longer than need be. The war never reached the American mainland - their cities were not bombed, no rubble in their streets, no unexploded bombs, nor were their factories destroyed. There had hardly been any appreciable difference in the plentiful life-style of American civilians as nearly everything they'd always enjoyed, was still produced for them - they had suffered no shortage of housing for returning servicemen. Here in England, most of our factories had been converted to war-time needs and it would take a considerable time for new jobs to be created when factories returned to peace-time production - raw materials from new overseas markets would need to be imported. We were millions of houses short already because of the bombing and all those service men who had got married during the war, needed a job and somewhere to live when they were demobbed.

When this posting came through, the war in Europe had been over for 15 months and I was still no nearer getting out or any indication when it might be. It was not surprising that George was beginning to have doubts as to whether I was really trying or that I was as anxious to leave the WAAF's as I intimated. A posting *instead* of demob seemed to convey that I might have had a hand in the decision and he too realised that I would not have been sent to another 'drome, *if* I was soon to be released.

Since the New Year's Eve Party at Hornchurch, Donnie and I still kept in fairly close touch either by letter or meeting on days off, as we had done since the Wittersham days and I met her in London on leaving Tolly with all my kit, en route for Honiton Clyst. She was on leave in civvies heading for Tidworth, where she was going to meet a G.I. boyfriend, so she said we could travel on the same train as far as Andover, which was fine by me and pleased to have her company. Tidworth Camp was where the English brides of American servicemen assembled before being dispatched to the States and Donnie's boyfriend, Jack, had said that he could fix her up with accommodation in the G.I. brides' quarters. On the way Donnie, listened sympathetically to all my recent problems - she'd heard nothing about demob either but was still quite enjoying herself and wasn't as desperately anxious as I was to become a civvie. Donnie was always full of of bright ideas . . . and in convincing me they were too, as well I knew from the times she had talked me into going places and doing things! "Why not come to Tidworth with me, stay the night and then continue to Devon tomorrow morning? I would be glad of a bit of moral support, as I don't know Jack that well and I'm not quite sure what the set-up will be. Come on, it will cheer you up" she said persuasively. The mood I was in, I couldn't have cared less if I never got to Honiton Clyst, so I was easily tempted! During our long association, Donnie and I had often embarked on 'spur of the moment' escapades together which were usually the ones that turned out to be the most fun and maybe this was just the tonic I needed to lift me out of the doldrums - so, throwing caution to the wind, I willingly replied "Why not?". American camps were well equipped and had every amenity for the

G.I's welfare - cinemas, dances, and a plentiful choice of marvellous food, as much as you could eat. Jack had a friend called Joe, who was married - I got the impression that his wife in the States had met someone else while he was overseas but he didn't wish to talk about it - all he wanted was a bit of companionship, which suited me too. He looked a lot like Danny Kaye, with short blonde curly hair and he was just as funny. The room that Jack had fixed up for Donnie in the Brides' Quarters conveniently had twin beds, so my arrival was no problem - we integrated in the female quarters and we were never asked for any identification. I wasn't at all anxious to leave such amenable surroundings for the dreaded Honiton Clyst, as I was quite enjoying myself and I did not leave the next morning as originally planned. In fact, I stayed a few more days until a nasty fright told me it was time to move on! The G.I's quarters were in long wooden huts with a central corridor and single rooms off on either side. One evening, when the four of us were in Jack's room having a snack of hot-dogs and coffee, there was a loud knock on the door, which wasn't locked and two burly American military policemen burst in, without waiting to be asked and I really thought we were all for the high jump for being in the G.I.'s quarters and Jack and Joe for having women in their rooms. They asked Donnie and I a lot of questions and we had to produce identification to confirm who we were. I was in uniform anyway but fortunately, the M.P's didn't scrutinise the dates on my documents too closely, otherwise they would have seen that by this time I was A.W.O.L.! I should have reported to Honiton Clyst several days ago. I also had to give my home address and I had visions of my parents being notified and having to explain what I was doing in a G.I's bedroom at Tidworth, when I ought to have been at Honiton Clyst - Father would do his nut! Donnie and I thought the M.P's would tell us to leave but they could see we weren't misbehaving and they seemed satisfied with our explanations. Before they departed they told us that the purpose of the swoop was to try and catch prostitute camp followers who were known to knock on the G.I's windows from outside and offer their services. That was a close one though and enough to make me realise I ought to be on my way, so I left for Exeter the next morning.

When I arrived at Honiton Clyst, the guards looked at my papers and wanted to know where I had been for three days. I told them I was on a D/F Station in Essex, a long way from Biggin Hill and I couldn't leave until they sent a replacement - then I had to travel to Biggin for clearance and travel warrants etc. which had already been made out. Luckily, they seemed to swallow that 'load of cobblers' but I sweated on top line for a week or more wondering whether the American Military Police were going to take the matter further and check on the details I had given, which would disprove the pack of lies I had just told. Thankfully, my parents were never contacted and neither was Honiton Clyst and that was indeed a lucky break I never expected and didn't really deserve!

I had no idea what sort of job I would be given at my new posting or whether it would still be connected with D/F work as there was far less flying now, so it was some consolation when I found out I would be working in a Homer - a totally new experience although theoretically using the same equipment and procedure in an identical Tower, situated on the far side of the airfield. As the word 'Homer' implies, we were involved with giving aircraft vectors/homings for returning to base. The only squadron I can recall at Exeter at that time was Treble Two (222) flying Gloster Meteors and the squadron had only recently arrived from Weston Zoyland in Somerset. We were now in the early years of the jet age but it had taken some time for the technology to evolve since Sir Frank Whittle had produced the proto-type jet engine in 1937. The German firm of Messerschmitt had introduced their first jet, the ME262 during the last months of the war but had either side seriously concentrated on developing the potential of the jet propelled aircraft earlier, it would have given the 'first in the field' an enormous advantage of speed and performance over conventional piston-engined aircraft but both the Gloster Meteor and the ME262 began operational service too late to make any appreciable difference in air warfare.

The Meteors flew at speeds of over 500mph and it was nigh impossible for D/F operators to keep track of their position and the noise when they flew low overhead while taking off or landing at Honiton Clyst was deafening. At Wittersham and Tolly, when tracking Spits or Mustangs etc., they were invariably south or south-east of us and the next bearing wasn't usually that far away from their previous transmission but working from a Homer in close proximity to the airfield, the Meteors could be north, south, east or west of us in seconds. By the time we had located them on our 360° wheel, ascertained whether it was a reciprocal bearing or not and passed it through to Air Traffic Control, the Meteor could be miles apart between voice transmissions. I quickly came to the conclusion that the equipment we were using was not up to the task of coping with the speed of the jets and there wasn't much job satisfaction for the operators either. I expect it was eventually superseded by an electronic system but during those war years, I am so thankful that we were able to hear and participate in what was happening in the air, which was a far more rewarding occupation than for those post-war D/F operators who came after - they had no interesting intercom to listen to and only a boring old 'blip' on a screen to look at!

I was mostly on duty with Pat Marriott, a popular buxom lass with lovely curly auburn hair, and full of fun - we lived in the same hut, spent off-duty pursuits together and became firm friends. Our Homer Tower was situated in a cornfield on the other side of the 'drome, far from anywhere, although we could just see the Control Tower in the distance. When there was no flying, we used to sit outside and laze in the sun, or at least one of us could - our summons to man a certain frequency was usually by telephone and we also had an extension of the Camp tannoy system. We were covered with embarrassment one day, when we heard a voice over the loud-speaker which would have been relayed all over the Camp - "Will the WAAF who is sunbathing outside the Homer in panties and bra, please return to her post immediately!" What we had not realised until then, was that the cornfield had recently been cut and the Peeping Toms in the Control Tower were now able to spy on us with their binoculars. We heard later that the guy who made the tannoy announcement wasn't very popular with his fellow workers for spoiling that bit of sport when things were slack in the Control Tower because thereafter, we made jolly sure we couldn't be seen from their direction!

The WAAF quarters were in an isolated rural setting among trees, far flung from the main Camp and had the usual cluster of Nissen huts, Ablutions, NAAFI and a Guard Room at the entrance. I had been lucky enough to be housed in civilian billets for most of my war service and I didn't much relish the return to communal living in a hut full of females, loss of privacy and only a few yards of floor space to call my own, but it did have its compensations. The girls in our hut were a lively crowd and with not enough work to keep us fully occupied, we larked about a lot and joined in any mischief that was going. As in a hospital ward, an Army platoon or a Forces hut, there is usually one joker who keeps the rest 'in fits' with an uncanny ability to see the amusing side of any situation. So many of our post-war stand-up comedians began their careers entertaining the Forces and what better audience could they have had to try their wit and humour on, than a captive bunch of blokes in a service hut. Our hut clown at Honiton Clyst was a bubbley WAAF called Babs, who had a mischievous sense of humour, an irreverence for authority and gave hilarious impersonations of the voice, walk and mannerisms of our N.C.O's and Queen B . . . .'s.

We were all required to take a turn of duty on a rota basis in the

WAAF Guard Room, checking anyone coming in and out. I never minded doing it, as I regarded those few hours as a welcome opportunity to write letters, away from the chatter of that noisy hut. One day when I was doing my stint, the telephone rang - it was S/0 Forbes who gave me a few things she wanted me to do, while I was on guard duty. Voices often sound very different on the telephone but I was slightly suspicious because I knew that Babs was at work on the camp somewhere, no doubt with access to an internal telephone. She also knew I intended to write some letters and it was just the sort of prank she'd think up to thwart me. Once she got going on some tack, her imagination knew no bounds and firing on all cylinders she could keep up the pretence at length - she used to crease me, although she could be such a pest at times, when she never let up. For the umpteenth time, I would put the 'phone down and in a few minutes it would ring again and she'd carry on where she left off, still impersonating S/0 Forbes, and keeping up the pretence. Eventually, I told her I was definitely NOT going to answer the 'phone any more and I thought she had finally got the message because there was a long break before it did eventually ring again. I let it continue for a while but I couldn't concentrate on writing with the constant ringing, so I angrily picked up the 'phone and began to reel off some of the unsavoury intercom language that had pervaded my ears but only passed my lips in moments of sheer exasperation . . . . like now! I ended by saying "Don't you ever give up woman, now pack it in for Gawd's sake" but the equally cross voice at the other end said "To whom am I speaking - this is S/0 Forbes and I have been trying to get through to the WAAF Guard Room for the last 10 minutes - the line has either been engaged or it rang and non-one answered. What do you mean by leaving the Guard Room unattended?" This was a typical Babs follow-up on our previous exchange and I told her in no uncertain terms to "Bugger-off and enough was enough". Even the shocked tone of voice in reply, didn't immediately convey to me that this time it really was the 'pukka' S/0 Forbes and that she had genuinely been trying to get through. Of all the people on Camp it might have been, it was my tough luck that the real Secton Officer Forbes should ring through, just when Babs was giving such a convincing impersonation. All I could blurt out was that a fella had been pestering me on the 'phone and in the end I decided not to answer. I put on my best grovelling act and apologised profusely, trying to convince her that I had been in the Guard Room all the time. She made no further comment but went on to the real purpose for her call. "I've received a report that airmen have been seen in the WAAF Quarters and I have contacted the RAF police, who are sending someone up to investigate. Keep an eye open if you notice anything suspicious". How strange, I thought as I replaced the receiver because I was in full view of the entrance and I hadn't seen anyone come in, except for those 2 RAF radio mechanics who were repairing our u/s radio in our hut . . . "Oh my Gawd" I mutttered, as it suddenly dawned on me that they could be in dead trouble being caught in a WAAF hut, even though they were only doing us a good turn, mending our radio. The back door of the Guard Room was only a few yards from the rear entrance of our hut, so I quickly dashed over and told them to scarper to the NAAFI because the police were coming. The Ministry of Defence staff who had quarters further up the road, used our NAAFI facilities and airmen were also allowed there. I had only just got back to the Guard Room when 2 RAF Regiment police rolled up in a Jeep, saying they were following up a report that airmen had been seen entering a WAAF hut. I said it was probably a hoax but I would get someone to show them around and indicated to Pam on the quiet to start well away from our hut to give the radio mechanics time to get to the NAAFI. Before leaving again in their Jeep, the RAF Regiment chappies said they'd had a good look round and found no sign of any intruders. As they disappeared from view, WAAF's on the site gathered outside their huts and wanted to know what the panic was all about - it seemed as though those two radio mechanics were the ones they were after but who would be so 'bitchy' as to deliberately tell tales to try and get the girls in our hut into trouble over such an innocent matter? Radios were a treasured possession during the war and had we sent it to be repaired in the RAF workshop, there was a good chance that it might disappear without trace. One of the girls asked her radio mechanic boyfriend and his pal to come and repair it 'in situ'.

Some of the WAAF cooks lived in the hut next door and we did eventually discover that one of them was the sneak, who was out to cause trouble but we did not establish exactly which one, so we had to let it pass unavenged. They didn't succeed and anyway, it wasn't worth getting on the wrong side of the kitchen staff because they dished out the meals in the Mess - you were liable to get short rations, custard on your kippers or an extra dose of salt or sugar on the wrong dish!

It was definitely not my day - after buying stamps for the letters I had written I was absolutely skint until next Pay Day. The rest of the hut were out for the evening, except for Pam and she was broke too. We soon got bored with reading and knitting and tried to think of something else to do to brighten up the evening. Then I remembered I had a bottle of whisky in the case under my bed (sent to me to cure a cold, but by the time I received it, the cold had gone) and I also found two packs of cards there. We both sat cross-legged on the floor on opposite sides of the case, which we used as a table and began to play Casino, passing the whisky back and forth, which we drank neat straight from the bottle. If we'd had a glass or cup handy, we might have thought of diluting it with water but as the contents of the bottle got less, the cheating got more outrageous and giggley. The numbers on the cards were becoming blurred and we swore black was white for whatever card we wanted it to be, trying to convince the opponent that they were too drunk to see it properly. By the time the bottle was empty, our sides ached from laughing. We ought to have just laid on our beds and slept it off but we decided a cup of coffee would help to sober us up, forgetting that we hadn't a bean between us. Then Pam had the bright idea of collecting all yesterday's papers and magazines from the hut, which we could sell at half-price outside our NAAFI, until we had collected enough for a coffee. We must have caused a bit of commotion outside the NAAFI shouting 'Express & Echo - Read All Abowd it'. I believe some kind soul took pity on us and paid for two cups of coffee but until I awoke the next morning, the rest of that evening remains a bit hazy. The girls from our hut took care of us and managed to get us into bed.

    I suppose I was drowning my sorrows and trying to blot out the fact that George and I had decided to part by mutual agreement. Since I first met him, we had only spent the equivalent of barely 14 days together before he went back to the States and we had now been apart for 15 months, which was not a very firm foundation on which to keep a romance alive indefinitely on such a brief acquaintance. That concerned me quite a lot and doubts did begin to creep in from time to time at the enormity of what I was contemplating - going half-way across the world to marry someone I'd only known for such a short time and how well did we really know each other? Those fears would probably never have arisen had we been able to see each other more often. Our romance was not standing the test of time and it was probably for the best that it was just fizzling out.

    I was on the early morning shift at the Homer and to get there from the WAAF Quarters, we cycled along the deserted Devon lanes with high hedges on either side. I must have been the first person to pass that way on that particular morning because the spiders' webs were still intact, stretching from side to side across the narrow lanes, their delicate strands glistening in the early morning autumn sunlight. Had anyone been within earshot, they would have thought I was totally bonkers because as I cycled along, I was shouting at the top of my voice - 'I'm free . . . . I'm free", breaking the

Battle of Britain Parade - Exeter Cathedral 1946

cobwebs as I went, with the dew on those silvery threads splashing my face. It was a most exhilarating ride and I felt on top of the world, as if a great burden had been lifted from me. As well as getting 'cold feet' at going so far away, I wasn't absolutely sure I really wanted to settle down and get married just yet.

I was quite expecting to be taken to task for my rudeness to S/O Forbes over the telephone but she didn't pursue the matter. Maybe she was near to getting demobbed too and let it pass.

****

My No. 3 WAAF sister, who was posted to Algiers, later went on to Rome, where she met her future husband and when they returned to U.K., they got married at Wembley in June 1946 and I was one of her bridesmaids. Husband David Eddie was a Squadron Leader and an RAF auditor. Two months after they married he had been assigned the audit at Honiton Clyst while I was stationed there. I attended my very last Church Parade at Exeter Cathedral on Battle of Britain Sunday 1946 and we paraded through the City. Being one of the tallest, I was left-hand marker in the front row, behind the N.C.O's and after the service, David and my sister took me to lunch at the Royal Clarence Hotel. A most welcome change to eat once more in such civilised elegance after the grab for grub in the Airmen's Mess - that was until I found a snail among my greens - uggh! Had it happened on Camp, I probably wouldn't have batted an eyelid because standards of hygiene were at a low ebb but I made the most of my disapproval and disgust that such a mishap ought not to occur in a first class hotel, if the kitchen staff had been more observant. The head waiter was full of apologies and we got VIP treatment from then on, as well as a reduction in the bill.

****

The Ministry of Defence civilian workers, who did the maintenance jobs around the aerodrome at Honiton Clyst had their living quarters beyond the WAAF Camp and the approach to both was a quiet country road, lined with trees and at intervals, there were closed five-bar gates, the entrances into various fields. The M.o.D. men mostly had motor bikes and they used to tease me that as they returned to their quarters at night, their headlights would pick me out saying 'Goodnight' to a different fella at a different gate - a charge I strongly denied! However, when I was posted from Exeter to Predannock in Cornwall (yet another posting), Bob Dunstan and Jim Lennon sent a message that they would like to see me in our NAAFI. When I appeared, they had arranged an investiture ceremony and presented me with a 'Snogging Medal' - a 7" diameter circular metal disc, hung on sections of red and blue material, fastened by a large 6" safety pin. Painted around the edge in blue and yellow on a red background were the words -

'FOR DEVOTED SERVICE TO THE CAUSE OF SNOGGING'
and in the centre
WOODBURY COMMON
DISTRICT OF AYLESBEARE
HOMER PRECINCTS
L. A. C. W   J O Y C E   M I L L A R D
1942   1946
DEER COPSE GATEWAY
FARRINGDON ROAD

The attached citation was then read out and presented to me with the certificate!

After the war, I was most disappointed that I was not eligible for the Defence Medal as I had not served for three years during the actual conflict in Europe. I missed out by a couple of months as the time I served after 8 May 1945 did not count. So even though I received no recognition from my country for my war efforts in the D/F field, I am consoled that I do at least have a medal and citation to record my talents at the gate!!

Maybe I'll confess to sometimes being at one of those gates with an RAF fella called Gray, inevitably nicknamed Dolly, who also owned a motor bike. We often met his best friend in Exeter and gave him a lift back to Camp, riding three on a motor bike with me in the middle which I suspect is quite illegal but we were never stopped. On our route, we passed a farmhouse which had been badly bombed, with only the outside walls still

Snogging medal and Joyce's WAAF money belt

CORPORATION OF HONITON CLYST

THIS IS TO CERTIFY THAT Joyce Millard W.441 OF THIS PARISH, HAS THIS DAY BEEN EXAMINED BY THE UNDERSIGNED & SHE HAS BEEN FOUND PROFICIENT IN THE ART OF SNOGGING.

This Certificate is granted with effect from this date & entitles the holder to Snog in the precincts of Honiton Clyst & its immediate contiguity on payment of a small fee.

RRP Dunston — Mayor, I.W.T.
JP W Lennon — Deputy Mayor, P.I.W.T.

Oct. 1st 1946

Presented to Joyce Millard W.H.H.F. L.A.C.W.
W.A.A.F.   L.A.C.W.
as a token of our complete amazement and incredulity at the skill and resource shown by her in a feat of arms on the evening of Sept. 26th at Deer Copse.

(Never in the field of human conflict was so much done in such little time by only two people.)

We feel that however we may try, it would be quite impossible for any of us to hold our own in competition with Miss Millard and we have therefore no alternative but to (sadly withal) gracefully retire from active snogging.

232

standing and of course uninhabited. Exeter and surrounding area had suffered many air-raids and the Town Centre had been flattened. On this particular farm, the outbuildings were still intact and contained many full milk churns, ready for collection in the early morning. One night we investigated and discovered that the metal drinking cans were conveniently and temptingly hooked on the side. We helped ourselves to this delicious creamy Devon milk and then we would replace the amount we had drunk with water, up to the original rim mark to cover our tracks. So hopefully, the customers never knew their milk had been watered down and the farmer did not lose out on the volume!

Once or twice I might also have been caught in the M.o.D headlights when saying Goodnight to Barrie Sheffield. We both liked classical music and used to attend organised Record evenings somewhere on the Camp.

I was unable to coax my memory cells into revealing any worthwhile details about my final posting to RAF Predannack on the Lizard Peninsula, but I know wasn't there long before my demob came through and in October 1946, after serving in the WAAF's for three years and ten months, I became a civilian once more.

****

Unless you experienced the comradeship of war-time service life, it is difficult to explain or justify saying - as so many of us now do - that despite the horrors of war, they were some of the best and memorable years of our lives. Class barriers fell away and the circumstances prevailing were a great leveller - the ordinary Tommy, the able-seaman and Johnny erk knew that their war effort was just as important. It was a time of great hardship but there was good neighbourliness, people spoke to each other on buses and trains, we had a common purpose and everyone pulled together with dogged determination in a justified struggle against an evil enemy, hell-bent on crushing the ideals of democratic rule. The best qualities of the British seem to surface when we are 'up against it'. We lived life at a different pitch, indulging in a lot of innocent fun and no way in peacetime would I have had the opportunity of meeting so many wonderful men from all over the world, that I feel privileged to have known. I freely admit that those years in the WAAF's were the most carefree and exciting of my young adult life and in comparison, I did find civvie street rather dull.

Chapter 24

AFTER THOUGHTS - THEN AND NOW

The opportunity to tie-up the loose ends of my war-time occupation and discover so many interesting background details, has given me immense satisfaction but among the trove of memories I unlocked, there was one I wish had remained concealed. In the early years after I was demobbed, I often wondered whether Peter Noble, the Beaufighter pilot (whose hand I got into trouble for holding at Cranwell) had survived the war. I lacked the courage to telephone his home in Dolphin Square for fear of embarrassment in case he had become engaged or married during the last two and a half years. The motive was only really to satisfy my curiosity that he had got through the war safely and not to dwell on the past - I thought I had found the answer because when I worked in London, I looked in RAF casualty records and in the books of aircrew K.I.A. in St. Clement Danes Church in the Strand but there was no Peter Noble listed, so it seemed that he had won through and all these years I thought that he had. At the end of 1943, we were still meeting occasionally and corresponding about once a month but when I was on sick leave in January 1944 after being in Hastings hospital, I believe he owed me a letter. The memory is a bit vague after all this time and I may well have written once more but if I got no reply then, I probably thought that I was being given the brush-off. In those days, girls didn't take the initiative, they waited for the fellas to do the pursuing. Of course, knowing that he was on dangerous flying operations, the thought did occur to me that he might have been become a casualty but had that been the case, I felt sure that having met his mother on several occasions, she would have let me know. Even without a recent address, his parents knew my surname, that I lived in Wembley and we were in the telephone directory.

In 1994, at the end of one of my research sessions at P.R.O. Kew, I had a brief look at 254 squadron records on microfilm but the only pilot named Noble I could find during 1943 when I knew Peter, was 118390 Keith W. Noble and he was also listed in the RAF Officers Year Book in January 1944 but not in March 1944, a likely indication that he might have been K.I.A. Unable to get to Kew again and thoroughly mystified in trying to reconcile that they might possibly be one and the same (his parents, brother and friends all called him Peter), I eventually telephoned the War Graves Commission, who gave me these details :-

F/LT. KEITH WELLS (PETER) NOBLE 118390 Aged 22. 9 February 1944. Buried Dunure Cemetery, Ayr, Scotland. Section E280. Parents - Major and Mrs. Frank Noble, M.C.

Further investigation has revealed that he was posted from 254 Squadron (the North Coates Wing) on 26 January 1944 to No. l Torpedo Training Unit, Turnberry, Ayrshire for a course and that on 8 February 1944, the engine of his Beaufighter cut and stalled on approach. The only remaining mystery is why the Noble family called him Peter instead of Keith.

The cream of our youth gave their lives to win the freedom that later generations have been able to enjoy but during the last five decades, it has saddened me that as each year has passed, their sacrifice has not been remembered and the anniversaries of the outstanding achievements of WWII barely warranted a mention in any of the news outlets. We were Europe's last and only hope of liberation from Nazi-ism and had that attempt failed, the Third Reich might well have lasted a thousand years, as Hitler boasted. It has taken 50 years to get any worthy recognition and during that time several generations of children have grown up in ignorance of the most important period of English history this century because it was left out of the school curriculum.

In the autumn of our lives, we are more inclined to take a backward glance at our younger days and make comparisons with similar age groups now but although I often regret that the years are passing by much quicker than before, I never yearn to be young again in today's world. During that formative period, I had the good fortune to enjoy the innocence of my childhood, free to play in parks or roam the streets in absolute safety and shielded from the unpleasantries of adult life. With the advent of television and exposure to scenes of appalling violence, explicit sex, rape, and drugs, children can no longer be protected from the decadent society now prevailing. Its a much tougher world for them and they have to be warned at such an early age of the evil things that might befall them and watchful parents feel it necessary to chaperone them wherever they go, whereas pre-war, many children had to walk miles to and from school, without any fear of being harmed. In my early teens, we met and played with boys of our own age, who were hardly aware that we were a different sex! Very young girls seldom knew the 'facts of life' - the first stage in the gradual process usually began with a platonic boy/girl friendship, leading to a more romantic relationship with a boyfriend to embrace on the dance floor or to indulge in mild 'necking' in the back row of a cinema.

    The girls who joined the Forces during the war had mostly been living at home under parental control, having to be in at a certain time at night. Fathers invariably ruled the roost and daughters defied his authority at their peril. Not many had branched out on their own because flats and bed-sits for single girls were scarce and hardly affordable on a low wage. So away from home for the first time, some girls did go a bit wild over their new-found freedom. I was only 18 when I joined the WAAF's a few days before Christmas and the high jinks that went on with airmen in the WAAF huts and beds, drunken females and the foul language, was a real eye-opener for an unworldly lass but I wasn't influenced to follow suit, as it wasn't exactly my idea of having a good time! It was Christmas and I didn't encounter such behaviour flaunted quite so openly again. The general mood was one of live for today - have fun, because there might not have been much of a future for any of us, had we succumbed to Nazi domination and been enslaved by the arrogant self-styled 'master-race'. Young folk in the Forces had a long interruption in their career prospects and it didn't concern us unduly that we were deprived of money to spend. nice clothes to wear, or being able to go on holiday - we had no difficulty in getting our priorities in perspective.

    We were certainly a tougher breed and had much more to endure than Service personnel in later war skirmishes, particularly some of the whinging Gulf War wives. Their menfolk were only away a matter of weeks or months at the most and they were able to speak to their husbands by telephone and exchange videos. People in our age group found the hype and lack of stamina, positively nauseating - Mrs. Miniver would have been appalled!! A lot of troops in the Far East in WWII were away for **years on end** (up to four in some cases) without getting any leave and many wives did not know whether their husbands were alive or dead, as ships carrying mail were often sunk and telegrams of 'Missing' or 'Killed in Action' were not sent unless officially confirmed. Most men in the Second World War were civilians, put into uniform and sent to fight in any theatre of war where they were needed but to the cosseted Gulf wives, it seems to have come as a tremendous shock that their husbands who, of their own free will, volunteered to serve and make a career in the Armed Forces, should be called upon to go somewhere and fight when a war situation arose. With casualties so infinitesimal in the Gulf War, how many troops would have even seen a dead Allied soldier, let alone one of his mates killed in action? And yet, so many seem to have returned suffering from P.T.S.D. - POST

TRAUMATIC STRESS DISORDER - one of those new-fangled terms that people cotton on to but if it had not been coined, would those soldiers ever have known they were suffering from it? Purported to be a medical condition, it seems it can best be cured by a large injection - not of drugs but Cash. There was no counselling for troops in WWII who experienced scenes of horrendous carnage or for those who suffered years of torture in Japanese PoW camps. Many civilians too endured great hardship but instead of moaning about their predicament, they tapped their inner sources of resilience to help them cope.

In the thirties, a University education was beyond the horizon of most women and training facilities were restricted to a few limited occupations but during the war, by proving that women could competently perform tasks equally as well as men, we paved the way for the tremendous post-war advances in broadening achievement prospects and equality for women in the field of employment. A good career and/or marriage is their choice but along the way, they have lost the freedom of movement we enjoyed, being able to travel in comparative safety, day or night, where there were no street lights and we didn't consider it a privilege - it should be a basic right for women to be entitled to both and not gain one advancement at the expense of another. It is hard to understand the underlying root cause for the upsurge in male violence against women and the increase in cases of rape, when there are far more willing females around today. Young men during the war had every reason to want to live life to the full because many knew they would have no tomorrow but cases of rape were extremely rare. Had we had the protection of the Pill then, no doubt our attitude towards sex would have been more liberal. The fear and shame of coping with an illegitimate child with no financial assistance and parents quite likely to disown you, were sufficient deterrents for most girls. Even so, the restraint on both sexes to generally wait for marriage, does not appear to have given us any long-term hang-ups - who can deny that, as a generation, have we not been more disciplined, law-abiding, honest and less violent citizens than those that have followed?

The geriatric brigade are sometimes accused of looking at the past through rose-coloured spectacles but the virtues of the society we grew up in, would seem to outweigh its shortcomings. It was far less stressful before we had to contend with each new menace which has gradually crept into our day to day living, since the war. Such as -

| Football hooligans, | Hi-jackers, | Pornography, |
| Drugs and related crimes, | Vandals, | Muggers, |

Acid House parties,	Paedophiles,	Rapists,
New Age travellers,	Lager louts,	Joy riders,

Race riots and the immigrant influx

If any of those can be regarded as 'progress', then many of us would like to return to some of Those Good Old Ways . . . now decried as The Bad Old Days.

At the end of WWII, with the idealogues of Nazi-ism suppressed for ever we hoped, we emerged full of optimism that the sacrifice of the millions upon millions who died would not have been in vain - this time lessons <u>would</u> be learned and the future must surely lead to a better world for everyone. Sadly, those aspirations fell far short of our dreams and the spread of so-called civilisation and improved education world-wide, has done little to curb man's inhumanity to his fellow man. Following in Hitler's wake, other evil Dictators have, unrestrained, attempted to emulate that heinous regime of conquest and genocide.

It is said that 'history repeats itself' and ours would seem to bear that out. An era of degenerative behaviour has usually been followed by a more puritanical, less tolerant period where the pendulum has swung to the other extreme. Ideally, a society balanced between the two is what is needed to make the world a better place than it is today.

Joyce in civvies

BIBLIOGRAPHY

The Right of the Line	John Terraine. Hodder & Stoughton.
The Doodlebugs	Norman Longmate. Hutchinson.
Action Stations	Bruce Barrymore.
The World at Arms	The Reader's Digest Association Ltd. 1989.
We Band of Brothers	Lloyd Hunt. Canadian Fighter Pilots Assoc.
Thorn in Rommel's Side	Laddie Lucas. Ulvescroft. 1994.
The Air Battle for Malta	James Douglas Hamilton. Mainstream. 1981.
The Road to Biggin Hill	(W/Cdr. Johnnie Checketts, N.Z.) by Vincent Orange. Airlife. 1986.
The 1,000 Day Battle	James Hoseason. Gillingham Publications. 1979.

ACKNOWLEDGEMENTS

It is impossible to name all those friends and ex-RAF personnel who gave me tremendous support and encouragement, although I would like to give special thanks to the following who have been instrumental in supplying additional details, which I might otherwise not have discovered and who have helped me trace those elusive 'ditchers' who called 'MAYDAY' over half a century ago. Ray Mills of Kent - Alan Smith of Ipswich - Sid Harvey of Beccles and Elward Burnside of Toronto.

INDEX OF SELECTED NAMES

Aguirre - Kattalin 92
Anthony - F/O B.W. 26,27
Atkinson - P/O Stanley Kyle 12,14,102/5
Bartholomew - Cpl. i/c 39,117,119,160
Beaumont - W/Cdr. R.P. 'Bee' iv,145
Belle - Marie van 73/74
Bellinger - Joan WAAF xi,208
Beurling - 'Screwball' George F. 27,106/10
Blanchard - S/Sgt. Stewart 41/43,77,160
Bond - Eileen xi,21,44,101,113,120,138,164/69
Bonnevaine family 85
Bowden - Sgt. I. 104
Brodie - F/Sgt. 79
Burkett - Cliff v
Butler - W/O 79
Bybee - M/Sgt. Sheldon 104/5
Carlson - Padre Don (Can.) 78
Carrington - Cpl. Muriel 204/5/9, 212
Carter - F/Lt. Arthur 129,133
Charles - Sq/Ldr. Jack 26,46
Checketts - W/Cdr. Johnny 47,71/4,100,106
Cheney - Joan 208
Cherwinski - Anje 86,95
Chubb - P/O Pat 102/5
Churchill - Winston 15,71,152,199/201
Clarkson - F/Lt. Dick 190/1
Clinker - Peggy xi,161,169
Cobb - Lady 39,111
Conrad - S/Ldr. Walter A.G. 29
Cook - F/Lt. Wm. Francis 'Cookie' iii,80/95
Cook - Sgt. L. 104
Coushane - Sgt. Frank 42
Daunt - Dr. 116
Davenport - P/O R.M. 31
Dawson & Deal - S/Officers 11
Deere - W/Cdr. Al 48,106
Dewan - F/Lt. Don J. 64

Dickinson - Elsie 110
Dorman - F/Sgt. Victor 52/65
Drobinski - S/Ldr. Boleshaw 'Gandy' 159
Duffy - Lt. George L. 202/12, 218/21
Dunsmuir - Curly xi,101,119,160,169
Eddie - Molly & David 207,230
Ewens - F/O Lionel 'Pop' 51
Farrow - Sgt. 161/2
Felice - Sous Lt. 171
Fiander - F/O Jimmy 50,78/80
Finucane - W/Cdr. Paddy 18
Forbes - Section Officer 226,230
Forrest - Sq/Ldr. Jack 51,69
French - John C. iii,123
Garrett - F/Lt. Ernest W. 129/133
Godefroy - W/Cdr. Hugh C. iv,80,110
Golding - David & Lorna 164/5,181,187,209,213
Göring - Riechsmarshall Herman 47,148
Grace - S/Ldr. Alan 28
Grant - Sgt. W. 'Bill' 104/5
Gray - Dolly 231
Grice - W/Cdr. Douglas 'Grubby' v,106
Hamilton - Lt. Derek 189/91
Hamilton - Joe 64
Hannay - F/O R.H. Bob 174
Harmer - June 181,185,187,195/210,212/18
Haw - F/O P.S. 'Lofty' 174
Haw-Haw - Lord (William Joyce) 72,195
Heap - F/Lt. Johnny 171/4
Hill - F/O Barry 53,64
Hilter - Adolph 47,152,176/79,198,235,238
Hodson - W/Cdr. Keith L.B. 33
Hoglund - T/Sgt. Norman 160,169
Horbacsewski - Sq/Ldr. Eeugeniusz B.H. 157
Howard - Sq/Ldr 17,119
Humphreys - Sgt. 78
Hunter - Sq/Ldr. 121

Hyde - P/O A.A.	170	Palmer - Joan Cpl.	xi
Johnson - W/Cdr. J.E. 'Johnnie'		Parks - P/O Tommy	27/8
	vii,18,29,38,67,80,106	Pollard - Polly	xi,149
Johnson - F/Lt. W.S.	78	Potocki - F/Lt.	156
		Rankin - Jamie	106
Jones - Capt.	111	Reynolds - Mary	xi
Jowett - Lord	40	Rommel - Field Marshall Erwin	99,176,178
Keefer - W/Cdr. George C.	29	Roosevelt - President Theodore D.	194
Keitel - Field Marshall Wilhelm	177	Ross - W/O Hugh 'Jock'	v,170/4
Kelly - F/O D.P.	31	Russel - W/Cdr. B. Dal	34
Kingcome - Brian	106	Saunders - A.V.M. Hugh W.L.	75
Kock - F/O Tom	32	Schofield - S/Lt.	30
Lacey - James 'Ginger'	107	Seager - Tony F/Lt.	171
Lamb - F/O Tony	52	Sheffield - Barrie	233
Lemp - Lt. Fritz Julius	90	Short - Connie	xi
Ligat - David	114	Skilton - Garland/Gay	4,5,10
Linton - Karl	82	Spundle - Sq/Ldr. Bob	171
Linton - F/Lt. Ozzie M.	79	Stauffenburg - Count Claus Schenk von	
Lucas - W/Cdr. P.G. 'Laddie'	iii,29,106		176/77
Macbrien - G/Capt. W.R. 'Iron Bill'	33	St. Denis - Jack	36/7
Malan - G/Capt. Adolphus 'Sailor'		Sugg - M/Sgt. Tommy	168,181
	18,47/48,106	Tamowiez - W/O	157
Marriott - Pat	225	Thatcher - F/O Dick	64
Martin - Doris	xi,14	Thompson - F/Lt S.T.	170
Matheson - F/Lt. Douglas R.	iii,33,35/37	Thornton - Lilian	xi,162/3,169
Mayhew - Donnie		Tippett - Michael O'Brien	14,112
	xi,42,77,101,133,149/52,169,181,219	Torre - Sq/Ldr. Spy de la	48
McNair - Sq/Ldr. Robert W. 'Buck'		Wallace - Lt. Robert D.	168/9,181/84
	vii,27/8, 36/7,81/2	Wedgebury - Joan	
McRae - F/Lt. W.R. 'Bill'	31,35		ix/xi,18/21,44,101,113,140,164,169
Meeklah - P/O J.E.	171	Wilson - F/Sgt. D.M.	79
Millard - Derrick (brother)	14,103		
Miller - Eileen	xi,220		
Mouchette - Rene C/dante	27,46/48,71		
Munson - F/Sgt. Rupert W.	26		
Murchinson - F/O	31		
Mussolini - Il Duce Benito	47,177,194		
Neal - Sq/Ldr. Jeep	34		
Noble - Kieth W. (Peter) F/O	4,9,29,234/5		
North - G/Capt.	73		
Ormston - Sq/Ldr. Ian C.	33/5		